D1594586

Seven Eggs Today

THE DIARIES OF MARY ARMSTRONG
1859 AND 1869

Life Writing Series

In the **Life Writing Series**, Wilfrid Laurier University Press publishes life writing and new life-writing criticism in order to promote autobiographical accounts, diaries, letters, and testimonials written and/or told by women and men whose political, literary, or philosophical purposes are central to their lives. **Life Writing** features the accounts of ordinary people, written in English, or translated into English from French or the languages of the First Nations or from any of the languages of immigration to Canada. **Life Writing** will also publish original theoretical investigations about life writing, as long as they are not limited to one author or text.

Priority is given to manuscripts that provide access to those voices that have not traditionally had access to the publication process.

Manuscripts of social, cultural, and historical interest that are considered for the series, but are not published, are maintained in the Life Writing Archive of Wilfrid Laurier University Library.

Series Editor
Marlene Kadar
Humanities Division, York University

Manuscripts to be sent to
Brian Henderson, Director
Wilfrid Laurier University Press
75 University Avenue West
Waterloo, Ontario, Canada N2L 3C5

Seven Eggs Today

The Diaries of Mary Armstrong
1859 and 1869

Edited by
Jackson W. Armstrong

Wilfrid Laurier University Press
WLU

This book has been published with the help of a grant from the Canadian Federation for the Humanities and Social Sciences, through the Aid to Scholarly Publications Programme, using funds provided by the Social Sciences and Humanities Research Council of Canada. We acknowledge the financial support of the Government of Canada through the Book Publishing Industry Development Program for our publishing activities. We acknowledge the Government of Ontario through the Ontario Media Development Corporation's Ontario Book Initiative.

National Library of Canada Cataloguing in Publication Data

Armstrong, Mary, 1819–1881
    Seven eggs today : the diaries of Mary Armstrong, 1859 and 1869 / Jackson W. Armstrong, editor.

(Life writing series)
Includes bibliographical references and index.

ISBN 0-88920-440-3

    1. Armstrong, Mary, 1819–1881 — Diaries. 2. Toronto (Ont.) —History— Sources. 3. Toronto (Ont.) — Biography. I. Armstrong, Jackson W. (Jackson Webster), 1978- II. Title. III. Series.

FC3097.26.A74A3 2004   971.3'54102'092   C2004-901977-5

Cover design by Leslie Macredie. Map of Yorkville, detail from *Illustrated Historical Atlas of the County of York* (Toronto: Miles, 1878). Courtesy Archives of Ontario. Text design by PJWoodland.

Every reasonable effort has been made to acquire permission for copyright material used in this text, and to acknowledge all such indebtedness accurately. Any errors and omissions called to the publisher's attention will be corrected in future printings.

∞
Printed in Canada

TABLE OF CONTENTS

List of Illustrations

PREFACE

✳

"Who is going to be interested in reading about the Armstrong family?" rightly asked my mother when this project began. Certainly very few will be drawn to these pages for the sake of our relatively bland family history, but I hope readers will be curious about the engaging glimpse of life in Victorian Toronto that my great-great-great-grandmother preserved in her diaries. What follows is an attempt to let Mary Armstrong tell her own story, and to this end my goal is to give context to her experience and to make her world accessible. Mary's writing records her daily life, covering a variety of topics including household work, family, and her strong female relationships; her emotions, faith, and identity; and the community networks and social events in which she and her family members participated, such as church services, lectures, meetings, and concerts. She also comments on events in the lives of her family members and records memories stretching back to her childhood. Mary's life writing is one of few published examples of diaries by middle-class Canadian women from the mid-nineteenth century, and this rarity magnifies its importance.

I have always been curious about family history, and that interest led me to Mary's diaries, which have been in our extended family for generations. In the summer of 2000, my father and I began to write a short synthesis, mostly for our own interest, of our genealogical discoveries—his from research in Canada and mine from research in the United Kingdom. In drawing together the story of two of our immigrant ancestors, Mary Wickson and her husband, Philip Armstrong, our attention shifted to Mary's diaries. Using a photocopy of the original, the two of us worked as a team and attempted a rough transcription of the earlier diary; I typed while my father read aloud what he could make out of his great-great-grandmother's handwriting.

We made it through the first diary by the end of the summer. I took the photocopy with me to Queen's University when the fall 2000 term began and continued to work on the transcription. It was Sandy Ramos, my instructor in a Canadian social history class, who first pointed out to me the importance of the documents and suggested that I try to make them available to others. Professor Jane Errington helped me set objectives, and the project grew from there. With the originals of the earlier and later diaries on loan from my third cousin Geoffrey Armstrong, and with the aid of a rough transcription of the later diary that he had had made over two decades before, I was able to make a faithful transcription of each. I could now begin to focus on "fleshing out" the raw diaries, providing a suitable amount of background information, and making them accessible to a wider audience.

That process took over two and a half years of additional research and was necessarily slowed by other commitments. However, it did lead me down an exciting path, the highlights of which included presenting a paper on Mary Armstrong at the New Frontiers Graduate History Conference at York University in February 2003 to an audience that had terrific questions and input. Along the way I met new relatives and friends, many of whom shared some wonderful information and pictures of the people that had become so familiar to me through Mary's writing. That process, I hope, is not over; though I have been able to locate a photograph or painting of almost all of Mary's family members, to my great dismay I have not yet found an image of Mary herself—but the search continues.

The introduction to Mary's diaries is divided into two parts. The first, "A Canadian's Story," is a narrative introduction that tells the story of Mary and her family in England and Canada. Here I have tried to ground personal life events within the broader context of the major social and political events of the time. The second part, "A Diarist's World," is an analytical introduction that examines, in the context of relevant secondary literature, the major themes of Mary's writing, which are addressed under separate headings. The objective of the annotation throughout the diaries themselves is to give reasonable contextual information on the events, people, and places that are mentioned, whether they play a small or large role.

As a first-hand account of the life of a wife and mother who lived on a small farm just outside Toronto, and whose close relatives included butchers, farmers, doctors, lawyers, academics, ministers, and local politicians, these diaries are a fountain of information and they should appeal to anyone interested in Canadian social history and the history of women, religion, medicine, immigrant experiences, local history, and, of course, family history.

✳

Acknowledgments

✳

I CANNOT EMPHASIZE ENOUGH how important the role of my father, Dr. Andrew Armstrong, has been in editing these diaries. Without his inspiration, interest, and help in the initial stages of transcription, this project would never have begun. My father's genealogical research that preceded and guided my own, and his vast knowledge and eagerness for discussion have proven invaluable to me and are a testament to his skill as a student of history. For this I owe him my thanks. I also owe thanks to my mother, Wynne Armstrong, for her guidance and encouragement, and to my siblings, Gary and Molly, for their moral support. I am grateful to both my parents for their financial support.

This project involved a geographically wide range of research, and it would have taken much longer to conduct without the kind assistance of many people. Geoffrey Armstrong of Toronto, who holds the original diaries, allowed me not only to borrow them and other family documents for a generous length of time but also to publish them. Alexander Baron, a private researcher in London, England, and Priscilla Lewthwaite, a professional genealogist on the Isle of Man, both spent hours searching through records that I did not have time to consult myself. Helen Cunningham provided a similar service through the Cumbria Record Office, and the other members of staff there were very helpful to me during my several visits. Marian Spence of the Upper Canada College Archives, Christine Bourolias of the Archives of Ontario, and Harold Averill of the University of Toronto Archives provided guidance in my primary research. I am also grateful to Liz Wylie of the University of Toronto Art Centre, Professor Jacalyn Duffin of Queen's University, Felicity Pope of the Canadian Museum of Health and Medicine, and Dr. John Fowler of the Toronto Academy of Medicine for their help at different stages.

Through this process I have discovered new relatives and friends. Marian Blott, another descendant of Mary Armstrong, shared some wonderful family stories and photographs. Ruth Wickson Newman welcomed my father and me into her home and not only eagerly shared her research and private archives with us but also allowed me to use many materials in this publication. Marg Deans of the Paris Museum and Historical Society was also an enormously gracious host who enthusiastically exchanged information on the Wickson family in Brant County and, with Bob Hasler, also of the Society, gave permission for the use of various materials. Professor Edward Alfred Allworth provided a great deal of valuable biographical information relating to Wicksons in Paris, Ontario, and the United States.

I owe a great debt to those who have provided feedback on my writing along the way. My thanks go to two anonymous reviewers from Wilfrid Laurier University Press and the Aid to Scholarly Publications Programme, and to my more informal readers and critics Mistine Webb, Robert Dennis, Anouk Lang, Dr. Alice van Harten, and Professor Robert Malcolmson. Sandra Ramos, Rob Dennis, and Professor Gregory Kealey all took the time to provide some wonderful feedback and information regarding the topic of the butcher trade. Elin Edwards of Wilfrid Laurier University Press lent her guidance and encouragement during the grant application and revision process.

It was Sandy Ramos, my instructor in a course at Queen's University, who first suggested that I find a way to bring these diaries to print. I sincerely appreciate her encouragement, valuable comments, and the opportunity to explore the diaries in class. I owe a great debt to Professor Jane Errington, who generously offered her assistance in the development of this project in its early stages, not only reading drafts but also eagerly giving her free time and advice to an inexperienced student. None of those people who offered help bears responsibility for any errors in this work, which are entirely my own. Finally, I cannot forget to thank Mistine for standing by me and indulging my strange interest in long-dead relatives.

✳

Editor's Note

✳

I N MOST CASES I HAVE CHOSEN to refer to individuals, notably Mary herself, by given name only. Though this is not conventional practice when referring to the author of a text, I have chosen to do so for two reasons. First, my narrative covers Mary's life before and after her marriage, and using Mary's given name provides continuity. Second, I aim to eliminate unnecessary confusion between the many individuals who share a surname. While this style is less formal, it is not intended to convey any less respect.

LIST OF ABBREVIATIONS

AAFP	Andrew Armstrong Family Papers
GAFP	Geoffrey Armstrong Family Papers
AO	Archives of Ontario
CHR	Canadian Historical Review
CRO	Cumbria Record Office
CTA	City of Toronto Archives
LAC	Library and Archives Canada
OH	Ontario History
TNA	The National Archives of the United Kingdom
UCCA	United Church of Canada/Victoria University Archives
WFP	Ruth Wickson Newman Family Papers
1833 Directory	G. Walton, ed., *York Commercial Directory, Street Guide, and Register, 1833-34* (Toronto: T. Dalton, 1833)
1837 Directory	G. Walton, ed., *City of Toronto and Home District Commercial Directory* (Toronto: T. Dalton & W.J. Coates, 1837)
1843-44 Directory	F. Lewis, ed., *The Toronto Directory, and Street Guide for 1843-44* (Toronto: H. & W. Rowsell, 1843)
1846-47 Directory	G. Brown, ed., *Brown's Toronto City and Home District Directory, 1846-47* (Toronto: George Brown, 1846)
1850-51 Directory	J. Armstrong, ed., *Rowsell's City of Toronto and County of York Directory for 1850-51* (Toronto: Henry Rowsell, 1850)
1856 Directory	W.R. Brown, ed., *Brown's Toronto General Directory, 1856* (Toronto: Maclear, 1856)
1859-60 Directory	W.C.F. Caverhill, ed., *Caverhill's Toronto City Directory for 1859-60* (Toronto: W.C.F. Caverhill, 1859)
1861 Directory	W.R. Brown, ed., *Brown's Toronto General Directory, 1861* (Toronto: W.C. Chewett, 1861)
1862-63 Directory	T. Hutchinson, ed., *Hutchinson's Toronto Directory, 1862-63* (Toronto: Lovell & Gibson, 1862)
1864-65 Directory	J.L. Mitchell, ed., *Mitchell's Toronto Directory for 1864-65* (Toronto: J.L. Mitchell, 1864)

1865 Directory	A.S. Irving, ed., *City of Toronto Illustrated Business Directory for 1865* (Toronto, A.S. Irving, 1865)
1866 Directory	*Mitchell and Co.'s General Directory for the City of Toronto and Gazetteer of the counties of York and Peel for 1866* (Toronto: Mitchell, 1866)
1867-68 Directory	J. Sutherland, ed., *City of Toronto Directory for 1867-68* (Toronto: W.C. Chewett, 1867)
1868-69 Directory A	*W.C. Chewett and Co.'s Toronto City Directory, 1868-69* (Toronto: W.C. Chewett, 1868)
1868-69 Directory B	H. McEvoy, ed., *C.E. Anderson and Co.'s Toronto City Directory for 1868-69* (Toronto: C.E. Anderson, 1868)
1870 Directory	W.H. Irwin, ed., *Robertson and Cook's Toronto City Directory for 1870* (Toronto: Daily Telegraph Printing House, 1870)
1871 Directory	*1871 Nason's East and West Ridings of the County of York Directory* (Toronto: Dudley & Burns, 1871)
1871-72 Directory	W.H. Irwin, ed., *Robertson and Cook's Toronto City Directory for 1871-72* (Toronto: Robertson & Cook, 1871)
1873 Directory	*Toronto Directory for 1873* (Toronto: Cherrier, Kirwin, & McGown, 1873)
1876 Directory	*Toronto Directory for 1876* (Toronto: Fisher & Taylor, 1876)
1877 Directory	*Toronto Directory for 1877* (Toronto: Might & Taylor, 1877)
1878 Directory	*Toronto Directory for 1878* (Toronto: Might & Taylor, 1878)
1879 Directory	*Toronto Directory for 1879* (Toronto: Might & Taylor, 1879)

INTRODUCTION
PART I

A Canadian's Story

MARY WICKSON, LIKE SO MANY CANADIANS, was an immigrant. With her family, she left England for a new land at age fifteen. She probably did not have much choice in the matter; as the head of his household, her father made the final decision to uproot and seek new opportunity and prosperity across the ocean.[1] Whether Mary was excited, reluctant, confused, or saddened at the prospect of leaving her home and friends is not known, but she probably felt a mix of emotions about the journey. Perhaps she had read about Canada or heard others speak of it, but no matter how much she thought she knew when she left with her parents, brothers, and sisters, she could not have expected what lay ahead of her. Over her lifetime she witnessed rebellion, the arrival of famine refugees, economic hardship and prosperity, the threat of invasion, and the creation of a new nation. She saw Toronto grow from a city of less than ten thousand to one of more than eighty-five thousand. She witnessed first-hand the changes that shaped Canada from a collection of disparate colonies into a confederation that dreamed of surpassing its southern neighbour. Her story is a revealing account of a time when most families kept their own livestock and made their own clothes. It is about life in a place that is familiar to many Canadians, but in a time that has now passed from living memory.

Mary was born on 18 February 1819. She was baptized at Mansion House Chapel in Camberwell, Surrey. Early nineteenth-century Camberwell was a community on the south side of the Thames that was quickly growing into a suburb of London. In the first three decades of the century the population of Camberwell quadrupled, and by 1837 it had reached about thirty-five thousand. A quiet countryside village in the middle of the eighteenth century, by the 1830s Camberwell was still discernable as a place distinct from London, but the coming of new people tied to the growing metropolis was altering its face forever. The expansion of transportation to the city, primarily through the erection of new bridges across the Thames, allowed the communities that lay south of the river to grow with London. The cutting of new roads enhanced overland communication, allowing people to reside in Camberwell and at the same time to conduct business in the city and have their daily needs supplied. The digging of the Grand Surrey Canal, which ran through the north of Camberwell, opened a route for trade in bulk goods such as coal and timber.[2] Mary's paternal great-grandfather, James Wickson, was one of many new arrivals to expanding Camberwell.

In the late eighteenth century, James Wickson, who was probably a butcher, brought his family south from Eynsham, a town about ten kilometres northwest of Oxford, to the dilating metropolis. His decision to uproot was probably made for reasons similar to those of Mary's father almost half a century later. James from Eynsham had a son—also named James[3]—who was a butcher and lived in nearby Walworth, a community adjacent to Camberwell. James the butcher's son, a third James (Mary's father), went into business as a merchant, no doubt making use of the new Grand Surrey Canal. Mary's father is listed in local directories from the 1820s and 1830s as a coal merchant and corn chandler. James and his family seem to have moved quite often, living over time at a number of addresses in the Camberwell and Walworth area.[4] Mary recalls in her diary living on not only Old Kent Road but also Mount Street and Rosemary Branch Lane, and her birth certificate indicates that she was born at Beckford Row.[5] This mobility was, perhaps, a function of the Wickson family's steady growth and need for more living space.

The growth of the family can be traced in the records kept by their local church. James the coal merchant married Jane Tuesman in 1814, and after their first three children—James (born 1816), John (born 1817), and Mary—they would have four others: George (born 1821), Jane (born 1823), Sarah (born 1824), and William (born 1830). These seven children were baptized in Camberwell at Mansion House Chapel, a Congregationalist church dating from the late eighteenth century. There were at least two other children, Arthur (born 1825) and Samuel (born 1828), who do not appear in the chapel records, though this is not surprising as the records are fairly sparse. By 1830 the evangelical chapel had a membership of 143 people, the Wickson family included.[6] The chapel was a meeting place not just for religious services but also for public lectures and discussions of current issues, such as the debate on the abolition of slavery.[7] As congregants, the Wickson family may well have attended such events.

Mary's parents raised their family in the period of economic booms and slumps that followed the victory over Napoleon in 1815. As industrial capitalism transformed the economy, the impoverished turned to dangerous employment in coalmines and factories to avoid the poorhouses, and the middling classes frantically looked for ways to maintain their income and social status.[8] These stresses generated public responses focused on specific issues. Between the 1810s and 1830s, topics such as abolitionism, Catholic emancipation, and parliamentary reform were at the forefront of British consciousness and often incited violence. A pro-reform demonstration held in Manchester in 1819 ended with soldiers killing eleven and wounding four hundred demonstrators when the local magistracy ordered them to turn against the crowd.[9] The following year saw a weavers' rising in Scotland and attempts to assassinate the cabinet. By 1829 Britain was strained with pronounced economic distress and increasingly frequent radical reform demonstrations. The Reform Act of 1832 redistributed parliamentary seats and extended the franchise, but the decade saw agitation by those discontented with its results, and also with grain import tariffs, slavery abolition, and the New Poor Law of 1834.[10] Times were uncertain in Britain, and it is not surprising that numerous families, like the Wicksons, were looking for more certain alternatives.

For many frustrated Britons, the answer to the economic and social situation was immigration to the diverse colonies of the Empire. Upper Canada, not as far away as Australia or South Africa and with vast amounts of arable land available at a low price, was one of the most attractive destinations. The Canada Company, a London-based firm that sold Canadian land to new settlers, sponsored lectures all over Britain in which Canada's pleasant climate, fertile soil, access to commerce and waterways, and opportunities for creating wealth were exaggerated and embellished. A number of "Emigrant's Guides" to Canada were published and circulated throughout Britain, all of which not only explained the details of how to get to Canada but also how new immigrants could expect to raise a log cabin in a single day with the help of friends and neighbours, and enjoy the easy profits of an industrious farming life. Immigrants, so the guides and lecturers explained, would find the society of the town of York (which later became Toronto) "equal to any provincial town in Britain." References to the nickname "Muddy York" were carefully avoided.[11]

Between 1829 and 1837 a wave of immigration to Canada rose, peaking in the years 1831–32.[12] Perhaps James Wickson was already thinking about leaving England in 1829 when he sold a lease he held on the Mount Street property back to the landlord, William Maidlow, for £155. This sum was considerable and could have purchased the warm clothes and sturdy boots the emigrant's guides said a family would require in the colony, or it could have been invested and held to finance a future land purchase in Canada. A large family travelling in a ship's cabin and planning to settle comfortably in the colony would have needed up to £500 to cover all expenses.[13]

In 1834 the Wickson family left England and sailed six or seven weeks across the north Atlantic to Quebec. From there they would have travelled by land and water to the recently incorporated city of Toronto, Upper Canada. Once settled, Mary's father took up the trade of his own father, James the butcher, and opened a meat business, which he later turned over to Mary's brother John. The Wicksons lived at a series of houses on Yonge Street, and they had a large family. Fifteen-year-old Mary had two older brothers, James and John, aged eighteen and seventeen, respectively. Her six younger siblings ranged in age from four to thirteen. With so many school-aged children to support, James and Jane senior were probably delighted when their older children began to marry. In 1836 James junior returned to Walworth and shortly came back to Canada with a wife. The next year, both Mary and John got married.[14]

On 22 August 1837, the Reverend Dr. Adam Lillie of Brantford, Upper Canada, performed the wedding ceremony for Mary and Philip Armstrong in Toronto. Philip was another English immigrant to Canada, though he had come over a few years before the Wicksons, probably in the late 1820s.[15] It is not entirely clear why Mary and Philip chose to be married by a minister from Brantford. The Wicksons seem to have had family friends and associations in Brant County, and Rev. Lillie, whom Mary wrote about in her 1859 diary, was probably connected to the family in this way.[16]

Philip Armstrong was baptized in Great Corby, Cumberland, on 3 July 1808.[17] Whereas Mary had grown up in the widening London sprawl with the bustle and noise of urban living, Philip was raised in a comparatively sedate, rural community. Great Corby, located on the River Eden eight kilometres to the east of the city of Carlisle, is a village in the parish of Wetheral that could boast a population of only 326 people in 1811. When Philip grew up there in the 1810s and 1820s, the local tenants paid to their gentry landlord, Henry Howard, Esq., a "boon service" of "one day's reaping, one day's ploughing, and one cart load of coals carried to the manor house, or two carts loaded with peat or turf." They were also bound to render a hen to their lord at Martinmas.[18] Philip Armstrong's father was John, a weaver, who died at age fifty-three on 4 December 1807. His wife, Dorothy (Philip's mother), had eight children. The last two were Thomas (born 1806) and Philip (born 1808). Philip was a "posthumous son," born after the death of his father.[19]

Though a search through land-related records does not reveal anything about where the Armstrong family lived in Great Corby, they probably resided in a weaver's cottage not far from Corby Castle, the manor house. Many of these cottages still stand today, though their thatched roofs are now shingled. The cotton industry at the start of the nineteenth century still relied on a significant number of handloom weavers. A loom cost forty shillings, and it was possible to eke out a living weaving cloth, especially when family members could be employed as assistants. However, the handloom was a tool that was gradually being displaced by factories and power looms. The families of factory workers, supported by relatively stable wages, had a chance of improving their standard of living, while handloom weavers' families faced fluctuating wages and a declining quality of life.[20]

Philip's first winter, 1808–1809, was severe, and because of the war with France, the cotton trade was seriously depressed.[21] Having three teenaged boys when her husband died, Dorothy Armstrong was not left entirely on her own to raise her five other children. She probably continued working at the loom after her husband's death, but at least some of her children sought other employment: one seems to have been a gardener and another a joiner.[22] The family was able to erect a headstone for John Armstrong in the parish churchyard, which suggests that they were probably able to manage financially without having to seek official poor relief.[23] However, for a rising number of their contemporaries, official poor relief was becoming the only means for survival in an increasingly unstable and uncertain society.

Cumberland was not immune to the violence bred by the instability of the times. A confrontation occurred in Carlisle during the 1826 election, only a few miles from where Philip Armstrong grew up. When the Tory candidate for Cumberland canvassed a suburban district of the city, the local weavers rioted. The military was called in and fired on the crowd, killing several people.[24] It may have been at this point that Philip recognized the future for handloom weavers was bleak, and the government did not care to protect them. Immigration to the Arcadian lands promised by the Canada Company lecturers, emigrant's guides, and newspapers must have seemed an increasingly attractive option.

Philip's mother died in March 1824, when Philip was fifteen.[25] The next fact known about Philip's life is that his ten-week-old infant daughter, Elizabeth, died in York, Upper Canada, and was buried on 25 July 1831, in a cemetery at the north end of the town.[26] What happened in the interim is unclear, and the only information available is oral family tradition. Supposedly, prior to leaving for Canada, Philip worked as a clerk at Farnham Castle in Surrey, the seat of the Bishop of Winchester. This story cannot be confirmed; however, it is a possible scenario.[27] The youngest of eight children would have had no inheritance—if there were much to be had anyway—and at age fifteen, with his parents dead, Philip would have been thinking of the opportunities realistically available to him. The idea of working to save enough to emigrate and buy some land in the colonies was, perhaps, appealing. If Philip ever went to Farnham, it was only a way-point on his voyage overseas.

Philip probably left England no later than 1829, as his first daughter, Anne, was born about the year 1830 in Upper Canada.[28] His first wife was Mary Calvert, who was born in England, but little is known about where they were married or where they had met. Philip and his first wife had three children, but the second two (both named Elizabeth) died in infancy. The first died in 1831, at ten weeks, of "bilious fever," and the second died in 1833, at nine months, of "water on the brain." Mary herself died in 1836, at age twenty-nine, of consumption.[29] A young widower with a young daughter would have been very keen to find a wife; it was not uncommon for economic and domestic concerns to hasten remarriage when a man or woman lost a spouse in Upper Canada.[30] In August 1837, twenty-nine-year-old Philip Armstrong and nineteen-year-old Mary Wickson were married in Toronto.

The Toronto directories for 1833 and 1837 list Philip as a butcher living on Yonge Street.[31] How he decided to become a butcher is unclear. Family tradition holds that upon his arrival in the town of York, a farmer hired him at the port. Supposedly he worked for this man until he was settled and had opened his own business and acquired property, which he seems to have been able to do quite quickly. Perhaps the farmer who hired Philip (or another member of his household) was a butcher who taught Philip the trade.[32] It was probably through the butcher business that Philip met James Wickson and his son John, both of whom would have eagerly facilitated an introduction between the ambitious widower and young and thoughtful Mary.[33]

The period in which the Wicksons and Philip Armstrong emigrated from England was one of uncertain social and political change, which often boiled over into violence. However, if Mary's family and Philip came to Canada hoping to escape instability and violence, they found themselves in a new land that had its own tensions. William Lyon Mackenzie's newspaper, the *Colonial Advocate*, had since 1824 been advocating responsible government and protesting the Tory oligarchy that ran Upper Canada. The week of Monday, 4 December 1837, saw the march of Mackenzie and five hundred rebels, mostly farmers, down Yonge Street towards Toronto in a disorganized and poorly led attempt to overthrow the government and establish an independent Upper Canada on an American model. The ragtag rebellion collapsed when local militia outnumbered the rebels and forced them to disband.[34]

Mary and Philip did not record their opinions on the rebellion, though a short posthumous biography of Philip notes that he was "a strong [Robert] Baldwin Reformer" in his early life, so he was not likely to have been part of the more radical uprising.[35] The couple may have stayed inside behind locked doors with little Anne; or perhaps they went to stay with Mary's family when things became tense. It appears that they conceived their first child in the same month as the rebellion. The following year, in the aftermath of the insurrection, while small-time border raids by "patriots" based in the United States were put down by local militia and regulars, and while Lord Durham came to Canada as Governor General and compiled his report of recommendations on colonial government, the people of the Upper Canada got back down to business.[36]

In August 1838, a year after their marriage, Mary and Philip's son, Thomas, was born. He would be a stepbrother to eight-year-old Anne. A local doctor delivered Thomas at Philip and Mary's house on Yonge Street.[37] While female relatives were probably present to assist Mary during her labour and recovery, the ability to pay for the services of an attending physician was a sign that Philip and Mary had achieved some financial security by this time; however, Mary's family may have helped cover the cost.[38] Thomas was an addition to the growing population of Upper Canada; the arrival of large numbers of British immigrants throughout the decade had increased the size of urban centres and driven the pioneer frontier further into the backwoods.[39]

In 1839 Philip acquired six acres of land in York County, not far outside of the boundary of Toronto. This was at lot twenty-one on the west side of Yonge Street, a few blocks south of the third concession line, or what is now St. Clair Avenue.[40] He bought the land for £200 from John Elmsley and his wife, Charlotte.[41] A Toronto directory for the mid-1840s records Philip and Mary as residents of York Township, and Mary's eldest brother, James Wickson, is listed in the same directory as a butcher on Yonge Street.[42] The 1850–51 city and county directory records Philip as a butcher with his residence on "Yonge-street road, north of the toll-bar," and both he and Mary are listed as residents of lot twenty-one in York Township.[43] In her diaries, Mary calls this property "Rose Hill," and the history of this name is easily deduced. The land across Yonge Street was owned by the wealthy tanner Jesse Ketchum. He built a house there in 1836 and gave it and the surrounding property to his daughter Anna, who married a private banker named Walter Rose in the same year. The house took the name Rose Hill, as it was situated on the hillcrest that runs east to west below St. Clair Avenue. The house gave its name to the area, and Philip and Mary seem to have adopted it for their property as well.[44]

In early 1841, two years after Mary and Philip bought their Rose Hill property, the provinces of Upper and Lower Canada were united under one constitution. However, in practice what was created was an almost federal union of two provinces, Canada East and Canada West, operating under a single legislature divided into halves. The franchise in the counties included those with land worth at least forty shillings a year, and in the cities those who owned houses worth five pounds a year or tenants paying ten pounds a year in rent. Landholders of Philip's stature, therefore, participated in colonial politics, but Mary, as a woman, was denied an independent political voice. The doctrine of marital unity, dominant at the time, meant that the male head of the household spoke for all his dependents, including his wife, who upon her marriage relinquished her legal sovereignty.[45]

The population of Canada West in 1841 had grown to 480,000, and that of Canada East to 670,000. In Canada West, about half of the English majority were immigrants from Britain, and the population of Toronto was 14,000. The city, which had been incorporated in 1834 and changed its name from York, superseded Kingston as the commercial centre of the western province even if, for a time, Kingston would be the new capital. In the meantime, Yonge Street had been "macadamized"—laid with interlocking stone or gravel—almost the distance to Lake Simcoe. Along this route and others the growing city communicated with the expanding network of rural settlements.[46] With their Yonge Street property, Mary and Philip lived on a main artery of the colony and within walking distance of the most important city in the region. By the mid-1840s Toronto had grown to a size of 20,000.[47]

In 1848, Anne Armstrong, Philip's first daughter, was eighteen years old. On 1 November that year, she married Robert Pallett in St. James' Cathedral in Toronto.[48] Robert was unable to sign his own name on the certificate, and not much is known of his origins. The 1851 census lists him as a butcher, a Wesleyan Methodist, aged twenty-four, and born in England. From the ages listed in the census for Anne and Robert's two children, William and Mary Ann, four and one respectively, it seems possible that they married because Anne was pregnant.[49] Neither Philip nor Mary witnessed the wedding, but Mary made reference in her diary to Robert and Anne "sitting down" with her the night they "went down to Mr. Grassett's to be married," so it does not seem to have been an elopement, but it does not seem to have been planned to any great extent either.[50] Anne Pallett would die in 1855. Afterwards, her son would live with Robert, and her daughter, Mary Ann, would go to live with Mary and Philip at Rose Hill for a number of years.

At the same time that Anne and Robert were married, events were taking shape overseas that would impact on the Canadian colonies. The failure of the potato crop in the British Isles caused unprecedented starvation and social upheaval in Ireland. In 1846 roughly 40,667 Irish came to British North America to seek food and work. The next year that number increased by more than two and a half times to 104,518—a number made more significant when one considers that the population of Canada West in 1848 stood at 725,879 persons. A great number of these immigrants came having spent most or all of their money moving their families to the New World.[51] Most came in a terrible state of health. "Coffin ships" carried immigrants afflicted with scurvy, dysentery, cholera, and typhus up the St. Lawrence River. The first stopping points for immigrants in Canada West were the port cities, such as Kingston and Toronto, and the reaction of locals was initially fear: a Kingston newspaper described the city as almost deserted in August 1847 for fear of "the emigrant disease."[52] The humanitarian disaster overwhelmed the government, churches, and charities. The Roman Catholic Bishop of Toronto, Dr. Michael Power, died of a fever he contracted while assisting the sick and dying. Fourteen hundred famine refugees died of typhus in Kingston and were buried there in mass graves.[53]

No record exists of how Mary and Philip reacted to the wave of immigrants arriving in Toronto. Did they lend assistance at the "emigrant sheds" or did they keep away from the sick? Did they make donations to help the newcomers or did they focus on their own lives? The impact of the arrival of so many people fleeing such a terrible situation shaped the end of the 1840s in Canada. As Mary and Philip and their young son moved with the city into the next decade, they could hardly have ignored the huge changes that were pushing Toronto and the colony towards maturity.

Philip was not only a butcher but also a small farmer. On his property at Rose Hill and his other land in York County known as Maple Woods, Hazel Dell Fields, and Woodhill, he cultivated oats, wheat, hay, potatoes, peas, turnips, rutabagas, carrots, clover, and wood for market.[54] He also kept bees and a fruit orchard for apples, and he kept horses for work and transportation and oxen for ploughing. As gender roles dictated, Mary took charge of the poultry and dairy; she had several hens and a few cows, and she sold calves, eggs, and butter at market. The Armstrongs lived a life that was dependent on agriculture, so it is not surprising that Philip became involved with local agricultural and horticultural societies at an executive level and attended the shows of these societies as both a contestant and a judge. In the two years leading up to his death he was heavily involved in the planning of the first Industrial Exhibition in Toronto, the forerunner of the modern Canadian National Exhibition, which took place in September 1879. Philip died in March of that year and never witnessed the culmination of his and others' efforts.[55]

While Mary's husband was a skilled and successful self-employed tradesman and an avid agriculturalist, her son, like her brothers Samuel and Arthur, chose a professional career. After first attempting to enter the bacon business in 1858 and taking a loss of eighty dollars due to his generosity in extending credit (which would have been difficult in the middle of the depression of 1857–1860), Thomas changed gears.[56] He entered medical school and graduated from the Toronto School of Medicine in 1862. In the following year he married Fidelia Jane Maughan.[57] Thomas and Fidelia lived first in Brougham, to the east of Toronto, but soon settled in York Mills, three and a half miles north of Rose Hill along Yonge Street, in the valley of the West Don River. In 1868 Thomas took over the practice of a retiring doctor in the area. In time, Fidelia and Thomas provided Mary with six grandchildren who lived to adulthood.

By January 1859, when Mary started her first surviving diary, she was thirty-nine years old, less than two months away from her fortieth birthday. She had been married to Philip for twenty-one years, and her only son, Thomas, was twenty years old and still a medical student. She was also a step-grandmother; eleven-year-old Mary Ann Pallett had been living with the Armstrongs since her mother Anne's death in 1855. Samuel Wickson, Mary's brother, had moved in with the family at Rose Hill and had gone into business with Philip.[58] Mary was a middle-aged woman who, by nineteenth-century standards, was entering her mature years.

Living on the Rose Hill property just north of Yorkville, Mary and Philip were a part of the city life of Toronto. Philip worked in the St. Lawrence Market, and their son, Thomas, attended medical lectures downtown while living at home. The family was involved with Toronto-based organizations like the St. George's Society and the Methodist Missionary Society. In the city they attended parties, temperance meetings, and public lectures by travelling speakers and professors. The Armstrongs were also members of the broader rural community of York Township, as Philip's involvement with the county agricultural society illustrates. Yorkville, the small "suburb" with a population of about eighteen hundred on the northern border of the city, formed the Armstrong's immediate community, their focal point being the Yorkville Church on Bloor Street. Yorkville maintained an identity distinct from Toronto itself. Beginning at Bloor Street and running north almost to St. Clair Avenue, Yorkville was incorporated into a separate village in 1853. The trip into downtown Toronto was facilitated by a horse-drawn omnibus that ran between the Yorkville post office and St. James' Cathedral four times an hour.[59]

Mary lived in a colony that was growing quickly. Canada West had a "well-knit agricultural community" of prosperous farmers, merchants, and professionals who were leaders of a largely agrarian society. Wheat farming was the backbone of agriculture, and the agricultural associations and fairs in which Philip Armstrong was so involved provided focal points for the improvement of produce and livestock breeds. By the 1850s, however, the pioneer era had ended and the role of towns and commerce in the development and organization of the province was becoming paramount. After economic depression and the strain of famine refugee immigration in the 1840s, the 1850s saw an economic boom for Canada and its trade partners. The spread of railway networks, enhanced trade ties with the United States, and the growth of the finance, timber, and steamship industries were signs of industrial capitalism taking root in the colony.[60] However, the boom broke in 1857 and a three-year economic depression took a heavy toll on smaller producers and large merchants while at the same time concentrating economic power around industrial capital.[61]

In the 1850s, the seat of government of the united Canadas rotated between Toronto and Quebec, and by 1859 the government had been in Toronto for five years. Debate on the question of the permanent location of the legislature filled the pages of the *Globe* in the early winter months of January and February 1859. Eventually Ottawa was decided on, but with the concession that until the parliament buildings there were ready, Quebec would be made the interim capital.[62] While internal politics rolled on, the colonial government was also planning for security. A voluntary defence force, the ranks of which filled quickly, was created in 1855, but the threat of invasion from the south was receding.[63] Perhaps of more concern was the threat of fire in expanding cities like Toronto, especially after the devastating blaze that destroyed many buildings around King Street East in 1849.[64] Meanwhile, the colony developed culturally. Newspapers like the *Globe* owed their continued existence to the economic growth of the 1850s. Despite the depression of 1857–60, permanent benefits of prosperity included public venues in Toronto like the Royal Lyceum Theatre and the St. Lawrence Hall, which became centres for concerts, lectures, and meetings. Canadian literature also blossomed with the publication in 1852 of Susanna Moodie's *Roughing It in the Bush*. Building upon publications in the 1830s by her sister Catharine Parr Traill and Anna Jameson, Moodie's work brought recognition to writing by Canadian gentlewomen about their experiences as immigrants to a new land.[65]

It was in this economic, political, and cultural world that Mary found herself when she began her first surviving diary on New Year's Day, 1859. Frustratingly, the diary concludes at the end of May, and we do not hear from Mary again until January 1869. In the intervening years, Mary probably carried on her life much as she had previously. As she took up her pen to write on New Year's Day, 1869, she was forty-nine years old and approaching her fiftieth birthday. She still lived with Philip at Rose Hill, but her brother Samuel, her son, Thomas, and her step-granddaughter, Mary Ann, had all moved out of Rose Hill. Thomas was a practising physician living in York Mills with his wife, Fidelia, and their first three children. Mary's health, a recurring theme in her writing, was comparable to what it had been ten years previously, though she seemed generally less confident of her strength in the wintertime.[66]

Philip, meanwhile, had left the meat business. After forming a partnership with another butcher at the St. Lawrence Market in 1864, Philip seems to have sold his share to his partner, John McCarter, by 1867.[67] He had also taken an opportunity to expand his landholdings and farming activities. He bought property from the Rose estate, to the east of Rose Hill, totalling thirty-three acres in two separate lots. It appears that this cost him £505.[68] This purchase is a sign that Philip had achieved some financial success and consequently had capital at hand. Land values were climbing throughout the nineteenth century and Philip saw that the real estate market was a profitable investment.[69] He did not just hold the land for speculation but put it to work. Hazel Dell Fields, which Mary referred to in her later diary, is the twenty-three-acre lot acquired in the 1864 purchase from the Rose estate. The Armstrongs built a barn on this property. They kept cows there and used the land to grow crops such as turnips and peas.[70] Additionally, in her later diary Mary mentioned that Philip employed at least four farm hands, whereas ten years before only two were mentioned. These hands may have been boarding with the family.[71] It seems that with the purchase of new property, Philip needed to employ more labourers to farm his different plots of land.

Another sign of the Armstrongs' increased affluence in 1869 is the fact that Mary no longer mentioned taking the omnibus to travel into the city, as she did in 1859.[72] Though a horse-drawn railcar had forced the horse-drawn omnibus service out of business in the early 1860s, Mary did not mention using this form of early mass transportation in her later diary.[73] Instead, she recorded more genteel "rides" or "drives" into the city in the family carriage or buggy, rather than praising the omnibus for its "great accommodation at a very low rate" as she had a decade earlier.[74] The purchases made by Mary and Philip at the bailiff's sale on 1 April 1869 also suggest a higher level of affluence. They acquired a "quantity of good furniture," including a bookcase, a toilette stand and mirror, a black walnut cupboard, a black walnut washstand, six volumes of David Hume's *History of England,* and five other books with a stand table for just over seventy dollars. Though they purchased these items at what Mary believed to be a bargain, the acquisition is still a sign that by this time they were comfortable enough to spend a significant amount of money when the opportunity arose.

While the Armstrong property grew, their colony underwent important political changes. The 1860s saw years of negotiation between the British North American colonies for a deal that would unite them into a confederate nation. These negotiations were set against the backdrop of the American Civil War, which touched even the Armstrong family when Mary and Philip's son, Thomas, was asked by the Union Army if he would serve as a medical officer, a request he turned down.[75] The mid-1860s saw tension with the United States over economic and military issues.[76] The Fenian Raids of 1866 and 1870 unsettled the Canadian-American border when militant Irish Americans sought to attack Britain by raiding the North American colonies.[77] Confederation was achieved two years before Mary's second diary, and during the late 1860s and early 1870s, Canadians were busy undertaking the task of assimilating laws and institutions and seeking the inclusion of the other colonies to the east and west as they attempted to build a nation that could compete with the United States.[78]

In these exciting years of change, Mary continued to run her household, tending to the hens and cows, cooking, baking, cleaning, and sewing.

Her world was not that of high politics but of daily chores, church, and social gatherings with family members and neighbours. Her involvement with temperance and educational lectures, missionary societies and the St. George's Society, so significant to her in 1859, seems to have tapered off, or at least these groups and events do not feature in her 1869 diary. Perhaps as Mary aged she found that she had less energy to remain as involved with the community as she had aspired to be ten years earlier.[79]

Mary and Philip would live long, but not lingering, lives. From at least 1866 Philip served as a justice of the peace for York County, and a county directory from the early 1870s lists Philip as a freeholder and a gentleman. He was still a JP when he died on 23 March 1879, at home, of congestion of the lungs. He was seventy years old.[80] After his death, his land on Yonge Street passed to his son, and in 1889 the city put a road through the dividing line between his property and the property to the north and named it Farnham Avenue.[81] Mary died of heart disease on 18 July 1881, aged sixty-two. She lived her last months in Paris, Ontario, and was buried beside her husband and grandchildren in Mount Pleasant Cemetery north of Toronto. She was living with her family in Paris when she grew seriously ill.[82] Mary's life was eventful but, in comparison with her contemporaries, not particularly unique. For those interested in the past, what is perhaps most significant about Mary's life is that she was able to record pieces of it in writing. Her two personal diaries are records of daily events and chores, the people she visited, and the tasks she completed, but they are also rich sources for historical analysis. They speak to broader themes of life in Victorian English Canada, which are the subject of the next section.

⁂

INTRODUCTION

PART II

A Diarist's World

M ARY'S DIARIES, OVER 25,000 WORDS IN LENGTH, are exactly the type of document that Barbara Maas was referring to in 1990 when she speculated that many female-related historical sources were probably still lying in private hands, their academic value unknown to their owners. As the private journals of an "ordinary woman," Mary's relatively brief diaries give us a rich glimpse of Canadian life in the 1850s and 1860s. While most published nineteenth-century life writing by Canadian women was written before 1840 or after 1870, Mary's writing fills a gap in this genre in the decades around mid-century. Moreover, her diaries are written from the perspective of a middle-class author rather than, as with most published journals, a member of the colonial elite. These valuable documents speak to themes of life writing, family, women's work, status and class, occupation, faith, social networks and community, and local and national identity for the author and her family.[1]

Life Writing

Diaries have been described as a "personal periodical record" in which an individual, usually on a daily basis, writes about some aspect of her or his life.[2] Scholars have generally used the terms "journal" and "diary" interchangeably, and this analysis does the same.[3] A diary, which can take a variety of forms, is a type of life writing, a genre that has been defined as consisting of fictional or non-fictional "documents ... written out of a life, or ... out of a personal experience of the writer."[4] Aside from their value as literary texts, diaries are valuable primary sources for historians.[5] In particular, women's life writing represents a rich field for historical inquiry into private life and an important source for recovering women's histories.[6]

The Anglo-American secular diary became a common form of life writing in the eighteenth and nineteenth centuries, reaching what some have argued to be its height in the Victorian period when private writing became a favourite pastime for many men and women. With roots in the spiritual autobiographies of early modern religious dissenters, and apparently even earlier beginnings in late medieval private prayer books in which owners made diary-like insertions, it is hardly surprising that the content of some women's diaries from the nineteenth century has a strong religious focus. Many authors wrote about their personal spiritual development and religious activities.[7] Conversely, women's diaries from this period can also record little personal inward reflection, being no more than simple account books. Most women's diaries tend to exist somewhere between these two extremes.[8] In their journals, women from this period tended to focus on other people, but they also filled empty pages with memoranda and miscellanea that included monthly accounts, information on animals, recipes, remedies, lists of social visits received and returned, as well as records of expenditures and daily activities.[9] The content of Mary's diaries is equally diverse. In the back of her later diary she recorded payments made on bills for "dry goods" and "small wheat," but she also mentioned that she kept a separate account book.[10] Otherwise, her writing varies from a descriptive tally of her daily chores to a commentary on the exciting and trying events in her life to a vehicle for her to formalize thoughts, recall memories, and express powerful emotions. It is not a spiritual diary, but it is more than simply lists of information. It served a number of purposes and incorporated different themes.

By the late eighteenth century, girls were frequently encouraged to keep a journal and to read their mothers' diaries, while published journals and advice manuals directed at women helped to shape the genre.[11] Women's diaries were very often semi-public family documents written for the benefit of a future audience, usually the author or her family members. It was not uncommon for diarists to use the personal pronoun "we" instead of "I," emphasizing the collective family identity as the subject of the narrative.[12] In this capacity, women played the roles of family and community historians and were the chroniclers of births, deaths, and marriages.[13] Mary may have intended her journal to be a family document. Certainly, she focused her writing on her domestic life and the lives of her family members, but her more personal emotional entries suggest that her writing served purposes other than merely being a family chronicle. It is clear that Thomas was aware of his mother's diaries, but it is unknown if he, Philip, Samuel, Mary Ann, or anyone else read the diaries during Mary's lifetime.[14] Thomas kept them when she died and passed them down to her grandchildren and great-grandchildren, keeping them in the family.

While a diarist's motives and intentions can change over time, female diary writing was frequently justified with an emphasis on the practical utility of the activity, such as self-improvement or the preservation of memories.[15] Though they may not have articulated such motivations, some diarists might also have written because of an urge to find a sense of control and continuity, preserve a part of the self for posterity, and give shape to the meaning of life.[16] Nineteenth-century "folk" diaries from the rural American Midwest, which Marilyn Motz has analyzed in detail, demonstrate that writers tended to make symbolic attempts to control the least predictable elements of life—the weather and death—by "imposing order on events" through repetition and recording patterns.[17] Mary's entries very frequently, though not always, included a comment about the weather and the number of eggs laid by her hens; some shorter entries contain little else. Her choice to repeat this information could be seen as a desire to trace patterns and to order these regular yet unpredictable parts of her daily life. While she mentioned the weather in a number of positions in her entries, she most often concluded with a tally of eggs laid. One gets the impression that this was something of a ritualistic closing that Mary practised—a regular habit that, like the tallying of eggs itself, provided a sense of daily continuity. If it was a habit, she had ceased it by 1869: in her later diary she only made one record of the number of eggs laid. Though she continued to note the weather in her entries, her reasons for no longer tallying her eggs are unclear.[18]

Mary made no formal statement of purpose in her diaries. She may have kept other journals that have not survived; indeed, she may have been a diarist for much of her life. The casual manner in which she began her earlier journal suggests that she was comfortable with this type of writing and was not embarking upon it for the first time. Though she did not mention any of her female relatives writing or keeping a diary, other family members might have had the same hobby: she made a number of ambiguous references to her brother Samuel's "writing," which may have been in a journal.[19] Mary did not attempt to justify her diary by claiming its utility, but she stated her "great fancy for old memorys" on two occasions, and this typically Victorian sentimentality seems to have been one of her motivations.[20] She frequently filled her entries with records of daily chores and activities, and though she does not tell us why she chose to record this information, it is plausible that she had a desire to preserve the details of her life from oblivion. Having time alone with herself prompted Mary to write. In one entry she recorded that "I may be said to be alone, which is the reason for my writing so much."[21] Solitude seems to have allowed her time to collect her thoughts and record the events of her day.

Self-improvement was another impetus for many nineteenth-century female diarists. The process of self-improvement involved self-criticism, and this was something that came easily to many Victorian women.[22] While religious faith could stoke an active conscience, guilt, low self-confidence, and low self-esteem were symptoms of the "cultural devaluation" that women faced in this period. Female diarists regularly searched for, and found, a myriad of personal flaws and faults. Moral failings were a common personal criticism, but so were neglecting household duties and neglecting the duty of keeping up the diary itself.[23] Unlike many women, Mary made no apologies for missing days in her journal, and she was comfortable making entries at intervals that suited her. Seldom self-critical, Mary did however feel the need to justify writing a long entry, which is evidence to support the claim that women have been historically uneasy about their personal writing.[24]

While women could be critical of themselves in their writing, they could also criticize other people. Mary was, on at least one occasion, critical of another woman's looks. In April 1859 she commented that she had been introduced to "a young Lady, who did not come quite up to my idea of elegance."[25] While hostility towards and criticism of other women was culturally discouraged, many Victorian women seem to have had an almost automatic reflex to evaluate and rank other women's looks, dress, and fashion choices. Though they eagerly acknowledged beauty when they saw it, female diarists could indulge an urge to identify a flaw in others.[26] Criticism of others could also extend beyond seemingly petty jabs at other women's appearances and take a moralistic tone—with drunkenness, for example, typically considered a moral failing open to censure.[27] Mary was highly critical of one of her deceased neighbours, Mr. Rose, whom she believed to have neglected his duty as a husband and father because of his intemperance.[28]

Alongside the important role criticism of self and others played in diary writing, self-affirmation was another significant motivation for diarists from Mary's period. A diary was a space where women were permitted and encouraged to indulge their sense of self-worth.[29] Women tended to commend themselves not for aggressiveness or competitiveness but for successfully completing a task, for charitable work, artistic talent, and physical accomplishments. Certain character traits were also frequently lauded,

such as loyalty, integrity, honesty, forbearance, prudence, resourceful-
ness, industry, determination, and adaptability.[30] Mary praised her own
economy and industry as a housekeeper. On different occasions she stated
that she felt satisfaction with completed work.[31] Mary affirmed her familial roles as mother, daughter, sister, and wife.[32] An expression of pride
and a sense of accomplishment in relation to these familial roles was typical of nineteenth-century diarists, many of whom defined their self-worth
by their gender roles and the esteem they received from their loved ones.[33]
Most authors held very conventional assumptions about their womanhood and aspirations, as Mary certainly did.[34]

Mary seems to have reread and edited her entries, a process that
implied reflection on her narrative and exploration of her evolving self
as portrayed within it.[35] Diaries allow authors an opportunity for such
reflection. An autobiographical "book of the self" that demands self-artic-
ulation and fosters self-exploration, diary keeping is an assertion of identity.[36] However, while Victorian women may have been interested in
themselves, they usually did not consider their self-interest to be an accept-
able reason for keeping a diary, and consequently, some diarists apologized
for being preoccupied with their own lives.[37] Without apology, Mary eval-
uated elements of her life. On New Year's Day, 1869, as if to make a fresh
start, she reckoned that all her debts were settled. She made a similar
entry on 6 January in her earlier diary, the day she bought the book in
which she wrote. Her stated aim in that entry was "to take stock, and see
how I stand in the world," and she proceeded to review the farm animals
under her care, her household stores, her wardrobe, the state of the carpets, and her son's decision to begin medical school. In such entries,
Mary examined and reviewed her life. Summary entries, usually made on
an occasion such as the new year or an anniversary and after a significant
event such as a marriage or a birth, were a common practice among
female diarists. These entries allowed the writer to assess her life, count
her blessings, evaluate her behaviour, and anticipate the future.[38] Mary's
birthday entry for 1859 was relatively long and concerned almost exclusively with childhood memories, but her entry on the same date a decade
later was much more concise. If Mary did not use her diary to explore her
inner self, she did use it to examine her outer life in more practical terms,
and by doing so she asserted and affirmed her identity.[39]

The desire for emotional sustenance and the relief that came from
translating feelings into words could make diary writing an addictive
hobby. A journal could contain an author's emotional record of her experiences.[40] One scholar has noted that remarks about the weather in some

diaries served as a symbol for the physical and emotional condition of the writer.[41] Through her writing, Mary was able to explore and express a range of emotions in her own terms. In one uncharacteristically expressive entry, she wrote about feeling anxiety, relief, joy, and excitement to the point of tears.[42] On other occasions, she recorded a number of positive emotions, such as being happy; feeling peace of mind, gladness, joy; enjoying herself; and feeling comforted.[43] Mary also wrote about her negative feelings, which included uneasiness with her father's illness, not feeling well herself, feeling poorly and fatigued, feeling restless and indisposed, being "much affected" by sad news, her heart feeling "very heavy," and recalling a "complete revulsion of my feelings" in response to a doctor's remarks.[44] She also recorded that her husband's bad temper affected her "a good deal," and caused her to feel "very poorly."[45] On one occasion she indicated a connection between the weather being gloomy and feeling "dull" herself.[46] Mary's response to negative emotions was often to ignore their cause in the hope that it would pass. In regard to her husband's temper, she stated, "I always mean, not to mind it," and on another occasion she wrote that she was "always for letting every thing alone."[47] After robbers had broken into her henhouse, she resolved that "the sooner I forget all about it the better." She noted at another time that she "felt much better" having distracted herself by going to town with her mother.[48]

While Mary recorded both good and bad feelings in her diary, she did not dwell upon her negative feelings. She did not seem to experience sustained depression or hysteria, which were evident in many women's diaries from her period.[49] The closest Mary came to exhibiting this type of behaviour was in May 1859, when her husband hosted potential buyers for divided lots of the property at Rose Hill. Mary was saddened at the idea of the division of the property, and though she must have understood the need for the sale, she objected to it and expressed her feelings in her diary, which were that Rose Hill was being unfairly "mutilated." During the sale, Mary retreated to "desired seclusion" in her bedroom with her window up and the blinds closed, so that she could "see all without being seen."[50] This was an isolated episode, and Mary did not record seeking isolation on other occasions.

While diarists actively expressed some feelings and emotions, they avoided certain topics. Scholars have argued that diarists' silences, created by both conscious and unconscious choices, reveal the censored nature of feminine thought. In choosing what to write about, diarists found themselves in a process of selecting different details in an attempt to create a persona, and this selection was shaped by the implied or expected presence of a reading audience.[51] For example, the body was treated circumspectly: sex, menstruation, menopause, and even childbirth were rarely discussed openly, if at all.[52] Not surprisingly, Mary did not write about any of these topics. Female Victorian diarists also avoided discussion of certain feelings, a practice that was related to a cultural tendency to control their own thoughts and repress strong emotions. Women may have felt shameful of putting their feelings into words; they may have been confused by their emotions or afraid of stirring up bad feelings (such as grief or wounded pride) that lay dormant. These factors contributed to the limitations on their writing. Some diarists chose to censor their emotional outbursts with punctuation, using exclamation marks in place of words.[53] While she did not record emotional outbursts or go into detail about tensions in the family (such as Philip's temper or a possibly strained relationship between Philip and Thomas), Mary had no problem recollecting her experience of grief at the death of her stepdaughter.[54] Mary did not use punctuation to mask her words, but she did use dashes or drawn lines to indicate emphatic pauses in her text. She does not seem to have sanitized her writing about the events she recorded; however, what she did choose to write about fits safely within the boundaries and conventions observed by other diarists of her period.

One of the boundaries that many women attempted to maintain in their writing was the line between the personal and the political. In most women's journals, political events usually appeared only as peripheral elements. Without the right to vote, women did not directly participate in government; but they did nonetheless tend to note particularly newsworthy events in their diaries, and some women spent a great deal of time writing about politics or business.[55] Mary made one of her few political comments in February 1859 when she noted the impending removal of the colonial government to Quebec City. Mary wrote that this debate generated "a great talk" in the community, and she expressed her own feelings on the issue, which were fairly detached: "it does not bother me, I expect there will always be people enough, to buy all the eggs and butter I have to spare, and if not we can eat them ourselves, the fields will look as green, the birds will sing as sweetly as ever and I shall not miss the passing of the Governor's Carriage."[56] Content with life as it was, Mary distanced herself from the "great talk" that was going on. Her concern was not for the colony at large but for her individual household.

Though she could distance herself from the world of politics, she found it difficult not to be moved by certain current events. Mary took time to write about the execution of two young murderers, John O'Leary and

James Fleming, in early March 1859. Despite the seriousness of their crimes, Mary felt "much affected" when she thought about their fate, and was quite touched by the story of O'Leary's sister, who had come from Ireland to Canada looking for her brother only to locate him in the pages of the *Globe* during his trial.[57] There seems to have been a large turnout of women to witness the public hangings of the two men outside the old jail. One is left wondering whether their sympathy was with the criminals, the sister, or the tragedy of the whole situation. Many women seem to have shared Mary's interest in the trial, which was far more pronounced than her concern over the removal of the government. It is clear that Mary was very aware of newsworthy events, information that she acquired both by word-of-mouth and through the newspaper. She paid attention to the broader world around her, and when she wanted to, she used her diary to comment on the events that she found noteworthy or interesting.

Health was a dominant theme in Mary's journals. During the course of the earlier diary, she recorded the progress of her fight with a winter case of influenza and a spring cold. In the later diary, she was disabled for a few days in January by a boil of some sort on her finger, which stopped her from doing certain chores. While taking these health problems in her stride, she frequently wrote about them in her diary.[58] Health as a theme also appears in her concern with her ageing father, then in his mid-sixties. Her entries for 13 through 24 January 1859 describe his illness, which appears to have been a severe fever causing temporary loss of consciousness and memory. As a caring mother, Mary also noted her son's health and her anxiety about a small operation he underwent to remove a neck tumour in May 1859.[59] She also made frequent mention of her step-granddaughter Mary Ann's well-being.[60] Health was a significant theme in nineteenth-century women's diaries. Like Mary, other diarists were not only preoccupied with their own health, but also that of family members. Mothers were especially concerned about their children and they often used their journals to monitor a child's illnesses. As sons aged and left their care, first for school and later for work, mothers seemed to be particularly interested in their condition.[61] Notes on health could also be a form of diary code for an individual's emotions, where the author or a family member was described not as being happy or unhappy but as being well or unwell.[62] Mary did not seem to use wellness and illness to indicate emotions, but her preoccupation with health was strong, and it was typical of female diarists of her period.

Related to the theme of health was Mary's perception of doctors. Doctors were people Mary held in awe and respect—they had the knowledge to tell her if her father was sick enough to die. Such awe was never-theless not incompatible with a degree of mistrust. When the doctor reported that her father's illness was "the breaking up of his constitu-tion," Mary felt revulsion and recalled the words of the doctor who had said her dying sister-in-law "was getting better till the night before she died."[63] Mary wrote about having similar feelings years earlier when another doctor had been unable to say with certainty that her father would recover.[64] In other instances, such as Thomas's neck operation, she revealed a nervous faith and "confidence" in medical wisdom.[65] Such a combination of awe, fear, trust, and mistrust defined Mary's view of doc-tors and medicine, and was not uncommon in her period.[66] In the early to mid-nineteenth century, physicians were considered by wives and moth-ers to be advisors in health matters.[67] However, nineteenth-century doc-tors were more often associated with death than with healing. A physician's treatments, which might include bloodletting or mercury medications, often unwittingly hastened the dying patient to his or her grave. Though women usually conceded to a doctor's authority, some resisted by quar-relling over medication and treatments, acts that have been interpreted as challenges to male authority.[68] While Mary did not challenge the mas-culine, medical authority of physicians, she was not particularly comfort-able with it.

Despite her misgivings about doctors, when Mary's own son took up the medical profession, she was very proud. In April 1859, Mary wrote that she felt a sense of peace and contentment "partly owing, to Thos having commenced his Studies which occupies all his time."[69] A decade later, when Thomas was a practising physician, Mary would delight in referring to him as "The Doctor (my dear son)." This delight was probably twofold: having a physician in the family not only reinforced her social status but also was a practical convenience. She did not have to call upon a local doc-tor to look after her aches and pains; now she could have her own son give her his expert opinion and care. In an age when illness was still in many ways a mystery and society was only just beginning to understand the importance of sanitation and public hygiene, the presence of a physician in the family would have been particularly comforting.[70]

A final theme of Mary's writing, notably in her earlier diary, is an apparent obsession with death, another typical characteristic of older women's diaries of her period.[71] Given the mortal dangers of childbirth and the amount of time women spent nursing sick and dying family mem-bers, it is hardly surprising that they should so frequently write about death.[72] More generally, a mid-nineteenth-century "popular preoccupation with death"—not exclusive to women—may have been associated with millenarian enthusiasm and religious revivalism, and may have been reinforced by the uncertainty and precariousness of life.[73]

In her writing, Mary often returned to the theme of death in different ways. She recorded her fear of her father's death, and similar fear felt by her siblings.[74] Her gloomy theme resurfaced when recollecting the death of her stepdaughter, Anne Pallett, Mary recalled Anne's unidentified recurring illness and concern about who would take care of her daughter, Mary Ann, after her death. The account is quite pitiable, especially Mary's description of Anne's conversation with her doctor, who "told her, she was dying, but she seemed to think not, she said ['] Oh Dr. you should not tell me so, you know I am so nervous [.']"[75] Well-constructed deathbed scenes involving dialogue, like this one, appeared frequently in women's diaries from this time.[76] Mary also explored death through her childhood reminiscences. She mentioned her first encounter with death, an incident in which a rocking chair crushed a guinea pig. She wrote, "my two other brothers and myself, did not make much noise after that, I question if we ever knew what death was before but I remember there was a silence in the kitchen then, such as had not been that evening before."[77]

Mary's emotion over the execution of Fleming and O'Leary, and over the sad story of O'Leary's sister, is another example of her morbid preoccupation.[78] About a week before the execution, Mary attended a concert where she responded favourably to a military band's performance, commenting that "I actually felt a desire to go to battle, not to hear the music but to gain a victory. I felt as if death would be glorious in such a cause."[79] On 1 May, she read about immortality, and the day before she had a "pleasant conversation" with her sister-in-law Mary Ann about death.[80] Some women used their diaries as a means to cope with grief and loss, and Mary seemed to use her diary to write about grief she had experienced in the past and her fear of her father's death in the future. It was not unusual for the passing of a loved one to cause a diarist to stop writing, and this is exactly what happened at the conclusion of her later diary, which ends abruptly in the middle of an entry that describes her father's death.[81]

Mary never discussed death at length, but it is a recurring theme in her entries, and it is interesting to observe her feelings about it at different times, addressed through different memories and events. Perhaps her later diary is the shorter of the two because by that point Mary no longer used writing as a way to sort through her apprehensions surrounding death, as she had so earnestly done ten years earlier. One does get the sense that by 1869 Mary had achieved a degree of serenity and in general was less anxious in her outlook on life and about her eventual mortality.

Mary's writing allows us to see only one part of a larger picture. Different perspectives on her experience, which might be yielded by other lost diaries, letters, or similar documents written by her or her family members, have vanished from record. Nevertheless, her writing reveals a great deal of information about how she perceived her self and her life. Overall, the reader is left with the impression that Mary's diaries are a strikingly typical example of the life writing of Anglo-American women of her period.

Family Relationships

The relationships that existed between the members of Mary's family are a major feature of her writing, and gender was a crucial factor shaping those relationships. The cult of domesticity; its close relative, the cult of true womanhood; and part of their supporting gender ideology, the doctrine of separate spheres, were paramount cultural elements of nineteenth-century Anglo-American gender relations.[82] The emerging middle class, which venerated domestic privacy and strong social relationships within the conjugal family as a bulwark against the uncertainties of market capitalism, championed this cultural phenomenon.[83] Women, it was argued, best occupied the private sphere of the home while men braved the public sphere of business and politics. The ideal woman perceived her social roles in the context of dependent relationships to the male relatives in whose homes she lived at different stages of her life. In childhood and youth, she was her father's daughter; after marriage, she was her husband's wife; and in widowhood, she was her son's mother.[84] The objective of these dependent female roles was, through "influence, tasteful economy, intelligent piety and faith," to aid, support, and inspire the men who crossed into the public sphere.[85] Domesticity was revered, and the ideal woman exercised her role as an "angel in the house," in which she sustained her male family members.[86]

Historians have argued that the doctrine of separate spheres served as a workable model for gender relations within the family and as a "cultural roadmap for private lives."[87] Gender roles were not defined in a fixed code, but rather were negotiated within accepted boundaries. Men were still involved in domestic life and women were often involved in the family business, but the essence of the doctrine of the spheres was that male and female roles were complementary. The gender ideology of the period explained this relationship by arguing that male and female characters were innately opposite.[88] Female nature was highly systematized in gender discourse: women were considered intuitive, gentle, modest, tender, pure, patient, unselfish, and delicate. On the other hand, male nature was more ambiguous; nevertheless, men were believed to have a natural ability for rationality, originality, and creativity of thought that women did not possess.[89] In her familial roles as wife, mother, step-grandmother, daughter, sister, and housekeeper, Mary embraced the private sphere of domesticity and the cultural expectations of womanhood.[90] In her diary, she noted a conversation with her nephew Rusby and recorded his comment that as of his twenty-first birthday, he felt he was entering a grave new social role that required him to take on the "serious responsibilitys of Manhood."[91] Even if she only indicated it indirectly in an example like this, Mary endorsed popular notions of distinct gender roles.

It is in the context of nineteenth-century gender ideology that we must consider Mary's family relationships. The focal point of these relationships was the busy Armstrong household. In 1859 Rose Hill was home not only to Mary, her husband, Philip, and hired employees, but also to Mary's step-granddaughter, Mary Ann, her son, Thomas, and her brother Samuel. In the earlier diary, both Samuel and Philip seem to have been out of the house at work during the day. Thomas also spent much time out of the house during the day, attending lectures or working at the hospital. Eleven-year-old Mary Ann was a student at school on weekdays.[92] For the great part of the day, Mary and her hired help girl would conduct household chores. In the evenings, her family members would return to eat and often head out again to meetings and social events, which Mary sometimes attended as well. At night, Mary made frequent reference to Philip, Thomas, Samuel, or Mary Ann sleeping in the armchair, rocking chair, or on the sofa, probably as they dozed off before retiring to bed. By 1869, however, Rose Hill was much quieter. Thomas, Mary Ann, and Samuel had all left the household. Samuel was living with his parents in Yorkville, and Mary Ann, now aged twenty-one and not yet married, was living with her father and brother.[93]

Philip Armstrong was the head of this household, and Mary's domestic role was shaped by her marital relationship with him. While some female diarists of Mary's period focused their writing on their husbands' lives and sought to live vicariously through them and their public careers, most often men featured only as marginal characters in women's diaries.[94] Philip appears regularly in Mary's entries, but he does so as one of many members of the Armstrong household and Mary's wider family, and certainly not as the special focus of her writing. She referred to Philip either formally as "Mr. Armstrong" or informally as "Papa," and she never used his given name. However, this was not a sign of distance or a strained relationship. It was common, until the late nineteenth century, for female diarists not to use their husband's given name, even in private journals.[95] Similarly, one mid-century journal by a Canadian male diarist suggests that men also referred to their wives formally in their writing.[96]

Within middle-class families, the domestic ideal generated an expectation that family members should have intimate bonds, such as close sibling and parent-child relationships, as well as strong love between a husband and wife.[97] The ideal matrimonial love was not erotic but tender; a mature husband was expected to support, guide, and advise his young wife, who reciprocated with her moral and spiritual influence.[98] Companionate marriages where—within the framework of masculine authority— couples respected each other and co-operated through illness, financial difficulty, and personal disagreements were the ideal, and many such unions did exist in the nineteenth century. On the other hand, marriages could also be patriarchal and authoritarian. In relationships like these, husbands exercised their full socially and legally endorsed control without consideration for their wives' wishes, happiness, or personal health and safety.[99] While marital tension was usually absent from women's journals and letters, and diarists often refrained from criticizing their husbands in their writing, some did express their frustration over marital troubles.[100]

Mary recorded nothing of her emotional relationship with Philip, so it is hard to clearly assess the nature of their marriage. Mary did take space to grumble about her husband's bad temper. In May 1859 Philip was "cross," and his anger affected Mary "a good deal," to the point where she called him a bully in her journal.[101] Nearly a week later she wrote that "Papa's countenance has once more cleared up a little, I think the clouds generally disperse about the third or fourth day."[102] Despite some infrequent strains in the relationship with her husband, Mary seems to have enjoyed his company and appreciated the full spectrum of his personality, which at times could be generous.[103] On balance, it appears that their marriage was companionate, and the two seem to have supported each other in their respective roles as husband and wife.

Mary was not only a wife but also a mother. She seems to have been very close with her son, Thomas, and her step-granddaughter, Mary Ann, whom she treated like a daughter. Both received frequent and favourable mention in her writing. Women were believed to be naturally suited to their role as nurturing mothers, and thus their duty to ensure proper physical, intellectual, and moral education for their children was perceived as almost instinctual.[104] Motherhood was an important part of a woman's domestic role, and some scholars have highlighted the ties between this element of domesticity and evangelical religion.[105] Methodism, which Marguerite Van Die has argued became a religion of the family from the 1840s, emphasized mothers' responsibility for the spiritual development of their children. Women were believed to have special Christian virtues that suited them to their role of providing moral training for children.[106] However, scholars such as Philip Greven and Jack Little have challenged the link between evangelicalism and domesticity in pre-industrial North America.[107] Even if it may not have been uniquely evangelical, Mary's role as a Christian mother was important to her, and to this end she embraced her role as step-grandmother to young Mary Ann. She noted on 3 April 1859 that she went to chapel twice, and she wrote, "I always take Mary Ann with me."[108] She was also the natural mother of Thomas and their relationship was, obviously, central to Mary's role as a mother.

Thomas was an only child, and it was very rare for a family to have just one child in the nineteenth century. Most women in this period first conceived shortly after marriage and kept having children regularly into their forties.[109] Mary offers us no explanation for her one-child family. It was probably not a deliberate decision, but it is possible that either she or Philip became infertile, perhaps through illness, after Thomas's birth. Nevertheless, Mary was very proud of her motherhood, and it was an important part of her identity.[110] Women often found a sense of purpose in their role as mothers. Female diarists used their writing to affirm their motherhood role and also to record children's growth, achievements, marriages, traits, behaviour, intelligence, looks, and popularity.[111] Mary was no exception. She frequently wrote about her son's progress through medical school as well as his social engagements. She seemed to be particularly fond of Thomas, commenting that his "likeness" in a medical school photograph was "uncommonly good."[112] As sons aged into manhood, it was their responsibility to break away from the "intense but dependent" relationships they had with their mothers. While this made the transition to independent masculinity uneasy for most children, it may have been even more difficult for an only child like Thomas, who seems to have been close with his mother.[113]

In 1859 Thomas was twenty years old. Rather than boarding in another household, which Michael Katz has shown was a normal transitory stage of semi-autonomy between adolescence and independent adulthood among males in Hamilton at mid-century, he lived at home while attending medical school.[114] Thomas would remain at home until he married

Fidelia Jane Maughan in 1863, a year after he graduated. Thomas was twenty-four years old when he married, and this was slightly younger than the average marriage age for men at this time, which was the mid-to-late twenties.[115] Katz has suggested that the 1857-60 depression may have been a factor influencing young men's decisions to stay at home longer.[116] Thomas may have chosen to live at home with his mother and father for economic reasons; if so, the money he saved may have allowed him to afford to marry at a relatively young age.

Living at home meant that Thomas stayed in the household and under the authority of his father. According to the doctrine of separate spheres, the role of fathers in child-rearing was to enforce discipline and teach practical skills like the handling of money, while mothers were expected to have the closest bonds with their children and were relied upon to give personal care and emotional support.[117] However, scholars who have challenged the ubiquity of this model of gender roles argue that in fact fathers often played a more active role in child-rearing than has generally been assumed.[118] For example, three pre-industrial Canadian fathers—Edmund Peel, Marcus Child, and James Reid—examined by Jack Little were very involved in the raising of their children.[119] Nevertheless, in contrast to these men, Philip's role as father to Thomas seems to have been much closer to the "cold and aloof" paternal stereotype usually associated with the doctrine of the spheres.[120]

Historians have found evidence of conflict between fathers and maturing sons, sometimes over education plans and career expectations.[121] Thomas's failure as a butcher may have been a source of tension between him and his father. Business failure was considered shameful and could be equated with character weakness, which might reflect poorly on other family members' businesses.[122] Moreover, Thomas's choice to attend medical school may have offended Philip. It appears that his maternal grandfather was far more supportive of Thomas's professional education than his own father was.[123] Philip "strenuously opposed" his son attending a ball for medical students in 1859, and Thomas dutifully acquiesced to his father's wishes by staying home.[124] Though Mary did not indicate her husband's reasons for demanding that Thomas not attend the ball, this episode is illustrative of some level of tension between Philip and Thomas. When Philip died two decades later, he left equal shares of his estate to his wife and son, so it does not appear that, if it did exist, any father-son tension endured.[125]

Outside of her household relationships, the most significant family bond Mary maintained was with her own parents, who lived only a few blocks away in Yorkville.[126] In both diaries Mary frequently noted paying visits to and dining with her parents, with whom she had a very close, loving relationship. She maintained a deep concern for her ageing father's well-being, and at the same time she respected him as an educated and successful man. Mary had a particularly close relationship with her mother. She recorded the content of a conversation they held in the winter of 1859, and of the things that Mary and her mother found important and enjoyable subjects, the most prominent was family.[127] Their relationship is an example of the strong bonds that frequently existed between female family members in this period. Female support networks were built among family relations, and members drew upon each other for guidance, advice, and emotional support in the female rituals of child-bearing, child-rearing, illness, and death.[128] In the words of Carroll Smith-Rosenberg, an "intimate mother-daughter relationship lay at heart of this female world."[129] Though tension in such relationships could occur, disagreements were often minor and readily patched up.[130] As daughters became mothers themselves, they frequently developed a new appreciation for their mothers' lives, and as their mothers aged, adult daughters fulfilled their reciprocal duties to their parent out of a sense of affection and moral obligation.[131] Mary's mother was a very important figure in her daughter's life. Mary was not only grateful for her mother's support and love but also enjoyed her mother's company.

Mary's father and mother were very involved grandparents. Historians have noted that grandparents commonly provided aid and support to their grandchildren as they grew.[132] James Wickson, Mary's father, tutored Thomas regularly while Mary kept her earlier diary.[133] Thomas's grandfather was probably teaching him Latin or Greek, which would be useful for his medical training. James Wickson taught Greek after his retirement from the meat business in 1840; his own educational background is unknown, but he certainly ensured that his sons received an excellent education.[134] In her later diary, Mary was herself a grandmother. She wrote about Thomas's young family, noting that she bought toys for his children and baked cakes for her grandson's fifth birthday, which she went to York Mills to celebrate.[135] Mary embraced her role as grandparent and seems to have been caring and affectionate towards her grandchildren. In doing so, she followed the example set by her own parents in their relationship with her son.

Mary maintained strong relationships with her siblings. Adult friendships were common between brothers and sisters, and were often reinforced by business connections between family members.[136] In light of his partnership with Philip, Samuel's residence at Rose Hill was by no means peculiar. It was, in fact, unusual for someone to live alone in a time when the cultural expectation was that all individuals should live in a family setting.[137] Samuel and Mary seem to have had a relationship that was as amicable and caring as could be expected between two mature siblings sharing the same house. When mothers had a large number of children, it was not uncommon for the youngest in a family, like Samuel, to be close in age to the offspring of their siblings.[138] Indeed, Samuel was only ten years older than his nephew Thomas, and the two seem to have been great friends.[139]

Mary was quite close with her brothers Arthur and John, and with their wives and children; they frequently made social calls and dined at each other's houses. John and Eliza lived on New Kent Road in Yorkville, and Arthur and Mary Ann lived in Toronto on Yonge Street.[140] Mary seems to have had a close relationship with Arthur's wife, Mary Ann, and their bond was an important part of Mary's female support network.[141] Samuel, who never married, had moved out of the Armstrong household at Rose Hill by the mid-1860s and moved in with his parents in Yorkville. In her later diary, Mary mentioned Samuel on several occasions, but she made no mention of John or Arthur, save a single reference to John's wife, Eliza.[142] This is not necessarily an indication of a soured relationship; compared with the earlier journal this diary is much shorter and sparser in its mention of other family members as a whole.

Mary also had sisters living in Paris, a town in Brant County to the west of Toronto. Jane lived there with her husband Rev. Edward Ebbs in 1859. Sarah, who lived in England with her husband Carruthers during the earlier diary, was by 1869 living in Paris with her new husband, the wealthy businessman Norman Hamilton. Toronto and Paris were connected by daily mail and Mary indicated in her diary that she and her other family members were in regular communication with her sisters in Brant County.[143] Mary reflected on the importance of family as a whole, and her sisters specifically. In one entry, she lamented their geographical separation. Addressing her sisters directly, she commented that "so late as six years ago we three sisters met and were happy [,] now one is in England and the other in Paris (C.W.)."[144] Historians have noted that ties between female family members were central in holding communities and kin groups together, and that strong ties between sisters, cousins, and sisters-in-law could exist across great distances.[145] By mid-century, married women who could afford the cost made regular visits to Britain to see their relatives. In this context, Sarah's stay in England was not peculiar. However, her sojourn might have been more than a mere visit; she may have been there for an extended period to study art.[146] Family and the bonds between relatives were important for Mary. Writing about Sarah, Mary felt her "dear sister's absence very much," and eagerly awaited her return to Canada.[147]

For Mary, family was a central element of her life. It was a bond not just of blood but also of community and identity.[148] The people with whom she spent the most time each day were her relatives living in her household and nearby. She accepted the dominant gender ideology of her period and embraced contemporary ideals of domesticity and womanhood in the roles of wife and mother. Mary's relationships with her siblings and parents were important, and through these bonds she fulfilled her role as an adult sister and daughter. Her intimate friendships with her mother and her sister-in-law were key local connections in Mary's female support network, which stretched across great distances.

Women's Work and Household Management

Gender ideology not only shaped family relationships, it also dictated a gendered division of labour. The doctrine of separate spheres held that a woman's role in the private sphere, in addition to providing emotional and moral support to the men in her life, was also to run her household. Women's household work was an integral part of the domestic duties and responsibilities of the "godly wife and mother."[149] To this end, domestic labour was revered and invested with a mystique as an elevated mode of work and "a labour of love" undertaken by the ideal woman.[150] The rhythms of domestic work dominated Mary's daily life, and in her journal she recorded her thoughts and feelings about them.

From mid-century, middle-class households in Ontario began to change from the almost self-sufficient unit of family production characteristic of the pre-industrial pioneer period to a "non-productive unit of procreation and consumption." In the decades in which Mary kept her diaries, this shift was underway but clearly not yet complete.[151] In this period of transition, women's household work also changed. More goods could be purchased rather than produced in the home. Carding, weaving, and spinning were abandoned, and assistance in domestic chores and the care of livestock and gardening could be more easily paid for as the colonial economy expanded. However, food preparation and the making of clothing remained features of female domestic life, as they had been from the early years of the colony.[152] A woman's primary responsibility was to meet family needs by preparing food and producing clothing and other household articles, and by performing services such as cleaning, laundry, and ironing. Fruit and vegetable farming, the raising of poultry, and dairy farming were considered feminine chores, and were by no means easy; the work associated with only a few milk cows was burdensome and back-breaking.[153]

Mary's household was her place of work. Her daily chores included churning butter, baking bread, cooking dinner and supper, tending the hens and cattle, making clothing, and working in the garden. Her daily tasks were laborious, and she often wrote of feeling fatigued or ill. Mary regularly performed work with her female family members. She recorded doing needlework with Mary Ann, which was part of her step-granddaughter's practical education. It was in their mother's house that girls learned domestic skills from an early age.[154] The practice also continued into adulthood: on two occasions Mary recorded sewing by the fire with her own mother, who was "a great help to her" in making a dress.[155]

Mary was often the last to go to bed in her house. She made many of her diary entries late in the evening, after she had finished her work, and frequently included descriptions of where the various members of her household were sleeping. Most entries made in the early evenings mention the men of the household being off at public lectures, meetings, or other engagements such as concerts, rehearsals, and parties. Mary attended these too, but not as frequently as the men. One entry reads: "I began to feel a little tired today of stopping home so many evenings by myself but being busy, I soon forgot it and I shall be out, for two or three [evenings] I expect directly."[156]

Mary's work kept her household running. Her primary task was to support the lives of her husband, her son, and the rest of her household, including farm hands, her brother, and her step-granddaughter. Weaving was not a part of her chores; at market she was able to buy clothing material, which at home she made into shirts for her son and husband, or aprons for sale at market. The transition away from the older pioneer family economy is also illustrated in her later diary; compared with 1859, her reliance on shopkeepers and credit to supply more of her household needs increased. In the back of her 1869 diary she recorded payments made on bills, and she also kept a separate account book. She did not write about making lard as she did ten years previously, but she was still occupied with sewing, churning, cooking, baking, washing, and cleaning.[157]

Mary's work had a weekly rhythm. It is clear that she assigned certain chores for different days of the week. For example, she usually did washing on Mondays, though if she could, she sometimes did this in advance.

On Mondays she also seems to have churned butter.[158] On Saturdays in 1859, Mary frequently left the house and went to market. While out she also made socials visits to family members. A typical Saturday in Mary's earlier diary went something like this: "Went to Market as usual weather moderate, dined at Arthur's according to custom, enjoyed a pleasant chat, stopped an hour at Mother's and reached home about five, bought more needlework, Calico for Shirts and pastellettes besides towelings."[159] In her later diary, she did not mention going to the market on Saturdays, although one entry suggests that she did go, as she noted the prices of butter and eggs. Mary may have continued to attend the market but simply decided not to record the event in her journal. Some women idealized Sundays as a day for rest from work, set aside for spiritual and intellectual activities and for social engagements with friends and relatives.[160] In her earlier diary, the entries Mary made on Sundays were generally very brief. She usually simply noted attending chapel and dining or having tea with family. It appears that Mary took time off from her diary writing on this day; some Sundays she did not make an entry at all, and in her later diary she wrote on only two Sundays in the space of eight months.[161] If Sunday was a day of relative rest from household work, Mary's choice to write little or nothing on this day suggests that her diary writing was something she may have associated with her housework on the other six days of the week.

We have seen that Mary sometimes worked with her female family members, but she also employed a "help" girl to assist her on a regular basis. Jane Errington has discussed help girls, who were regularly hired by Upper Canadian homemakers to assist with domestic chores. Errington distinguishes between "helps" and "servants," where helping was characterized by a more informal relationship between employer and employee, and the help girl did not require the special living quarters or uniform of a servant. Moreover, in rural areas, "farm mistresses assumed that help girls would share the living conditions of the family."[162] Mary regularly employed a "girl." At times some girls might stay with the family, and at other times they might travel to work each morning. The latter option would have been feasible considering how close the Armstrong property was to the city.[163] Katz's analysis of Hamilton in 1861 found that 21 percent of families in that city had a servant living with them at the time of the census.[164] Errington concluded that full-time female help received between three and four dollars per month plus room and board in the 1830s.[165] Mary hired her girl on an annual contract and paid her six-and-a-half dollars per month in 1859, a figure she thought was reasonable, as she hoped to have "three or four cows to milk."[166]

Help girls certainly earned their monthly salaries. Errington's description of the workday of a help girl, taken from the diary of Mary O'Brien, is consistent with what is recorded in Mary Armstrong's diary. O'Brien's girl got up before dawn to start the meal preparations and was soon joined by her mistress; the women would have breakfast ready for the family at 6 a.m. Throughout the day the two would iron, make meals, and clean.[167] Like O'Brien, Mary Armstrong described her servant rising before everyone else in the morning and also assisting with chores during the rest of the day. One illustrative entry in her later diary reads:

> My Girl, Mary Ann Shields, gets up without any trouble in the morning and gets the men their breakfast which is a great blessing to me then she starts out to milk and I get papa's breakfast and my own ready then we feed the calf & fowls [.] I set the upstairs in order and she clears up below, then we both hurry the dinner as we get our's [*sic*] at half past eleven so it can be removed for the men at twelve—I can truly say I am as happy as the day is long.[168]

Mary wrote about needing a girl present to be able to keep up with her chores. When her girl Bessie was unable to come to the house to work, Mary was grateful that her son brought buns from town, "to save me the trouble of cooking much dinner."[169] Three days later, when Bessie was still not able to come to the house, Mary wrote about her relief when her mother's girl came to help her in the morning "for," she said, "I was almost worn out with the work."[170] Mary had a trusting relationship with her girl. When she was out, she often left the house in her girl's care. On one occasion, she chose not to leave home because she "could not leave the dear old home to the care of a stranger (Bessie being away, and another in her place for this day)."[171]

Managing help girls and other domestic servants was an important skill for middle-class homemakers. Marks has observed that a "major social gulf" existed between mistresses and their girls in the later nineteenth century, demonstrated by the relative absence of female servants from church membership rolls.[172] In light of differences in social status, maintaining a maternal attitude towards help girls was an important part of middle-class household management.[173] Mary played a motherly role in her relationship with Bessie, who by April 1859 was wearing her patience thin. Mary was critical of her girl's behaviour, attitude, and reputation: "five months passed in taverns, have altogether spoilt her," Mary reasoned before she asked God to give her strength.[174] In addition to hired female labour, the

Armstrongs had male farmhands living with them in both 1859 and 1869, but their work was on the land, not in the realm of household chores, and it was Philip, not Mary, who managed them.[175]

How busy Mary and her girl were seems to have varied with the seasons. On St. Patrick's Day, 1869, she wrote that "housework will soon increase." This is probably in reference to spring cleaning, an annual top-to-bottom scrubbing of the house that lasted several days. This massive project involved taking curtains, rugs, and bedding to be beaten, washed, and hung to dry; thoroughly sweeping and dusting behind and underneath furniture; and painstakingly cleaning windows, walls, and floors.[176] Despite an increasing level of work, spring was an important time of year for Mary; she recorded the signs of its arrival in both her diaries.[177] Margaret Conrad has argued that the rhythms of seasonal work often regulated women's sense of time and place.[178] The change of season was a significant marker of time for Mary, as it meant a change in her work habits. In the cold days of February, she speculated that "when the fine spring season, brings back the flowers" she would be able to work outside.[179] By mid-April she was eager to get her indoor work out of the way: "I want to get all my needlework done, before the fine weather sets in."[180] During the warmer season, Mary was able to spend her time outside doing work in the garden or, when she had a moment, taking walks with friends and family. After a long and cold winter, Mary had an understandable desire for the freedom and change of pace that accompany the spring and summer months.

Housework could be an uninspiring occupation, and in reaction to its monotony some women became restive. Some found their lack of time and energy, and their limited sense of self, which was confined to a domestic identity, frustrating.[181] Mary cannot be described as restive, but in her journal she grumbled about the physical strain of her work. The last pages of her 1869 diary record in detail the needlework she completed each month. Endless hours of sewing took a toll on her eyes. She described reading as "the principal pleasure of my life," but observed that she would have to give it up (at least temporarily) after sewing twelve shirts in the parlour by the light of the fire, which caused her sight to grow "dim."[182]

Housework could also bring a sense of fulfillment, competence, and usefulness.[183] In February 1859 Mary reflected that her knitting and sewing had "caused me more satisfaction than anything I have done for the last week and yet I had the greatest disinclination to set about it."[184] Mary looked at her work positively and identified part of herself in it. In the earlier diary she commented that "as half of my probable stay upon earth has now been spent in unceasing efforts to keep a tidy house and every thing mended up and made the very most of, it is now time, that I should enjoy the fruit of my labour." These fruits seem to have been the ability to enjoy the warm spring weather outside, and to take a break and "look round me a little."[185] Ten years later, Mary penned, "I think I could not live without work (in more senses than one) but I do really like it."[186] Mary strongly disliked being idle and only felt content when she was occupied with one of the many tasks that had to be done each day.[187] Mary was also possessive of her work. In both diaries she referred to the dairy cattle as "my cows" and the chickens as "my hens," living in "my fowl house." She felt a personal loss when robbers broke into her henhouse and stole some of her chickens, though she wrote that she bore "no malice to the thieves."[188] The lists of needlework found at the back of the later diary were perhaps a way in which Mary could catalogue her unceasing work and look back on it with a sense of achievement.

Related to Mary's housework, and as much a part of her identity, was the way she managed finances. As a married woman under the English common-law doctrine of coverture and the legal fiction of marital unity, she forfeit her right to contract and to sue or be sued in her own name. She was able to own real estate, but only her husband had the right to manage it or claim the rent or profits from the land. She was permitted to carry on a business of her own only if she had the formal consent of her husband. All her personal property, and any wages she received, legally belonged to her husband, who was liable for all her debts, torts, and contracts.[189] For centuries a wife had traditionally been entitled to inherit, during her lifetime, one-third of her deceased husband's estate as dower right, but the inviolability of this practice was formally repealed by statute in 1833. Increasingly, trusts were used to provide for a widow's use of her own property.[190] In January 1859 Mary indicated that she hoped to claim some of the proceeds from a sale of Philip's real estate as dowry, but exactly what she meant by this is unclear.[191] She seems to have expected to be able to put this money to use immediately, but it is unlikely that she anticipated her husband's death in the near future. She may have been referring to a trust that she and Philip had arranged to handle property.

Despite the legal restrictions on married women, it seems that Mary acted quite autonomously in financial matters, and this was probably the result of an agreement between her and Philip, another sign of a companionate marriage.[192] Mary referred to her own "exchequer," or her private savings, and observed that "I could have bought very nice hens at a quarter of a dollar each but my exchequer has had so many drains upon it, I was forced to forgo that pleasure."[193] She wrote about or referred to her own money on other occasions. In April 1869, when she and Philip purchased furniture at a bailiff's sale, they took home a forty-eight-dollar bookcase that Mary promised to pay for with her own money. Philip bought the rest of the furniture "on his own account."[194] Mary did not expect Philip to pay for her if they went out together. She noted in her diary that Philip was kind enough to treat both her and Thomas to the omnibus fare and admission price for a lecture the three of them attended one spring evening, suggesting that it was not normal for him to do so.[195] Responsibility for her own finances, through an arrangement with her husband, lent a degree of control and independence to Mary's life.

It was common for wives in the nineteenth century to have their own money, earned by the sale of surplus household produce, which they used to manage household expenses.[196] Indeed, the role of a wife as an economizing homemaker and efficient household manager was an important part of the maintenance of a family's financial security and middle-class status.[197] We have seen that women produced a variety of foods and clothing items in their daily work. Any surplus production could be traded or sold, but this objective was secondary to the maintenance of the household and, some historians have argued, would only be significant when a large number of daughters or servants were present.[198] With the assistance of one help girl and her step-granddaughter, Mary made a profit from her surplus production, of which she kept account, at one time noting in her diary the profit from making lard.[199] In 1859 Mary was at market at least once a week, where she bought and sold food, and sometimes chickens and material for clothing. She also sold the calves from her dairy cows, eggs from her hens, butter, and lard; oats, hay, fruit, and vegetables grown on her property; and aprons and other articles of clothing that she made on her own. Female market vending at mid-century has been described as the "most marginal of businesses," where women were subjected to taunts and abuse and even assault from young roughs.[200] Mary's experience seems to contradict this interpretation. While her vending was marginal, she never recorded receiving abuse while at market, and she certainly regarded it as a respectable way to spend a Saturday morning.[201]

Mary had a keen business sense, and she carefully followed market changes, sometimes recording the price of butter and eggs in her journal.[202] In January 1869 she chose to sell butter at her house rather than to shopkeepers, presumably so that she could receive maximum profit from prices, which she speculated were about to rise. She wrote, "there is no demand for butter round here just now people have mostly laid in a winter supply [.] Gibson [a shopkeeper] of course would take it but I prefer selling it at the house & I think the price may go up."[203] Mary did not only deal in cash; she also used her surplus produce to barter for goods that she needed. She did this on one occasion when she sent her girl to a shop with eight pounds of butter "to help pay for the fowls feed."[204] She was responsible for managing household expenses and settling her debts, and she commented in 1859 that she found it "it more difficult to keep house" than she had in the past, as her expenses seemed to be increasing.[205] Mary was also responsible for paying her help girls, whose salary came out of the income generated by the sale of produce.[206]

The day-to-day running of Mary's household involved a vast range of time-consuming and difficult chores that had a weekly and seasonal rhythm. She managed her massive workload with the assistance of her female family members and her help girl, and through a financial arrangement with her husband, she had a large degree of autonomy over her own finances and her productive household activities. Despite its physical toll on her body, housework was something that Mary enjoyed and from which she derived a sense of satisfaction, accomplishment, and purpose. Her personal responsibility lent her a degree of control and independence, and consequently, being a middle-class homemaker was an important part of Mary's identity.

Status and Class

Mary's text and other sources relating to her life and the lives of her family members reveal a great deal of information about social status and class in nineteenth-century Ontario. In her earlier diary, Mary clearly identified herself as middle class, but contemporary definitions of social status changed over her lifetime.[207] Before 1850, the Upper Canadian economy was relatively underdeveloped compared with industrialized Britain.[208] Small artisan workshops were prevalent, and through working towards and achieving self-employment, a man could achieve economic independence.[209] This pre-industrial society was divided into different "ranks" or "sorts," but in a colony without a landed aristocracy, even these divisions were not firmly fixed.[210] Prior to 1840, as Peter Russell has argued, three major ranks defined the social structure of Upper Canada: the "respectable," who were the wealthy, well-connected, and powerful leaders of society; the "independent," who were able to support themselves economically; and the "dependent," who relied upon being employed by others to earn their wages. Additionally, two intermediate ranks existed— the "quasi-dependent" and the "marginal-respectable"—as transitional regions between each of these levels.[211]

The middle decades of the century proved to be a crucial period of transition for the colonial economy.[212] Fears previously expressed —that industrialization would upset the social balance—were gradually realized once early industrial capitalism took hold and began to transform the economy after mid-century.[213] Economic class began to determine social structure, replacing the older hierarchical order described by Russell.[214] Marxist historian Bryan Palmer has argued that in the 1850s, the expansion of industrial capital was encroaching upon independent artisans and petty producers, a process that was exacerbated by the depression of 1857-60.[215] Gregory Kealey has shown that this trend continued in the following decade in Toronto as modern factories replaced hand manufactories.[216] In smaller towns like Brantford, self-employment in craft production declined, and the size of the business population shrank. Beginning at this time, economic class relations and class structure began to become more clearly defined.[217]

While others have observed a "broad agrarian middle class" of small-farm proprietors existing in the rural context in this period,[218] Andrew Holman has argued that from the 1850s, a new middle class began to emerge and define itself in small towns, sustained by new waves of British immigrants coming from a similar economic class in their industrialized homeland.[219] This middle class forged a place for itself in the social structure of the province. Over the second half of the century, new class-based identities came to define the boundary between workers and the middle class with reference to manual labour and non-manual work, and to define the barrier between the middle class and the upper class with reference to wealth, occupational prestige, and lifestyle.[220] This argument builds upon Alison Prentice's earlier assertion that the major status distinction at mid-century was between those who were educated and those who were not, as one's level of education dictated the type of labour one was able to perform in the new industrializing economy.[221]

Scholars have looked at certain aspects of the developing middle class in Victorian Ontario. Such work includes Lynne Marks's study of protestant culture, gender, and class, and Barbara Maas's published doctoral research on gender ideology among immigrant women at different times in the nineteenth century.[222] Though he chooses not to use the term "middle class," David Burley's study of the community of small businessmen in Brantford and their adaptation to industrial capitalism makes an important contribution to our understanding of class development.[223] However, in the Canadian context, as Holman observes, academic research has largely neglected the middle class.[224] Nevertheless, excellent studies of the nineteenth-century middle class in the United States and Britain have been completed. These include Mary Ryan's examination of the role of the family in maintaining and reproducing the values and economic behaviour of the middle-class in New York State, and Leonore Davidoff and Catherine Hall's exploration of gender, economy, and identity among the same stratum in Birmingham.[225] Their work provides important comparative reference points for the Canadian experience. To date, Holman's analysis of middle-class formation in Victorian Ontario towns is the most thorough investigation of the structure and ideas of this social group.[226]

The social structure of Mary's colonial world changed over her lifetime. By the decades in which she kept her diaries, early industrial capitalism had overturned the more static and hierarchical structure of ranks and orders that had delineated the society of Upper Canada. Economic classes were now emerging and defining themselves and a new social structure. An examination of social mobility illustrates how Mary and her family fit into these changes to social structure.

Social mobility, or movement up and down the ranks of social and economic status, is a topic that historians concerned with social structure have addressed.[227] Mary and members of her family seem to have experienced upward social mobility during their lifetimes; however, such mobility is harder to gauge when the social and economic developments outlined above are taken into consideration. The definition of social status groups changed over time; consequently, not only did the status level of Mary and her family change but so did the very social ladder itself. While Mary identified herself as middle class in 1859, in the same year she also used the term "rank" in reference to status.[228] Alison Prentice has shown that the old hierarchical model of social structure died hard, and that prominent members of colonial society still spoke about social "ranks" in 1849.[229] Mary's use of the same term ten years later, coupled with her use of the term "middle class," suggests that perceptions of the old hierarchy persisted into the early industrial capitalist period, competing with new concepts of economic class. This blending of status concepts informed Mary's experience of social mobility from the time of her immigration to the dates of her dairies.

Mary's social mobility was tied firmly to the occupational status of her father, and later, to that of her husband. Prevailing gender ideology dictated that this was the case for the majority of women in the nineteenth century.[230] While Mary's birth family was part of the British middle class in the 1820s and early 1830s, upon their arrival in Upper Canada and James Wickson's subsequent opening of a business and purchase of a house in the city, the family can probably be considered, in Russell's terms, to have been "marginal-respectable."[231] Mary's brothers William, Samuel, and Arthur attended Upper Canada College in the early 1840s, and Arthur later went on to study at King's College, earning four degrees.[232] For Mary's brothers to receive this level of education, her family must have been wealthy enough to support them. James Wickson was financially secure enough to retire from his business six years after first opening it.[233] Mary's marriage also positioned her within this status group. In the early years of her life with Philip, a self-employed tradesman, Mary and her husband were probably also in the "marginal-respectable" rank of Upper Canadian society. In addition to owning his own business, Philip had two hundred pounds with which to purchase six acres of land to cultivate as a small farm in 1839, and this transaction, the first of many land acquisitions for Philip, can be seen as securing the couple's position at this status level.[234] It does not appear that the Armstrongs' status level changed over the next decade.

By mid-century, as we have seen, the traditional hierarchical ordering of ranks was increasingly anachronistic, and new definitions of class were gradually taking shape. In the transitional middle decades of the century, the intellectual leaders of the colony urged all members of society to "improve" and advance their "condition," a message coupled with the perception that the only alternative was to fall behind.[235] Those who have examined social mobility quantitatively in this period have observed that quite a lot of mobility occurred in what was a very fluid society, that most social mobility was incremental, and that the amount of upward mobility roughly equalled downward mobility.[236] Burley argues that two criteria were vital for upward social mobility among Brantford's small businessmen: persistence in business over time and accumulation of wealth.[237]

Philip's business and investment activities allowed him to persist in the market and accumulate wealth. In the 1850s and early 1860s he was a self-employed butcher with a market stall, and he was also a small-farm owner. Land investment contributed to Philip's ability to survive as a tradesman despite the adverse impact of early industrial capitalism.[238] In 1859 Philip owned two plots of land at some distance from his residence. These were Maple Woods and Woodhill, described in both of Mary's diaries. In 1864 Philip purchased more land from the nearby Rose Estate, land that Mary called "Hazel Dell Fields" in her later diary. Philip farmed some of this land and also grew oats at Maple Woods and wheat at Woodhill.[239] Burley has argued that for retail grocers and shopkeepers, profits could not be easily reinvested in their smaller businesses, and real property served as an attractive alternative investment. Butchers may have found themselves in similar circumstances. While Philip does not seem to have rented out his real estate investments and instead hired labourers to farm them directly, the potential to generate rental income served as a financial cushion should his fortunes sour.[240] Interestingly, he chose to sell part of his land at Rose Hill in 1859 rather than rent it out.[241] This choice may have represented financial scrambling during the economic strain of the 1857–60 depression and Philip's intention to use the proceeds from the sale to support his business. On the other hand, the funds could have been earmarked to finance another land purchase. It was the wealth Philip accumulated through real estate investment that probably went a long way in allowing him to persist as a businessman over time and comfortably to exit the business world in the mid-1860s.

Philip's business and investment strategy allowed him and his family to achieve not only financial survival but also, as we have seen, increased affluence throughout the 1850s and 1860s.[242] However, the improved fortunes that Mary recorded in 1869, as compared with the more straitened circumstances of a decade earlier, are probably partially explained by the better economic times of the late 1860s and the depression years of the late 1850s, respectively.[243] Nevertheless, a rise in social status seems to have occurred for Philip and his family in these decades. In 1866 he was appointed to the public office of justice of the peace for York County.[244] It is probably not a coincidence that within a year he had left the meat business behind, selling his share in his relatively new partnership, "Armstrong and McCarter."[245] He may have felt that to continue in trade was beneath the status of his new appointment.

Philip was also involved with a variety of agricultural and related societies that will be discussed in detail below.[246] His involvement in these societies from the early 1850s was a reason for his successful rise in status. These associations allowed Philip to work with and socialize among the provincial elite, including leaders such as Robert Baldwin and George Allan. Holman has noted that voluntary societies gained respectability through avenues of public visibility, such as newspaper announcements and events that drew spectators, and that they "borrowed status" from the individuals who served as their officers.[247] No longer described as simply a butcher as he had been in previous directories, Philip is listed in the 1871 County of York directory as a "freeholder" and a "gentleman." While by this time "gentleman" was a self-assumed title that anyone could aspire to, it indicated the social position to which Philip had risen: as an "educated agriculturalist" and horticulturalist, and an independent and prosperous landowner, Philip was living the ideal farmer's life.[248] In the time that Mary's husband rose far enough socially to feel comfortable styling himself a gentleman, the Armstrongs remained prosperous members of the middle class.

For those who were concerned with advancing their social position, paying attention to the habits and lifestyles of their "betters" was an important consideration. It was also a middle-class preoccupation. In the British context, Davidoff and Hall have discussed gentry emulation by members of the middle class. Observant eyes took regular advantage of large parties held at the homes of the local gentry, which afforded a select group of curious guests a look at elite tastes and styles.[249] While there was no hereditary aristocracy in Canada West, a "self-fashioned local gentry" existed in some communities, composed of very wealthy residents leading visibly extravagant lifestyles. For example, some wealthy officers of the Canada Company laid claim to elite status in the decades after mid-century, and among them was Frederick Widder, a company commissioner.[250] In 1859 the Widders gave a party at their house on Front Street; the Armstrongs were in attendance and Mary commented on the evening in her earlier diary. The Armstrongs knew the Widders through the St. George's Society and the Toronto Horticultural Society.[251] In this entry, where Mary identified herself as middle class, she expressed her "great desire to be introduced to the arrangement of a great house" and carefully recorded the decorations and tastes of the elite household, comparing them directly with her own.[252]

On another occasion, Mary again indicated a curiosity with her social superiors. She eagerly recorded in her earlier diary that at one evening lecture, she and Philip sat just in front of the wife of the Honourable Peter Boyle de Blaquière, a member of the legislative council. Mary commented that Mrs. de Blaquière "is of higher Rank than any other families at Yorkville or indeed at Toronto," and happily noticed the hair, "delicate complexions," and bonnets of de Blaquière's two daughters, as well as their expression of "great pleasure" at the meeting.[253] That Mary found the details of this occasion, as well as those of her visit to the Widders' party, worthy enough to record in her diary indicates that she had a strong awareness of those above her in the social structure. It also indicates that she admired and perhaps aspired to their genteel public self-presentation, both of which were typically middle-class preoccupations.

We have established that Mary and her family were prosperous and upwardly mobile members of the middle class, and that, in typical middle-class fashion, she observed in detail the lifestyles of her social superiors.

Another distinctive element of middle-class status abundant in Mary's writing is the pursuit of respectability. Those who have studied nineteenth-century middle-class ideology have recognized the central importance of the concept of respectability.[254] A positive cultural value, respectability was a tool that the middle class used to shape the world to its own interests.[255] The concept of respectability was dynamic, and it was defined through various roles, behaviours, and activities that were collectively acknowledged to represent different aspects of the ideal middle-class lifestyle. Unsurprisingly, respectability was not something that the middle class invented after mid-century; it was in fact an adaptation of an older social theme. In Upper Canadian society, as we have seen, "respectable" was another word for the elite social group, but an individual's chances at rising in status towards that elite were closely connected to his or her character, the "constellation of moral virtues" that included industry, honesty, moderation, temperance, loyalty, and strict sexual mores.[256] Moral character in Upper Canada was an important element of new concepts of middle-class respectability after mid-century, and this connection has been explored in Errington's study of women in Upper Canada, in which she observes conceptions of respectability among what Russell would call the "independent" status level.[257]

Respectability was certainly a dominant concept in Mary's life. She even used the word in her writing. It appears once in her earlier diary, when she wrote about acquaintances that were "respectable but poor," as if to make the point that despite their financial misfortune, these people were of good moral character and were upstanding members of society.[258] Mary's comment reflects a distinction, made by the middle class, between the "worthy" and the "unworthy" poor. This distinction was based, Holman has argued, on an explanation of chronic poverty as a consequence of moral failure, where it was believed that hard times could be overcome by embracing the values of industry and thrift. The worthy recognized this tenet and deserved assistance in the form of food and clothing, while the unworthy did not and instead needed moral correction.[259] In this instance, Mary used the word "respectable" to illustrate that the acquaintances she spoke of were impoverished but worthy of the credit her son extended to them.[260] This distinction between the worthy and unworthy poor was just one aspect of respectability, which was a concept with a subtle range of meanings that were manifest in different aspects of Mary's life.

We have seen how the cult of domesticity shaped Mary's family relationships and working life.[261] Female domesticity was closely related to the concept of respectability. Historians have observed that gender ideology, ideals of womanhood, the doctrine of separate spheres, and belief in the sanctity of family life were central to the way in which the middle class upheld its status.[262] While women derived the bulk of their status from the public-sphere occupations of their male family members, it was widely accepted that through their influence in the private sphere and their household management, women generated middle-class respectability by constructing and perpetuating distinct behavioural norms, moral values, and ideals.[263]

Child-rearing was a role in which women were expected to implant respectable morals and values in their children.[264] Motherhood was considered not only a vocation in itself but also a central part of middle-class respectability.[265] Mary was concerned about her step-granddaughter, Mary Ann. She remarked that after the early death of Mary Ann's mother, the young child was "anything but interesting," had forgotten her letters, and was generally untidy and poorly raised. Mary took it upon herself to live up to her promise to the child's dying mother and look after Mary Ann. To that end, Mary seems to have been very conscientious in ensuring that Mary Ann received proper schooling, and domestic and moral instruction.[266] In a moment of self-congratulation, Mary commented that her young charge was "very much improved" since she had moved into the Armstrong household.[267]

Mary Ann's education was also an indicator of respectable middle-class status. She probably attended a fee-charging grammar school in 1859, and earlier might have attended classes taught by Mary's sister Sarah Carruthers who was, for a brief time in the 1850s, a common-school teacher in York County.[268] Though in the 1840s Mary Ann's education could have indicated genteel status, by the 1850s formal schooling for girls was increasingly prevalent. It was not, however, designed to prepare young women for business careers or professional training, but rather for a good marriage and for proper feminine behaviour in the roles of wife, mother, and household mistress. This change was partially influenced by the development of the economy, the ending of the frontier period, and the declining need for child labour at home.[269] As a middle-class child in Britain in the 1820s, Mary had herself received an education, and she now ensured that her step-granddaughter would receive the same.[270]

Middle-class respectability was also defined by the social activities of those who claimed this status. For a middle-class woman, daily activities could include visits, drives, shopping, self-learning, and, of course, inevitable and unending household duties.[271] Mary occupied herself in exactly this way, throughout her diaries describing drives, visits, teas, shopping for household items, reading, and sewing.[272] Reading in particular was a respectable middle-class pastime. It was not only a leisure activity but also a serious pursuit aimed at moral and intellectual growth, self-discovery, and self-definition. Books on history and biography were considered to be particularly instructive and enriching. In addition to being read, books were also items for displaying in parlour bookcases.[273] Mary and her family actively engaged in reading a wide range of material, from newspapers to the Bible, devotional exercises, and David Hume's *History of England*. Mary also borrowed books from the Yorkville Library.[274]

Attending public lectures was another important social activity of the middle class. These were often hosted by local self-improvement societies, and respectable public speakers were invited to give talks on a wide range of subjects that had general appeal.[275] Mary and her family attended a wide range of lectures, and the topics she recorded include "ancient amusements," "the curiosities of chemistry," "cities of antiquity," the moon, and a reading of dramatic performances.[276] Mary also recorded that an "interesting" lecture for men only took place in February; this entry supports Holman's point that propriety was a concern in the selection of lecture topics. Temperance lectures were also attended by the middle class and will be discussed below.[277] Lecture attendance reflected the practical, useful, and self-improving aims of respectable members of the middle class.[278]

An emphasis on the cultivation of one's personal deportment, behaviour, and conduct was a further aspect of respectability. Proper cultivation, Holman argues, was essential to middle-class self-identity; it was "a tool of class distinction."[279] Middle-class families, as Davidoff and Hall have pointed out, perceived themselves to be surrounded by external threats, including poverty, disease, death, sexuality, brutality, and political unrest. Fixed styles of behaviour, speech, and dress were some of the practical and symbolic shields relied upon to protect middle-class domesticity from these outside threats.[280] Inward achievement and outward appearance of gentility were not only respectable goals; it was widely believed that a respectable exterior was a reflection of a respectable and morally strong interior. In a period of rapid social change, an "identifiable middle class appearance was a measure of trust."[281]

A middle-class concern with cultivation is apparent in Mary's writing. Clothing and jewellery were highly visible indicators of a refined lifestyle, but these were not things about which Mary wrote a great deal. However, she did include comments, at Thomas's request, about "a beautiful gold watch" that he had purchased, recording details about a church engraved on one side and its "exceedingly elegant gentleman's chain."[282] While this entry reveals an interest in appearance, a concern with personal carriage can be detected in Mary's thoughts on Mary Ann after the death of the child's mother.[283] Cultivated demeanour meant proper self-control over emotions, and when Philip lost his temper, Mary criticized his anger in her diary and recorded her resolution to "let it pass."[284] A final point of cultivation detectable in Mary's writing is speech content, which, as Holman has observed, was ideally to be focused on elevated topics and not stained with the vulgarity of shop talk concerning business stocks and goods, or household servants.[285] Reporting in her earlier diary on a conversation she'd had with her mother, Mary wrote about speaking of family, friends, and neighbours, the merits of a cup of tea, and of roast beef and mashed potatoes, all of which were respectable topics for polite conversation. Interestingly, she proudly admitted to speaking about "the troublesome qualities of servants," and she clearly did not think this to be an unsuitable topic.[286]

Related to cultivation and the outward appearance of personal respectability was the presentation of middle-class homes and yards. Measured, but not ostentatious, decorations were considered to be appropriate inside a home.[287] Certainly, Mary's happy recollections of "old fashioned dressers" and the floral patterns on her bed curtains in her childhood homes illustrate this point, and so do her comments on the new items purchased for the rooms at Rose Hill in 1869, including a walnut cupboard for the breakfast room, a toilette stand and mirror, a black walnut washstand, a "splendid" bookcase, and a "common" table.[288] She was very attached to the entire Rose Hill property, which she hoped would "go down to my descendants unmutilated."[289] Her eagerness to compare her home with that of the Widders, discussed above, also highlights the importance of home decoration to Mary.

Next to the home, a garden was an outdoor symbol of the middle-class values of privacy, taste, and appreciation of and control over the natural environment.[290] Mary fondly wrote about the "little garden" at her childhood home, which had a holly tree with scarlet berries that was "trimmed over the sitting room window."[291] On Dominion Day, 1869, she noted that she heard "endless exclamations of delight" from "holiday folks" passing by and catching view of her garden at Rose Hill, exclaiming in pleasure at its beauty.[292] Her garden was an important symbol and a source of pride for Mary, publicly proclaiming her respectability and domesticity.[293]

The size of middle-class households was also an important indicator of status and respectability. A large household that contained servants and boarders was an important element of middle-class lifestyle, distinguishing respectable homes from those of the working class.[294] Katz, in his quantitative study of social structure in Hamilton, argues that wealthier households tended to be larger. His statistics for 1851 show that the mean size in Hamilton for households whose heads were the same age as Philip (in their forties) was 6.5 people. For the same group, 3.3 children was the mean.[295] Mary and Philip had one child in 1859 and their household included at least seven people, depending on the number of hired farm hands.[296] The large household was a surviving ideal of the early nineteenth century, when prominent Upper Canadians had a more inclusive definition of the family not confined exclusively to blood relatives.[297]

At mid-century a distinction was made between family size and household size, and at this time elements of male culture promoted smaller family size. A man seeking credit for his business could be denied a loan if he had too many mouths to feed, and a large family was considered a waste of resources for a businessman.[298] However, to have one child, as Mary and Philip did, was rare for middle-class parents.[299] Interestingly, Davidoff and Hall noticed very little evidence in the English context to suggest that large families were discouraged among the middle class in that country.[300] While numbers of children were small, the size of the household was usually increased by the presence of boarders and servants. Contrary to Katz's conclusion that urban landlords infrequently employed their boarders, Philip's boarders seem to have been working for him as farm hands. That the Armstrongs did not actually live in a city may partially explain this arrangement.[301] While having only one child was not a typical trait of middle-class families, Philip and Mary's large household certainly fit the middle-class mould and was another element of their lives that demonstrated respectability.

William Westfall has suggested that religious change, rather than social change, may have lain at the root of the middle-class concept of respectability.[302] Church attendance was certainly an important part of respectability, and so were church-sponsored concerts, lectures, and picnics.[303] The Armstrongs and Wicksons were frequent and eager churchgoers—sometimes attending three services in a single day—and recorded trips to chapel are almost as common in Mary's diaries as her references to the number of eggs laid by her hens. The families' active involvement with their local Methodist church was an important symbol of their respectability and middle-class status.[304] Marks observes that family church attendance was a visible extension of the private Victorian family into a "public yet sacred space," allowing members to demonstrate their respectable status and "to see and be seen by their neighbours."[305] For a married man, attendance at church with his family reinforced and reflected a Christian masculinity that included a commitment to domestic life and his role as "respectable family provider."[306] Both Mary's father and husband were frequently at chapel, and a safe assumption is that among their motivations was a desire to affirm and demonstrate their social position.[307]

Neil Semple and Lynne Marks have both noted an increasing connection between religion and wealth after mid-century. Protestant churches, particularly the Methodists, attributed a religious quality to the wealth of prosperous members who were, in return, expected to share that wealth with the church.[308] Moreover, Van Die argues that by the end of the nineteenth century, at least in Toronto, Methodism became closely identified with upper-middle-class respectability.[309] Mary's record of sharing some of her wealth through a subscription to a "chapel fund," which may have been a contribution to the trust fund of a Wesleyan Methodist church on Queen Street, can be interpreted as an example of this connection between religion and wealth.[310]

Respectability, in its different manifestations, was a dominant concept in Mary's life, and she and her family members in myriad ways aimed to publicly demonstrate their respectable status. As we have seen, Mary identified herself as middle class.[311] By this, she meant to indicate her place in the new social structure that was gradually emerging in the context of early industrial capitalism. However, she certainly had not yet shed pre-industrial ideas of "rank" and hierarchy. Mary and her family were prosperous members of the new middle class that experienced gradual upward social mobility over many decades. Like other members of this class, Mary was aware of and curious about the lifestyles and public self-presentation of her social superiors, and she took note of them in her diary as she strove to define her own place in a changing social structure.

Occupation and Trade

The occupations of Mary's male family members, and the more specific topic of the butcher trade, tell us more about Mary's status and class.[312] Occupation has been cited as the most important factor determining middle-class status, and by this measure the Armstrongs and Wicksons were certainly middle class.[313] While industrial capitalism began to challenge independent butchers from the early 1860s, the Armstrongs and Wicksons maintained strong social and business ties with each other. Their young male relatives attempted, independently, to try their hands in the business. Census data on national origin and religious affiliation present a picture of Toronto's butchers at this time, and evidence from Mary's diaries illustrates the importance of kinship bonds in cementing business alliances.

Holman's three main categories of middle-class occupations are a useful framework with which to examine Mary's family. In his first, most populated, category are the merchants, manufacturers, and master artisans who comprised the business community. He devotes a second category to white-collar workers, including clerks and assistants employed in private businesses and in government offices. These individuals claimed middle-class status on account of their non-manual labour, their respectable dress and manner, and their perceived potential for advancement in business. In Holman's third and final occupational grouping are professionals, including members of the clergy, medical doctors, and lawyers. From mid-century, middle-class Victorian professionals were seen as "masters of bodies of useful knowledge," and their social responsibility, financial independence, and non-manual work, all of which derived from their education, were what distinguished them from wage labourers and the idle rich.[314]

Mary's male relatives could be found in at least two of these middle-class occupational categories. Some of her family members found their way into professional careers. Her youngest brother, Samuel, only ten years older than her son, Thomas, became a barrister and solicitor in the 1860s. Directories from the end of that decade list him as living in Yorkville, with offices in the city.[315] Another of Mary's brothers, Arthur, was a scholar and a minister. He received his M.A. and LL.B. from the new University of Toronto in 1850 and subsequently became a Congregational minister and a lecturer in classics, mathematics, and Hebrew at the Canadian Congregational Theological Institute. In 1856 he was appointed classical tutor and registrar of University College. In 1860 he received an LL.D. from the university. From 1863 to 1872 he was rector of the Toronto Grammar School, and during this time he continued to act as a matriculation examiner for the university and to sit occasionally on the university senate. In 1872 he returned to England and became a Congregational minister in London, where he died.[316] As professionals, Mary's younger brothers were clearly members of the middle class.

Mary's son, Thomas, was a medical student in 1859 and graduated as a physician in 1862.[317] As he entered middle-class adulthood, Thomas's choice to pursue a medical education seems to have been encouraged and possibly even financed by Mary's father, James Wickson, whom Mary frequently recorded as tutoring Thomas.[318] Education was increasingly seen as a gift of power that a father could provide for his children, and in some cases even as an appropriate substitute for inherited property. From the 1840s education was emphasized as a necessary tool for young men seeking self-sufficiency and a means to manage social change. Mary Ryan has examined what she calls a "family strategy" towards finding a career for young adults, where family members would contribute to funding an education or setting up a position in business.[319] Thomas's pursuit of a professional education and career, and the support he received from his family in this decision, illustrate the desire of the Armstrongs and Wicksons to maintain and reproduce their status across generations.

Though some members branched off into different, but typically middle-class, career routes, the backbone livelihood of the Wickson and Armstrong families was the butcher business. Mary's father, James Wickson, was a butcher. Her brothers James and John were butchers, and so were her nephews Rusby and, later, Henry. Her husband, Philip, was a butcher and for a time he went into business with her brother Samuel. Before going into medical school, Mary's son, Thomas, tried his hand in the butcher business. Robert Pallett, who married her stepdaughter, Anne, was a butcher too. Among the butcher businesses listed in the 1859–60 Toronto directory, one was Armstrong & Wickson (Philip and Samuel's short-lived partnership), one was John's business, and a third was Rusby's. All three had shops in the St. Lawrence Market.[320]

As land and business owners in the food-processing industry, self-employed butchers would fall most closely into Holman's first occupational category as master artisans. Mary's male relatives who were butchers seem to have networked and married into each other's families. Historians have observed that family members were an important resource of labour, credit, and capital investment for family businesses.[321] Davidoff and Hall argue that the daughters and sisters of small businessmen often married their fathers' and brothers' present or future business partners, an arrangement that served to bind the fortunes of different families together.[322] When Mary and Philip were married in 1837, these considerations probably played a role in bringing the couple together. The Wickson family quite likely saw Philip as a future partner (and certainly an ally) in business, and encouraged a union between him and Mary.[323]

If partnership was an expectation when the couple got married, in 1859 it was a reality: Philip and Samuel were in business together, advertising in the city directory as "Armstrong & Wickson, butchers." Mary's diaries give the impression that Samuel did much of the paperwork at home, while Philip attended market.[324] In the 1850s, Burley has noted, men with inadequate capital means banded together to pool their resources in the face of expanding industrial capitalism, and it may be that this spirit of partnership propelled Philip and Samuel into business together.[325] For an unknown reason, Philip and Samuel's business alliance did not last more than one year, and upon its conclusion, Samuel left the meat business altogether and became a lawyer.[326] By 1864 Philip had formed a new partnership with John McCarter, another butcher, which lasted for three years. As we have seen, Philip left his second partnership by 1867, leaving for good the trade that had been his primary occupation for almost forty years.[327]

In light of Philip's openness to enter into partnerships, it is interesting that when starting out in the meat industry (before he chose to begin medical school) Thomas did not join his father's business. Instead, he attempted to start independently, and failed.[328] John Wickson's son Rusby also began his own meat business in the late 1850s, but he too did not persist. He was out of business by the early 1860s, though he eventually moved to Buffalo, New York, where he found success as a butcher. Like his cousin Thomas, when Rusby started out in Toronto he did not enter a partnership with his father.[329] These business decisions were not as peculiar as they might at first seem. Burley has noted that after mid-century few enterprises were big enough to support a new partner who brought no additional capital, and consequently, many tradesmen's sons chose alternate careers.[330] It is apparent, however, that Thomas and Rusby were encouraged to try their hands in the trade before moving on.

The main Wickson family butcher business, begun by Mary's father in 1834, was taken over by her brother John in 1840.[331] While Mary kept her earlier diary, John and his wife, Eliza, lived in the city on Church Street, and he kept a stall in the St. Lawrence Market.[332] In the 1860s, John moved up to Yorkville and lived a little to the south of the Armstrongs on New Kent Road (subsequently Wickson Avenue and now Alcorn Avenue). There he owned and operated a slaughterhouse, which represented a large investment in his enterprise. His operation was big enough to necessitate employing a clerk.[333] It is probable that Philip and Rusby both made use of this slaughterhouse for their own businesses through some arrangement that may or may not have been formalized within the family.[334] John's slaughterhouse was strategically placed. Situated very close to Yonge Street, a main thoroughfare for farmers bringing livestock in from York County and beyond, it was also north of the city toll bar, and market regulations forbade the slaughter of animals within the city limits.[335] These advantages must have attracted a substantial number of farmers to the business.

While butchers in Victorian Ontario have not drawn much attention from historians, geographer Ian MacLachlan's study of meat-packing in Canada addresses the economic history of this industry from its development in the nineteenth century and through the twentieth century.[336] As well, south of the border, Chicago is a city in which the expansion of the meat-packing industry has been examined in depth.[337] No detailed study of the impact of industrialization on Toronto butchers will be undertaken here, but a cursory overview of some patterns among these artisans may be offered. The industrial competition that butchers faced came from meat-packing companies like Wilson & Co. and William Davies Co., the latter being the direct corporate ancestor of Maple Leaf Foods. These were Toronto's first meat-packing companies, and they appeared in city business directories for the first time in 1862 and 1864, respectively.[338] It was in these years that Philip must have begun to consider leaving the butcher business, which he did in 1867. However, the immediate impact of industrialization on Toronto's butchers is ambiguous. The number of butchers appearing in city directories between 1856 and 1876 fluctuated significantly and, if anything, grew. This expansion might indicate that the strains of early industrial capitalism were not felt as harshly in this area of the food industry as they were elsewhere.[339]

The index to the 1871 Ontario census reveals significant patterns of national origin and religious affiliation among butchers in Toronto and York County. Of a total of 243 butchers that appeared in these districts, 75 percent were of English national origin. The next most common nationality was Irish, at about 16 percent. Scots made up less than 5 percent. Not surprisingly, in light of the high level of immigration at mid-century, almost 85 percent of all butchers had been born overseas. In terms of religious affiliation, just over 50 percent were Anglican, 20 percent were Methodist, about 9 percent were Catholic, 7 percent were Presbyterian, and 5 percent were Baptist. If these approximate numbers reflect the composition of the trade in the preceding decades, as a Methodist of English origin Philip would have been among a group that comprised 16 percent of all Toronto butchers. On the other hand, the Congregationalist Wicksons were perhaps the only members of that denomination to be in the meat business, as John's son Henry was the only Congregationalist butcher listed in 1871.[340]

Historians have observed a close link between religious affiliation and business partnerships. Generally, family businesses operated in an overlapping network of kin, friends, and religious community. In these circles of family, congregation, and voluntary organizations, individuals were able to raise credit and capital from mostly personal sources.[341] Among the vast majority of butchers, who were Anglicans of English origin, these networks may have existed and may have been cast more widely than the compact Armstrong-Wickson nexus. Interestingly, the Armstrongs and Wicksons, as members of smaller religious groups within the butcher population, appear to have preferred to keep their business networks within their kin group and among those of the same national origin. Of course, there is the exception of Philip's eventual partnership with John McCarter,[342] but the blood connections between the Armstrong and Wickson families, which stretched across denominational lines, support the argument that kinship was more important than religious affiliation in determining business networks.[343]

Mary's diaries flesh out an analysis of the occupational positions of her male family members. While other primary sources provide much of the information in this section, it is Mary's writing that offers a close perspective on the professional careers of her son and brothers. She also sheds light on Thomas's attempt at the meat business, and the very close social and economic connections between her marital and birth families. The occupations of the Armstrongs and Wicksons were clearly middle class, even typically so, and their professional careers, businesses, partnerships, and concern with setting up their young adult male children in similar livelihoods demonstrate this point. The social connections between these two families were strong, and this tends to emphasize the point that kinship and co-nationality were important factors in the creation and maintenance of business networks. Mary's diaries will be an important source for any future study that, building on MacLachlan's work, examines independent Toronto butchers at the time of industrialization.

Faith and Religious Practice

Faith and religious practice are significant themes in Mary's text, and they were essential elements in the lives of Mary and her family members. The cultural relationship between evangelicalism and Anglicanism in nineteenth-century Ontario is the background against which were set the faith and religious practice of Mary and her family. Westfall and Van Die, in particular reference to Methodism, have examined the major changes in the protestant culture of this period. Westfall argues that early in the century, two distinct protestant cultures existed: that of established

Anglicanism, based on rationality, order, and a systematic understanding of God and the world; and that of evangelicalism, based on intense personal experience, emphasis of emotion over intellect, and belief in God as an active power in daily affairs.[344] By the middle decades of the century, these two extremes began to find a new cultural middle ground. From the 1840s, the Anglican Church slowly underwent a series of changes that dismantled the apparatus of its establishment and transformed it into one of many competing denominations.[345] At the same time, the material success of many Methodists who had assumed important positions in society generated a sense of optimistic confidence in that rapidly growing church. In response to this social change, and to changes in the old religious order, Methodism sought a more moderate interpretation of Christianity. The church shifted its focus away from conversion and revivalism and transformed itself into a moral social institution that nurtured the faith of its members through churches, Sunday schools, and voluntary organizations.[346] By 1870, Westfall argues, Methodist evangelicalism had moved closer to disestablished Anglicanism.[347]

In the dynamic religious and cultural environment of the mid-nineteenth century, Mary and her family actively participated in organized religion. While Mary kept her diaries, she and Philip and several of her Wickson relatives who lived nearby attended the Central Methodist Church, which Mary refers to as the "Yorkville Church," situated at the northwest corner of the intersection of Bloor and Gwynne Streets, just east of Yonge Street.[348] However, not all of Mary's family members were Methodists. In England the Wicksons had been Congregationalists, and many of her family members maintained their involvement with that church in Canada. Mary's brother Arthur became a Congregational minister, and both of Mary's sisters, Jane and Sarah, were of the same faith. Jane married the Reverend Edward Ebbs, who was pastor of the Paris Congregational Church from 1858 to 1865.[349] Notably, it was Edward Ebbs and Arthur Wickson who performed the marriage ceremony of Thomas Armstrong and Fidelia Jane Maughan in the Eglinton Methodist Church in 1863.[350] Notwithstanding his Congregational ministry, Mary noted that Arthur sometimes attended the Yorkville Church. Mary's brother John and his family were Congregationalists, and she happily recorded in her earlier diary that they invited the Armstrongs to the baptism of their twins.[351] The Armstrongs and Wicksons maintained strong family connections across membership in different denominations.

Conversion was a recurring event in the religious life of Mary's birth and conjugal families. Though born an Anglican, Philip Armstrong married in the Congregational Church and later both he and Mary after him converted to Methodism, as did Mary's brother Samuel and her father and mother. Mary's stepdaughter, Anne, wed a Methodist, but they were married in an Anglican church. Thomas married a Methodist, but they later became Anglicans. The conversion experience lay at the core of Methodist piety; indeed, all evangelical churches had some form of this experience as a precondition for membership.[352] Conversion was a personal "spiritual and emotional force" that drew people into a faith for more than just worldly reasons.[353] While it could be a "radical disjunction" with one's past, for individuals raised in an evangelical family, the conversion experience could be intimately associated with their childhood years and perceived as a spiritual return to that period of life.[354]

For Mary's family members who left an evangelical faith for Anglicanism, they may not have experienced an emotional conversion so much as made the decision to switch churches for other, more worldly, reasons.[355] However, for Mary, we are left to speculate on her personal reasons for leaving Congregationalism and becoming a Methodist. We do know that she probably converted sometime between 1851 and 1855, but we do not know how her conversion occurred.[356] It very well may have been at a lively outdoor revival that she found her new faith. However it was accomplished, Mary's conversion to Methodism was not a major break with her past, or with her other family members who did not convert. Indeed, Mary seems to have converted once more before she died. The 1881 census lists her as an Anglican living in Paris, Ontario, with her widowed sister Sarah, a Congregationalist, and her two nieces, Lizzie, also a Congregationalist, and Fannie, a Presbyterian. We have seen that the Wickson family remained close despite their participation in different churches, and Congregationalist Arthur Wickson's performance of Thomas and Fidelia's marriage ceremony in a Methodist church underlines this point. Moreover, Mary expressed in her diary that her faith was something she saw as lifelong, and she traced her belief back to her childhood.[357]

Aside from the personal conviction of a conversion experience, membership in a church was governed by a variety of motivations. Faith and religious belief were obvious factors, but worldly considerations were important too. Religious practice reinforced a sense of identity and community among congregants.[358] As we have seen, church attendance was also a public demonstration of respectable social standing in the larger community. While the concept of respectability was emerging as an important element of middle-class ideology after about 1850, at the same time new patterns of belief and styles of religious practice were materializing within Methodism.[359]

After mid-century, Methodist revivals and camp meetings were in decline, while an enthusiasm for building new churches and a focus on Sabbath services, Sunday schools, and missionary activities was growing within the denomination. In this process, Westfall argues, the new concept of respectability forced successful and status-conscious Methodists to reject their "rather tacky past" of rambunctious outdoor revivals and seek to adapt to new codes of social and religious behaviour.[360] Equally, the outward appearance of Methodist religious practice was becoming more refined. Ministers adopted a more pleasing and respectable manner of speech and tidied up their personal appearance, while at the same time church members were instructed to sing hymns with decorum.[361] Reason and moderation began to be emphasized in religious belief, and religious experience became more temperate and internal than it had been at the excited camp meetings of previous decades. The faithful were expected to connect with a powerful sermon by feeling the words of the preacher deep in their souls.[362]

Mary's comments on religious practice and experience bear out Westfall's analysis of this change. She did not describe revivals or camp meetings, but instead regular and frequent attendance at chapel services. Mary wrote about her very intense faith and claimed to feel the "spirituality of Divine things" during the reading of the liturgy and a "fervour of devotion" during prayers. Attending the St. George's Day service at St. James' Cathedral in 1859, Mary felt "inspired with Holy feelings" that stirred the articles of her belief in her "inmost recesses."[363] She was clearly a woman of deep personal piety, but one who experienced her faith with internal reflection and not through uncontrollable public exclamations of devotion. The intensity of Mary's faith had perhaps lessened when she kept her second diary in 1869. She generally quoted less from scripture and made far fewer, if any, attestations of her religious conviction, though she frequently referred to the goodness of God and "His blessing," and she often noted her thanks to God for her good fortune.[364] A lessening of the intensity of Mary's faith may, however, be interpreted as a further "refinement" of her expectations of religious practice and belief, and not primarily as a reduction in her personal piety.

Personal piety was important to Mary, and belief could both inspire and exalt her. Faith was something she took quite seriously and, as we have seen, was something she traced back to her childhood.[365] Nineteenth-century female diarists frequently made reference to and directly addressed God in their journals.[366] In her earlier diary, Mary did this often: she called directly on God to have mercy on her family; to express her thanks and gratefulness; and to reassure herself that God not only heard but also answered prayers.[367] Family prayer, which was part public worship and part private devotion, was an important feature of middle-class life.[368] While Mary did not record her family praying together, she did mention that on at least one occasion she spent a Sunday afternoon at home reading devotional exercises out loud with her son.[369]

Religion could also be a consolation in difficult times.[370] During her father's illness Mary regularly mentioned God in her diary, and she and her family relied on faith in God's will, "whatever," she said, "that might be."[371] Mary turned to her faith when she felt troubled. While criticizing the morally questionable behaviour of her help girl Bessie, Mary took time in her diary to reconcile herself with God's plan. She wrote, "I pray God to give me faith in his promises … especially in that one,—'Whatever ye shall ask the Father in my name, he will give it you' On Lord God I ask for Jesus Christ[']s sake convert my dear child, and make him a living epistle."[372] Mary believed that God could help not only her but also those for whom she prayed.

For some nineteenth-century women, faith was also essential to one's well-being.[373] For Mary it could be a source of contentment. Reflecting on her life in April 1859, she wrote that she had "enjoyed more peace, the last three months than at any former period of my life" in part because she had resolved "not to worry myself over things of which I had no control but to trust in God."[374] God was a being on whom Mary could rely in times of confusion. She believed wholeheartedly in God's promises, which she took personally, and this belief gave her a sense of relief and peace.

Mary and her family's faith was shaped by the feminine quality of Protestantism in the nineteenth century. Women were twice as likely as men to be church members in late nineteenth-century Ontario.[375] Marks has shown that membership rolls reflected the dominant evangelical theory of the period, which represented the ideal of Christian tenderness, love, and submission "in terms that had much resonance with contemporary feminine ideals."[376] At the same time, this ideal was less easily—but not impossibly—reconciled to contemporary notions of strong, autonomous, and virile masculinity.[377] Women were commonly viewed as being naturally more religious than men, and for many women, the conversion experience symbolized entrance into a "sisterhood of shared belief beyond the bonds of home and family."[378] While Mary did not address this subject in detail, on Easter Sunday, 1859, she noted that she went to church with her mother while her father instead went to town.[379] This was unusual, as Mary usually went to church with most of her family, and both her husband and son seem to have been quite religious. Among men, those who were married were in some cases three times more likely to be church members than those who were not.[380] In the case of Mary's son, Thomas, he was not only a frequent congregant but also attended Bible meetings, presumably held at the Yorkville Church.[381] Thomas's active church membership was not typical of young men his age, and this suggests that his motivations were based less in social considerations than in a personal faith that was reinforced by his pious mother.[382]

During the decades in which Mary wrote her diaries, in the context of a gradual cultural rapprochement between Methodist evangelicalism and Anglicanism that was influenced by middle-class ideology, the Armstrongs and Wicksons maintained strong family connections across different denominations. Conversion was a recurring event within the family and was perhaps a contributing source of the intense faith that Mary traced back to her childhood. She was deeply pious, she turned to God for comfort in difficult times, and her faith was ultimately a source of contentment and structure in her life.

Social Network, Community, and Local Identity

Social network and community are important aspects of Mary and her family's experience, and both are important to the construction of local identity. Social networks are defined here as overlapping and interconnecting circles of family, friends, and acquaintances. In aggregate, these overlapping circles create community, which is an abstract sense of fellowship or friendly association with others based in shared experience and, to varying degrees, location. It is possible to speak of an individual belonging to different communities at the same time, such as a local neighbourhood, city, or county community, and also a religious, ethnic, or professional community. Mary and her family were part of different circles of social contacts, and they belonged to different communities in which they became involved through church membership and participation in voluntary societies. While they belonged to different communities, Mary and her family assumed local identities derived from those communities.

Voluntary societies and associations were an integral part of social life in the nineteenth-century Anglo-American world. Middle-class men sought to demonstrate their social power and responsibility in the public sphere through involvement in voluntary associations.[383] Holman has argued that in mid-Victorian Ontario, voluntary organizations were focal points around which the middle class assembled and developed ideals of "proper public conduct" and determined its "role as a public guardian and model of moral rectitude." A phenomenon related to middle class formation, from mid-century participation in voluntary associations was an important expression of respectable male involvement in the local community. However, while the majority of voluntary organizations were male-dominated, women also participated in some of these societies.[384] As middle-class families, the Armstrongs and Wicksons actively participated in this "age of societies."[385] They did so through membership in their local church, and in church-related organizations. They were also involved with temperance reform, national, and self-improvement societies, and some of Mary's relatives took on leadership roles in agricultural associations and local government. Such involvement shaped the social networks and communities to which Mary and her family belonged, and in turn these communities shaped her local identity.

Religion in the mid-nineteenth century was not just about personal faith; it was also about community. As we have seen, church attendance was a family affair. When Mary went to chapel her husband, son, step-granddaughter, and brother frequently accompanied her, and upon her arrival at the Yorkville Church she usually met her father and mother there as well.[386] Family togetherness at church was important to Mary, a sentiment she expressed at the thought of her wider family gathering for the baptism of her nephew and niece in the spring of 1859.[387] In addition to fostering family ties, church services allowed Mary to participate in a local community of faith, where she shared her religious practices with other members of her congregation, many of whom were probably her neighbours. Moreover, historians have noted that going to church was one of the few opportunities middle-class women had for leaving their domestic surroundings.[388] For Mary, church attendance also meant an enjoyable walk through her neighbourhood, which in itself was a welcome break from her household duties.[389] Membership in the Yorkville Church was an important aspect of Mary's local identity as a member of her village community.

Another local church community that was of great importance for Mary's family was centred on the Paris Congregational Church in Brant County, to the west of Toronto. It is clear that shortly after their arrival in Upper Canada, the Wickson family forged links with fellow Congregationalists in Brantford and Paris.[390] Mary's sister Jane married Rev. Edward Ebbs, who from 1858 to 1865 was pastor of the Paris Congregational Church.[391] Edward Ebbs's sister Elizabeth was the second wife of the wealthy local businessman Norman Hamilton. In 1884 their daughter

"Lizzie" Hamilton married Paul Wickson, the son of Mary's brother Arthur. By 1865 Elizabeth Ebbs Hamilton had died, and Norman Hamilton took as his third wife Mary's widowed sister Sarah Wickson Carruthers. That same year, Edward Ebbs resigned as pastor and was succeeded by Rev. William H. Allworth, whose son Alfred Adolphus Allworth in 1882 married Fannie Wickson, the daughter of Mary's brother George.[392] This convoluted web of intermarriage between the Wicksons, Ebbs, Allworths, and Hamiltons, families that were among the prosperous elite of the small town of Paris, illustrates how close a church community might be. Though she lived in Yorkville, Mary was still involved with this group in Paris. She attended the church meeting at which Edward Ebbs resigned as pastor, and like her mother, Mary died in Paris at her sister Sarah's house.[393] Her connections with this network of Congregationalists in Paris lasted for almost the entirety of her life in Canada and no doubt expanded her sense of place and belonging in her adopted land.

While religion could serve as a focal point for family and neighbourhood, it also linked broader communities, providing a wide social network of friends and acquaintances.[394] Mary's first entry for her 1859 diary records that Philip attended a Primitive Methodist tea party that day. Small gatherings like this were common, but so were larger ones, such as the opening of a new church in the surrounding community. On Sunday, 1 May 1859, Mary wrote, "the Opening of A New Church was attended with invitations for us to four different familys." Though Mary and Thomas stayed home that day for want of transportation, Philip, Samuel, and a family friend attended the dedication ceremony for Cooper's Church at Davenport Station. The Methodist weekly newspaper, the *Christian Guardian*, reported, "crowds of worshippers covered the road leading to the church," and the building was filled to capacity. "At least two hundred visitors were entertained during the day" under the "hospitable roof of Davenport House." It was an all-day event. Services began at 10 a.m. and the last one of the day started at 6:30 p.m.[395] Mary's receipt of invitations to various receptions held by friends and acquaintances after the event (on which she commented as a point of pride) illustrate the social nature of the day. The dedication of a new church was cause for celebration and hospitality, through which the bonds of community were reinforced among the broader Methodist community, which spanned Toronto and the surrounding region. Participation in this city-wide community contributed another part of Mary's local identity.

In mid-nineteenth-century Canada, religion went beyond church membership. It was the basis for the activities of a number of voluntary organizations. Van Die argues that in the first three decades after mid-century, the Methodist church was "transformed from a select body of converts into a far reaching social institution."[396] This transformation, associated with the influence of new ideas about respectability on religious practice, was achieved through the expansion of church-related organizations.[397] Similarly, Westfall argues that in this process Methodist leaders asked church members to become more "usefully" involved in their world, promoting activist and Methodist religious causes such as missionary work, benevolent societies, and temperance reform, among others.[398]

In 1859 church-related organizations were an important part of Mary and her family members' lives.[399] Her brother Arthur, a Congregationalist, was minute secretary of the Upper Canada Bible Society during 1859.[400] The goal of this non-denominational organization and its kindred associations in other countries was to translate and distribute bibles as widely as possible, spreading the scriptures with a passive and co-operative missionary agenda. Mary and her family members were also involved in other religious organizations, such as the Wesleyan Methodist Missionary Society, which had been formed in 1819 and was divided into conferences around the world. The Canada Conference of the society held regular meetings for the Toronto district, and Mary made reference to these meetings in January and February 1859, which she, her parents, Philip, and Thomas attended. The depth of involvement that the Armstrongs and Wicksons had with the society is unknown, but their membership and attendance at meetings reveals that they identified with and supported this cause.[401]

Historians have examined women's involvement in church-related organizations. While power in these organizations lay mostly with male leaders from the church community, enthusiasm for social reform and evangelicalism prompted women to become involved with missionary societies and benevolent associations, where they often took on leadership roles.[402] The work of women in these organizations was perceived as a "public extension of their separate sphere," and their encroachment on the male-controlled space of the church was sometimes perceived as a threat to the authority of its male leaders.[403] While the dominant involvement of middle-class women in the philanthropic work of these societies was a reflection of their respectability, it also allowed women to be socially active beyond the boundaries of their family networks.[404] Benevolent societies such as the Ladies' Aid that co-ordinated poor relief were a major philanthropic avenue for women, but Mary was apparently not involved in this type of group at the Yorkville Church. In contrast, Mary and her female family members were involved with the missionary society. While they sometimes attended meetings with their male family members, the missionary society was an organization that the Armstrong and Wickson women sometimes attended on their own, without male accompaniment. This occurred in February 1859 when Mary recorded that she, her mother, and Mary Ann intended to go to a meeting together one evening.[405] They do not seem to have played leadership roles in this organization, but their involvement suggests that regular attendance at meetings was perhaps a mostly female activity, not requiring the presence of men. As such, Mary's participation in and identification with the Toronto area Methodist missionary community was something she shared with her female family members.

Temperance reform was a quasi-religious cause that attracted Methodists such as the Armstrongs and Wicksons. From mid-century, alcohol was increasingly seen as an unhealthy, immoral vice and a collective social problem. The movement for temperance reform became, not surprisingly, a prominent middle-class cause that was driven by a sense of social duty and collective responsibility to correct the moral failings of society.[406] Indeed, the colony came very close to legislating alcohol prohibition in 1855, but the bill was rejected on a technicality. Quasi-religious organizations such as the newer Sons of Temperance and the older Temperance Reformation Society promoted abstinence from drink and taverns. The Sons of Temperance and its affiliate groups for women and children, the Daughters and the Cadets, had low fees, open membership policies, and were known for large public gatherings and street parades in fancy regalia. Members and their families were entitled to financial support in case of bereavement, and funding for elaborate funerals. In return, members signed pledges of sobriety in family groups, which were proudly displayed on parlour and dining-room walls. Those found to have broken their pledge forfeit their membership and entitlements.[407] Members of temperance societies were not necessarily church members, but some, particularly women, came to these societies with evangelical faith and a belief in the conventions of churchgoing respectability.[408] It is not clear whether Mary and her family were full members of these temperance societies, but even if they were not, they still participated in the societies' social events. Though Mary made no corroborating record in her diaries, family tradition holds that Philip was an avid teetotaller who would go into taverns and invite anyone who wished to renounce alcohol to spend a night sobering up at Rose Hill.

Tea meetings, soirees with vocal music, and lectures were typical activities of temperance societies.[409] Mary and her family attended various temperance lectures during 1859. In April, Mary went with Samuel, Thomas, and Mary Ann (whom she had "promised" to take to the lecture) to hear the Scotsman Peter Sinclair, a travelling temperance lecturer from Edinburgh, give a talk hosted by the Temperance Reformation Society at Temperance Hall on Temperance Street. Sinclair gave a series of lectures in Toronto in the month of April and drew "good attendance" and an article in the *Globe*. Mary apparently believed that, like regular attendance at church, hearing about the evils of drink was good for eleven-year-old Mary Ann's development; she took her to another of Sinclair's lectures on 12 April, held in the Yorkville Church. Mary quoted in her diary an inspirational phrase from Sinclair's lecture that she thought to be "well worth remembering." Mary, Philip, Samuel, and Thomas attended a tea party at Temperance Hall in Sinclair's honour on 19 April, which was addressed by Colonel Playfair, who was involved with the Sons of Temperance.[410] Much like the lectures on more general topics that the family attended, the temperance-related social events that Mary and her family members frequented were an important aspect of her community. Going beyond the merely "practical" or "useful," temperance lectures combined a sense of occasion with moral conviction and inspiration.[411] They were a public environment in which Mary could identify with and feel personally connected to her wider local community and the social issues affecting it.

Besides religious and social reform organizations, Mary and her family were involved with other voluntary associations. The St. George's Society, established in the 1830s for the charitable assistance of English immigrants in need of relief, was, like the Irish St. Patrick's Society and the Scottish St. Andrew's Society, a focal point for recent and more settled immigrants, providing them with a venue to connect with fellow English people in their new land.[412] Mary often mentioned the St. George's Society in her earlier diary and also the regular attendance of Thomas, Samuel, and Philip at rehearsals for a concert put on by the Society in March.[413] The St. George's Society, while it had a charitable aspect, was for Mary less about benevolence and morality and more about large social events and respectable entertainment. A hint of irritation may be detected in Mary's comments about not being able to attend the concert in March because her husband had, after weeks of rehearsals, "taken offence at something."[414] Certainly, Mary enjoyed going to the party hosted by the Widders that coincided with the last rehearsal for the concert.[415] She also recorded the details of the St. George's Day choral service hosted by the society at St. James' Cathedral in 1859, an event before which she dined with family friends and after which she noted the performances of members of the Yorkville Church.[416] The St. George's Society events were a significant part of Mary's social life. Membership in this community contributed to Mary's local identity by reinforcing bonds with networks of friends and acquaintances from both her Yorkville neighbourhood and across the city.

A different non-religious organization with which the Armstrongs and Wicksons were involved was the Yorkville Debating and Mutual Improvement Society (YDMIS). Self-improvement societies were created in Victorian Ontario as part of a middle-class effort to provide young males with venues for intellectual activity aimed at guiding them into responsible adulthood. Organizations such as the Young Men's Christian Association (YMCA), mechanics institutes, and debating societies provided lectures, readings, and debates as activities designed for cultivated self-improvement.[417] While it is not clear if Thomas and Samuel were individually involved with such societies, Mary recorded in April 1859 that both young men as well as her parents and Philip attended a "soiree" held by the YDMIS that was, as advertised in the *Globe*, "complimentary … to the gentlemen who delivered the late course of Lectures in connexion with the society." One of these lecturers, Mary noted, was Mr. Ash, the young minister at the Yorkville Church. Mary does not say whether or not Thomas or Samuel had also given lectures.[418] While the activities of this debating society were directed at Mary's son, brother, and minister, the organization served, on occasions like these, as a social venue within the local community of Yorkville that involved entire families and reinforced bonds between them. In this smaller association the Armstrongs seem to have been more prominent than in the larger city-wide organizations discussed above. The family's prominence may have served to underline the importance of the Yorkville community to Mary's local identity.

Though other family members were not directly involved, Philip's involvement with exclusively male agricultural and horticultural societies and Mary's brothers' service as local politicians in Yorkville were important aspects of the Armstrongs' and Wicksons' roles in both their immediate and wider communities. Philip was an eager participant in agricultural and related societies. Prior to legislation for public grants passed in 1830, agricultural societies had been private social clubs for the colonial elite, but throughout the 1830s and 1840s, middling farmers, merchants, and businessmen became involved and these organizations grew.[419] Philip entered and won prizes for his produce at the County of

York Agricultural Society (CYAS) show in the 1850s. By 1859 he was president of the society, and in April of that year he organized a ploughing match at Yonge Street and Eglinton Avenue, which was attended by George Allan and two MPPs.[420] He was intermittently a judge at the Provincial Agricultural Exhibition and was also very involved with the Toronto Horticultural Society (THS) from the 1860s, often serving as vice-president of this society in the 1870s.[421] In 1866 and again in the 1870s he served as president of the City of Toronto Electoral Division Society (CTEDS), which held a summer horticultural exhibition and a fall agricultural and mechanical exhibition. With the CTEDS, he was heavily involved in the development of the Industrial Exhibition in Toronto, the forerunner of the Canadian National Exhibition (CNE).[422] Philip's leadership role in these societies connected him with both the Toronto horticultural-agricultural community and the wider York County agricultural community.

Some of Mary's brothers served as municipal politicians on the Yorkville council. The Baldwin Act of 1849 encouraged municipal incorporations, and this level of local government came to be dominated by middle-class interests.[423] Yorkville was incorporated as a village in 1853, and in the 1860s Samuel served as village clerk. In 1873, 1875, and 1876 he was deputy reeve, and he was elected as reeve in 1878. Mary's older brother John also served in the village government. He was a councillor in 1855, 1856, 1868, and 1870.[424] The Wickson family were active in local politics, and their public service illustrates their very middle-class concern with actively shaping the welfare of their local community.[425] While not a voluntary organization in quite the same sense as a temperance or a missionary society, local government was nevertheless similar in that it was an organized cause to which Mary's brothers chose to devote their time and energy. Even Philip became politically active as a member of the York county council at some point, probably in the 1870s.[426] Participation in local government and agricultural and related societies by her male family members had an indirect influence on Mary's social network. The prominent activities of her husband and brothers widened their network of social contacts and also widened the communities of which they and Mary, by association, were a part.[427] Consequently, these activities involved Mary and her family members in the Yorkville political community, the Toronto horticultural-agricultural community, and the county agricultural and political community, each of which made a distinct contribution to her local identity.

For Mary and her family, a typically middle-class involvement in a variety of organizations shaped the social networks and communities to which they belonged. We have noted above that by 1869 Mary was less involved in voluntary societies than she had been a decade earlier.[428] Her cooled enthusiasm may reflect the achievement of a degree of upward social mobility in later life. Having successfully demonstrated her respectability, status-driven motivations for her voluntary activities may not have been as strong as they had been.[429] In general, Mary's experience confirms what Holman, Marks, and others have determined about middle-class formation, respectability, religion, and social networks elsewhere in the province.[430] It is clear that the same processes were underway in Yorkville at mid-century. Involvement with the various organizations discussed above gave Mary and her family members a connection to the broader communities of which they were a part. They identified not only with people from their immediate church and neighbourhood but also with people from across the city and across the ocean. For Mary, this community involvement was a vital extension of her life beyond her household.

Community involvement creates a sense of identity. Mary and her family were involved in Toronto-based communities, as their involvement with city-wide organizations illustrates. Nevertheless, despite this involvement in different city communities and Mary's regular attendance at the city market on Saturdays, Mary did not identify herself as a Torontonian.[431] Toronto was a distinct place for Mary, and she referred to it as such in her diaries. She wrote about Yorkville residents bringing news from the city, speaking of it as a different place.[432] On a number of occasions she specifically recorded that she had taken a ride to "the City" on a leisure excursion, or that a male household member had gone there on business.[433] It seems that though Mary lived in York County, near to both the village of Yorkville and the city of Toronto, and though she belonged to a number of different communities that all contributed some element of her identity, her local identity was predominantly shaped by her connections to and involvement in the Yorkville community.

National Identities

National identity and British imperial history are related topics that have drawn a great deal of academic attention in the last quarter century. The concepts of nation, nationalism, and national identity have been explored by scholars who tend to define identity as a cultural phenomenon that is not static but dynamic.[434] Moreover, Anthony Smith has expanded the concept of identity and argued that an individual can have multiple identities that exist in layered, concentric circles, an idea that is useful for examining Mary's experience.[435] At the same time, imperial history has grown as a discipline in response to decolonization and the end of empire. Scholars of imperial history, many connected with the Manchester School, have focused on categories of cultural difference in the three themes that have dominated social history since the 1960s: "race," class, and gender. More recently, some historians, notably Catherine Hall, have paid particular attention to the culture of the colonizers, as opposed to the colonized, and to the cultural relationship between the imperial metropole and the colonies.[436]

Scholars of literature have approached the cultural questions of imperialism, and their work has produced some very interesting results. With a focus on travel literature, Mary Louise Pratt's examination of the cultural representation of European expansion from the eighteenth century and after has produced important ideas about the interplay between different cultures in the colonial context. Historians like Hall have taken up Pratt's ideas about "contact zones" (social space in which cultures meet and clash in relationships of dominance and subordination) and "transculturation" (the ways in which subjugated peoples influence and shape the dominant culture's constructions of periphery and metropole).[437] Sara Mills has also focused on travel writing and has engaged questions about gender and space in the context of colonialism.[438] Her work on Fanny Parkes, an English woman who wrote about her experiences in British India during the nineteenth century, argues that women could exist in the colonial world as "spectators of empire" and portray themselves as "transcendent observers," but not directly participate in the system of colonial dominance.[439] It is with this historiography in mind that we approach Mary's national identity, and her experience in a British colony.

Mary's sense of national identity was complex. It can be described using Smith's model of concentric layers.[440] At one layer was, perhaps, her sense of being a part of empire. In the 1860s, the British Empire claimed dominion over 200 million people around the globe, and the idea of the English metropole and its colonies was firmly established in the imaginations of Englishmen.[441] Hall has examined the lives of some colonial administrators and argues that they developed an "imperial identity" that was derived from experiences in different "sites of empire," where distinct relations of power, subject positions, and cultural identities were articulated.[442] While Mary was not an imperial administrator, her national identity was, at one level, imperial, and her identification with the empire was on cultural terms. In a colony of white settlement, Pratt's concept of transcultural contact zones is not readily applicable to Mary's experience or the evidence of her text. However, women's historians concerned with the development of conceptions of femininity in the Victorian period have highlighted the existence of a "transatlantic community of culture" between Britain and North America.[443] Mary's imperial identity can be examined in the context of a transatlantic, and imperial, cultural community.

Newspapers and other printed materials played an important role in the construction of national and imperial identity. Benedict Anderson has argued that the development of commodified print-capitalism in the eighteenth century allowed the nation to be imagined in the minds of readers.[444] Others have extended this argument to include the idea that newspapers and other printed materials fostered readers' imaginative participation in the economic and political world of empire.[445] More specifically, scholars have argued that the nineteenth-century newspaper and periodical press facilitated a transatlantic cultural transfer between Ontario and Britain, in which a middle-class gender ideology was disseminated through texts that shaped ideas on womanhood and domesticity.[446] It has, however, been argued that print culture was directed at "masculine political subjects" primarily concerned with the public sphere.[447]

Not surprisingly, Mary's husband, Philip, read the newspaper.[448] More interestingly, whether or not it was directed at her as a reader, Mary recorded that she too "enjoyed [reading] the paper exceedingly."[449] Though she did not state what papers she and Philip read, it is safe to assume that they included the *Globe*, as Philip placed advertisements in this paper on different occasions.[450] Being members of the Methodist church, Philip and Mary may also have read the Methodist *Christian Guardian*. By advertising in the newspaper, the Armstrongs participated in the economic and social community that they shared with their fellow readers. Beyond this engagement, simply through reading these papers they accessed information on the economy, politics, and culture of their local community, their colony, their English homeland, the empire around the globe, and the rest of the world.[451] This point of access was one way in which Mary's imperial identity was constructed.

Religious and voluntary organizations were other mechanisms through which Mary's imperial identity was constructed. Simply being a member of the Methodist Church meant some level of participation in the "transatlantic fellowship of evangelicalism" that Van Die has described.[452] Participation in missionary societies meant identification with "England's social mission to the rest of the world."[453] Likewise, the temperance reform movement was a transatlantic phenomenon, drawing speakers from across the ocean. Mary and her family eagerly listened to the speeches of the touring Scottish temperance lecturer Peter Sinclair in 1859.[454] The organizations to which Mary belonged existed in an imperial context, and through her membership Mary connected with the world of empire and shaped her imperial identity.

Personal connections with family members in England also served to maintain a sense of imperial identity. Transatlantic letters exchanged between relatives could be an important part of colonial life for some women.[455] Mary recorded exchanging correspondence with her married sister Sarah Carruthers, who was in England during 1859 and whose return to Canada she eagerly awaited.[456] In the 1870s, Mary's younger brother Arthur returned to England, taking up ministry in a London Congregational church.[457] No doubt he kept in touch with Mary and the rest of his family that remained in Canada. These transatlantic family connections between the colony and the English homeland were another means by which Mary's awareness of her identity as an imperial subject was maintained.

Beneath the layer of her imperial identity, Mary was very much aware that she was an Englishwoman. Rather than identifying herself as "British," or as explicitly "Canadian," it was her Englishness that stood out for Mary and constituted the core of her national identity. This was not an unusual conceptualization in the context of Victorian imperialism. Proponents of empire in the mid-nineteenth century conceived the English people as sharing a common imperial destiny in which English men and women could share pride in the greatness of their colonies and the spread of their institutions, laws, principles, and language around the world.[458] Within the imperial project, it was the dominance of Englishness that stood out as a point of pride for English people. Mary's personal sense of Englishness is illustrated in her comments about the Yorkville Debating Society soiree held in late April 1859, which Mary and Philip attended.[459] Patriotic songs were part of the entertainment of the evening, and with regard to one song—the lyrics of which were: "I'm an Englishman, Deny it who can?"—Mary commented, "I felt that nothing could so effectually raise the Loyalty of a people as heart stiring [*sic*] Music set to such sentiments." Mary also recorded that Philip and Mr. Ash, the minister of Yorkville Church who was "not long from Merrie England," cheered loudly and were joined by an Irishman in expressing sentiments "against the Yankees" and in support of the English system of government.[460]

Almost all the family friends Mary mentions in her diary seem to be of English origin. The bonds between fellow English immigrants were important to maintain. For those living in a colony and city that was occupied by people from all over the British Isles, Europe, and North America, a sense of connection with one's homeland was essential. National societies like the St. George's Society, to which the Armstrongs and Wicksons belonged, facilitated the maintenance of that connection. Membership in the St. George's Society was not only about reinforcing bonds with networks of friends and acquaintances but also about proclaiming a distinct English identity and difference from the Scots, Irish, and other nationalities represented in the colony.[461] Mary made reference to individuals from other nationalities in her writing. She noted that her hired help girl Bessy, whose morally questionable activities Mary frowned upon, was a "Scotch girl."[462] Mary also made note of Irish individuals on different occasions.[463] To her, national origin was an important element in the identity of individuals she mentioned in her diary, particularly if they were not English.

Englishness was not just about nationality; it was also about "race."[464] In a colony of white settlement, "race" does not feature as a major theme in Mary's text. It does, however, play an implicit role in her membership in the Methodist Missionary Society. Marks noted that women's involvement in missionary societies partially reflected an affirmation of superiority over the non-Christians and non-whites that were being sought out for conversion.[465] In terms of concrete reference to "race," Mary spoke of the "pure Saxon descent" of her husband and son, an idea that implied a belief in an inherited racial identity.[466] The "Anglo-Saxon race" was closely associated with English national identity, and those who believed in the imperial destiny of the English people were also likely to believe that that destiny was rooted in Anglo-Saxon racial superiority.[467] Anglo-Saxons believed themselves to have the capacity to embrace political freedom and self-government, which were supposedly "Teutonic virtues" that distinguished their "race" from others.[468] In contrast, Irish Celts were denigrated and deemed to be unfit for self-government.[469] Fenianism, the Irish republican movement, adopted the racial distinction between Celt and Anglo-Saxon and chose the slogan "death to the Saxon."[470] While the theme of racial differences among the peoples of the British Isles can be detected in Mary's writing, it does not play a major role, and there is no reference to racial difference between the broader categories of white Europeans and "other" racial groups. However, Mary's comments on the Saxon lineage of her family underline her awareness of "race" and racial "others," and her need or desire to define herself as Anglo-Saxon.

If Mary was both an Englishwoman and an imperial subject, there are signs that her national identity was still more complicated. Another layer, certainly not as fundamental as her Englishness, nor perhaps even as apparent as her identification with empire, was her Canadian identity. What did being Canadian mean in Mary's period? Then, as now, it meant (at least partially) that one was not American. A negative definition of Canadian identity—contrasted with American identity—can be detected at least as early as the 1830s, when prominent individuals in the colony complained that the adoption of American spelling was promoting an anti-British idiom in Upper Canada.[471] The societal differences between Britain (chiefly England), the United States, and Upper Canada were indeed perceived and debated before 1840, and the debate continued into the middle and later decades of the century. American society was considered vulgar, with manners and morals that had been degraded by democracy, in comparison with English refinement.[472] Mary's disparaging comments about American "mobocracy," which she contrasted with English "aristocracy," illustrate the currency of these perceptions among her family members and acquaintances.[473] By 1870 some commentators had refined the relationship between Canada, England, and the United States to an assertion that Canadian was "a sort of middle term between the Englishman and the American."[474] It was in this context that the Canadian identity both grew and came to be adopted by immigrants such as Mary.

Some immigrants in this period were quick to establish their sense of being Canadian, but it seems that "Canadianness" never completely overshadowed a newcomer's national origin.[475] Such was also the case for Mary, who observed in May 1859: "The grass is brightened with the gay dandelions and though it may be treason I hail their coming as much, as I used, the buttercups in the rich pasture grounds of Old England."[476] After a quarter century in Canada, Mary's new national identity was evolving. By 1869, on the second anniversary of Confederation, she noted Dominion Day in her journal, and the various holiday events and celebrations that were going on around the city and countryside, such as picnics, trips to the Toronto Islands, general "merrymakings," and a parade of the band of the Queen's Own Regiment. Though she never specifically called herself Canadian, Mary's changing sense of national pride is apparent in the time she devoted in her diary to the Dominion Day celebrations.

Mary's national identity can be perceived as comprising three layers. Most dear to her was her identification as an Englishwoman. The overwhelming majority of the individuals she mentioned in her diaries were English, and this probably is a reflection of the composition of her social networks. Mary recognized the nationalities of other individuals and was proud of her own Englishness. Her involvement in the St. George's Society underlined this fact. Her English identity was very closely related to her racial identity as an Anglo-Saxon, something that she also embraced. While Sara Mills and Indira Ghose have argued that some women may have existed as mere spectators of empire, Mary was a participant in it.[477] She was a part of the culture of empire, and participation in this culture through reading newspapers and working with religious, missionary, and temperance societies shaped her imperial identity. Her transatlantic family connections also reinforced an imperial consciousness. Beyond her English and imperial identities was a more ambiguous sense of Canadianness. It is clear that for Mary this was not a central part of her identity, but it was growing, and certain indications in her text suggest that the decade in which Confederation occurred made a significant difference in its development.

Conclusion

All of the themes that have been drawn out of Mary's diaries and discussed above relate, in part, to her overall sense of self. Her writing, family relationships, work, status, faith, community, and local and national identities all constitute different elements of her comprehensive personal identity. Mary was a wife, a mother, a grandmother, a daughter, and a sister, and her ties with female family members were particularly strong. She was a homemaker and household manager with financial responsibility. She was an employer. She was a neighbour. She was a Methodist, and her faith was personal and important to her. She was middle class, but her social status rose over her lifetime. Her male family members were butchers, farmers, academics, doctors, ministers, and local politicians. She was a member of different communities and had different local identities. She was an English immigrant in a colony of the British Empire, but she increasingly came to see herself as Canadian. She had her own preoccupations, fears, feelings, comforts, and hopes. She paid attention to what was going on in the world around her but, like many other women of her period, spent most of her time focused on her family and her domestic responsibilities.

Nevertheless, the themes that Mary touches upon in her writing are worth more than what they tell us about the elements of her identity. They relate to important areas of historical inquiry into mid-Victorian English Canada, and to this wide range of scholarly interest her diaries contribute new information from a new perspective. While Mary's experience in many ways "fits" into the broad conclusions that historians have reached on the themes of her period, it is significant that this fit comes from the first-hand perspective of a middle-class "ordinary woman" who wrote during the decades in which only a very small amount of English Canadian women's life writing has been published.[478] Mary's text is a valuable primary source on its own account, and it bears much further scrutiny than has been offered here. My goal in the preceding analysis has not been to reach any "final" conclusions. Instead, I hope that my investigation has stimulated new questions. At this point, rather than reiterate the various preliminary conclusions drawn above, I would prefer to let Mary's diaries stand for themselves and to invite others to examine and reflect on them with their own interests in mind.

A Note on the Text

Some of the features of Mary's writing cannot be conveyed through transcription alone, and so it is useful to address her diaries from an editorial point of view. Cynthia Huff has observed differences between diaries written in books formatted explicitly for diary keeping and those kept in a more makeshift, self-determined format. She argues that the formatted diaries impose rules of spacing and dating on the diarist, though the writer can freely chose to ignore or violate these rules. Conversely, a self-determined diary, in which the writer works in a bound volume of blank pages or loose papers that are assembled together, allows the writer to set (and change) her own rules of format.[479]

Mary kept her earlier diary in a 16 cm × 19.5 cm unlined notebook, which she purchased "down town" on 6 January 1859.[480] In this self-determined-format diary she usually included the date at the start of each entry, as part of the first line. In doing so, she relied on no fixed style for giving the calendar date, the day of the week, or the month, which she would sometimes also write at the top of the page. Mary's entries are almost all horizontal; that is, not overlapped with vertical writing to save space. Her right-sloping handwriting is small, and she emphasizes ascending and descending strokes while keeping the body short and consistent. Some of her minim strokes are very tiny and difficult to distinguish. Mary filled her pages almost entirely, taking anywhere from a few lines to a few pages to cover one entry. Occasionally, Mary would leave a full blank page between entries.[481]

Mary's later diary took a different form. It filled the pages of a 15 cm × 20.5 cm formatted book entitled "Diary for 1861," which presumably she had acquired years before and not used until 1869. In this formatted diary, the facing pages have spaces for six days of the week, with three on each page (excluding Sundays). Mary's entries are again almost all horizontal, and her handwriting is the same as it was in the earlier diary, though at times it becomes larger. If she needed more space, she freely redated the three daily header spaces on each page by crossing out the printed dates and writing in the appropriate substitute. Sometimes she would insert her own headers between days, in the same style as the printed dates in the book. On many pages she repeatedly redated the year 1861 to 1869. Mary seems to have attempted to stick to the weekly structure of the diary, even if she found herself falling a few weeks behind. Mary also tried to stick to the space allotted for daily entries, and she changed the spacing and size of her writing to accomplish this. The impressions of pressed tree leaves are apparent on some of the pages.[482]

Huff argues that in formatted diaries, where publishers often included pages for regular financial accounting, the distinction between the monetary and the personal can become blurred, especially when diarists entered comments along with their accounts.[483] In the back of Mary's later diary, in a printed "cash account" section, she chose not to keep financial accounts except for two entries of amounts she owed. Instead, she kept in these pages lists of needlework done each month. It was here that she made her entry for New Year's Eve, 1869, which was a summary of needlework done since June, and later a similar entry for the month of January 1870. The blank pages at the back of the later diary were filled with lists, not in Mary's handwriting, of prize winners. Philip perhaps made these entries while judging agricultural competitions at some point.

Margo Culley and others have pointed out that the publication of a diary necessarily involves the process of editing, in which small changes can alter the impression of a passage or the text as a whole. She has highlighted the editor's challenge to render the original text as accurately and accessibly as possible while clearly stating the methods used in so doing.[484] I have made several choices in trying to strike this balance. I insert punctuation in square brackets where I feel it is necessary to clarify my interpretation of unclear phrases. I have tried to do this sparingly, in order to change the original text as little as possible. Additionally, I have used square brackets to insert any explanatory comments on format that are not placed in the notation. I attempt to reproduce Mary's inconsistent dating methods for her entries as accurately as possible while providing full date information in square brackets. I have chosen to space out separate entries, something that Mary did not do in her earlier diary. She usually started a new entry on the line immediately following her last, a format that does not lend itself readily to the eye of a reader who is quickly skimming for different dates. I have only followed her line breaks if a series of dashes—something that Mary used to indicate a long pause between ideas—is used at the end of a line. I have tried to follow her infrequent indentation as much as possible, and I have only otherwise changed her paragraph structure when she uses dialogue in order to improve the readability of these passages. I have followed Mary's page breaks and inserted and numbered these in the text.

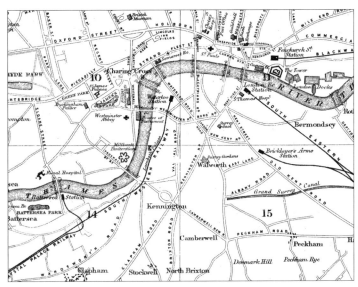

FIGURE 1 Walworth and Camberwell, where Mary Armstrong spent her childhood, are on the south side of the Thames River. New Kent Road and the Grand Surrey Canal are clearly marked. ~ Extract from the *Stanford's Library Plan of London and Its Suburbs*, 1862; reproduced by kind permission of the publishers, Harry Margary, London, and www.harrymargary.com , in association with the Guildhall Library, holder of original map (republished London 1980): Key map (detail).

FIGURE 2 Jane Tuesman Wickson, Mary Armstrong's mother. She was eighty years old when this photograph was taken in 1870, a year after her husband's death. ~ Courtesy Ruth Wickson Newman of Parry Sound, Ontario.

FIGURE 3 John Wickson, Mary Armstrong's brother. He was seventy years old when this photograph was taken in 1887. ~ Courtesy Ruth Wickson Newman of Parry Sound, Ontario.

FIGURE 4 Eliza Chilver Wickson, John Wickson's wife and Mary Armstrong's sister-in-law. No date. ⌒ Courtesy Ruth Wickson Newman of Parry Sound, Ontario.

FIGURE 5 John Rusby Wickson, son of John and Eliza Wickson. Mary Armstrong was close to her nephew, who, upon his twenty-first birthday, told her that he felt it "a very serious thing" to "take upon him the serious responsibilitys of Manhood" (17 March 1859). This photograph was taken in Buffalo, New York, in 1899, when Rusby was aged sixty-one. ⌒ Courtesy Ruth Wickson Newman of Parry Sound, Ontario.

FIGURE 6 A view of Toronto at mid-century (lithograph). St. James' Cathedral can be seen clearly as the tallest spire near the centre, and just to its southeast are the St. Lawrence Hall and the St. Lawrence Market, extending down to Front Street. ⌒ From Whitefield's original views of North American cities, no. 30: *Toronto, Canada West: From the Top of the Jail, 1854*, Miscellaneous Map Collection, C 279-0-0-0-42, Archives of Ontario.

FIGURE 7 Calendar "Commemorating the 100th Anniversary of the Founding of the Business John H. Wickson." This calendar was made in 1934, and it shows Mary Armstrong's father, James Wickson, her brother John, her nephew Henry, and her great-nephew John H. Wickson. The family business was sold in 1949. ～ Courtesy Ruth Wickson Newman of Parry Sound, Ontario.

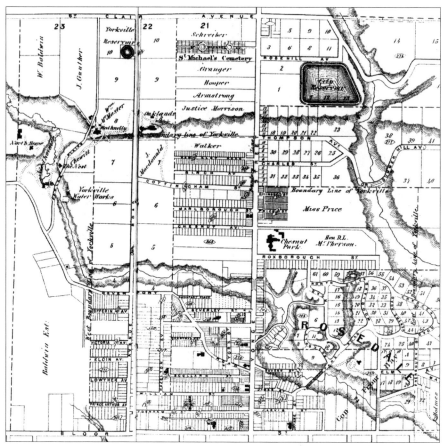

FIGURE 8 This map of Yorkville shows the Armstrong property on the west side of Yonge Street, opposite the reservoir and Rose Hill Avenue. New Kent Road and William Street, where Mary's family members lived, are also shown. The Yorkville Church can be seen at the corner of Bloor Street and Gwynne Street. The property Mary calls "Hazel Dell Fields" included lot 14, where the ravine meets St. Clair Avenue. ∿ From *Illustrated Historical Atlas of the County of York* (Toronto: Miles, 1878), 22–23 (detail), atlas 79, Archives of Ontario.

T. ARMSTRONG,

Physician, Surgeon &c.

CORONER FOR THE COUNTY OF YORK.

Office hours : 8 to 10 a.m.

YORK MILLS, ONT.

FIGURE 9 Thomas Armstrong's business card advertising his office hours as county coroner in 1878. ∿ From *Illustrated Historical Atlas of the County of York* (1878; reprint, Campbellford, ON: Wilson's Publishing Co. & APMIST Enterprises, 1996), 60 (patrons' business cards, detail).

FIGURE 10 Philip Armstrong, Mary Armstrong's husband, painted in the 1870s, when he was in his sixties. Artist and date unknown. ~ Courtesy Geoffrey Armstrong of Toronto, Ontario.

FIGURE 11 Thomas and Fidelia Jane Armstrong, Mary Armstrong's son and daughter-in-law. Photograph taken in 1913. ~ Courtesy Marian Blott of Dunnville, Ontario.

FIGURE 12 Fidelia Jane Maughan Armstrong and her son Thomas Norman Armstrong c.1867–70. The writing on the back of the card on which this albumen print is mounted is in the hand of Mary Armstrong. It reads: "The dear little Tommy & my dear daughter in law." ~ Courtesy Geoffrey Armstrong of Toronto, Ontario.

FIGURE 13 Paul Wickson's painting of a country doctor may in fact depict his own cousin Thomas Armstrong, a country doctor who made house calls by horse-drawn sleigh. ∼ Paul G. Wickson (1858–1922), *The Country Doctor,* 1980. Courtesy the Academy of Medicine, Toronto, Ontario. Photo: Dr. John Fowler, president of the Academy.

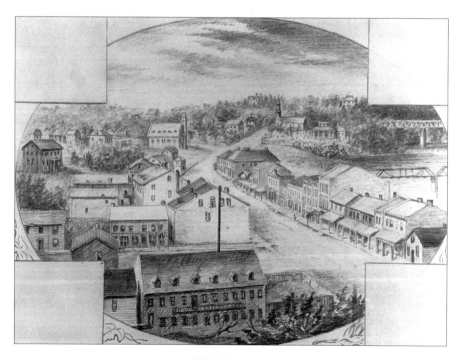

FIGURE 16 Paul Giovanni Wickson, son of Arthur Wickson. In her diary, Mary Armstrong refers to Paul as "Arthur's little boy." He became a prominent painter and lived most of his adult life in Paris, Ontario, after marrying Lizzie Hamilton, the daughter of his new uncle Norman Hamilton. This photograph was taken in about 1890, when Paul was in his early thirties. ⁓ Courtesy the Paris Museum and Historical Society.

FIGURE 15 Reverend Dr. Arthur Wickson, Mary Armstrong's brother. ⁓ Paul G. Wickson (1858–1922), *Portrait of Arthur Wickson,* c.1881, oil on canvas, 20 in. × 12 in. (50.8 cm × 30.4 cm), University College Art Collection, University of Toronto Art Centre. Photo: Tom Moore.

FIGURE 14 (opposite page) Crayon sketch of Paris, Ontario, by Sarah Wickson Hamilton, c.1882. Mary Armstrong's sister Sarah, an active artist and teacher, was married to a Mr. Carruthers in 1859 but was later widowed. In 1865 she married the Paris businessman Norman Hamilton. Their home, Hillside (now Hamilton Place), can be seen clearly on the top of the hill at the right, near to the bridge. This house is probably where Mary and her mother died. ⁓ Courtesy the Paris Museum and Historical Society.

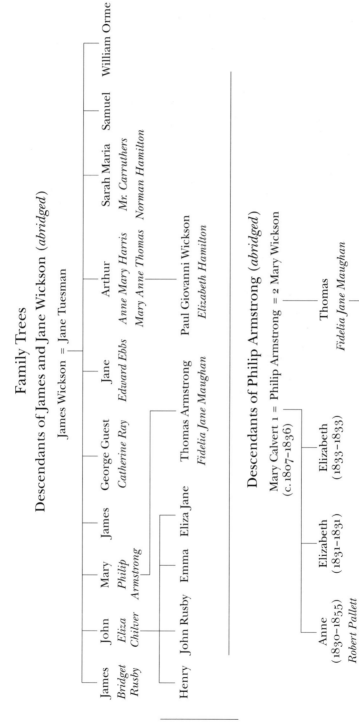

Family Trees

Descendants of James and Jane Wickson (*abridged*)

James Wickson = Jane Tuesman

James	John	Mary	James	George Guest	Jane	Arthur	Sarah Maria	Samuel	William Orme
Bridget Rusby	*Eliza Chilver*	*Philip Armstrong*		*Catherine Ray*	*Edward Ebbs*	*Anne Mary Harris* *Mary Anne Thomas*	*Mr. Carruthers* *Norman Hamilton*

Thomas Armstrong Paul Giovanni Wickson
Fidelia Jane Maughan *Elizabeth Hamilton*

Henry John Rusby Emma Eliza Jane

Descendants of Philip Armstrong (*abridged*)

Mary Calvert 1 = Philip Armstrong = 2 Mary Wickson
(c. 1807–1836)

Anne Elizabeth Elizabeth Thomas
(1830–1855) (1831–1831) (1833–1833) *Fidelia Jane Maughan*
Robert Pallett

William Pallett Mary Ann Pallett

Philip Thomas Albert Arthur Ada Fred Mary Emily

86

DIARY OF MARY ARMSTRONG

1859

PAGE 1

1859

Ebinezer [1]

January 1st At home all day, Mr. A[2] at Primitive[3] tea party, Saml.[4] and
Thomas[5] tea, at John's [,][6] Mrs. C in England,[7] Arthur[8] making calls,
Father and Mother[9] at John's ----

January 3 Small party to tea, Mr. Ross, Hausman [,][10] Rusby & Emma,[11]
Arthur and Mary Ann,[12] Misses Robinson's and Givens,[13] very pleasant.

January 4th All of us to tea at mother[']s, social,

January 5 Mother & father to spend the day

"[*January*] *6:* I have been down town to day, partly to bye this book, and
partly to treat Mary Anne[14] to a ride in the Omnibus[15] ---

Recollecting the old adage, ["] better late than never ["] I proceed
to take stock, and see how I stand in the world — through the Goodness
of God, I have met with no losses in the year, that has past,[16] although
I did not make so much, as the preceding one,[17] I had but one calf, consequently could not have so much butter to sell, this year I expect
two --- The following is a list of my cows [:] Daisy, Short Horns, Butter Cup, and a young heifer Shamrock. ---

Short Horns (MacKenzie's Heifer)[18] is to Calf next March If Patrick[19]
is correct, and Daisy some time in

PAGE 2

the fall, [.] Butter Cup is one, I traded lady Maud for, as it suited Pa,[20]
to do so, [.] It was her calf that I mentioned as having had, and as she
is a new Calved Cow I expect to do well with her — My stock of fowls is

87

increased by about a dozen pullets which make the whole number near thirty, only one hen is laying at present, they have never entirely ceased laying, since last February twelvemonth it will hardly be worth while, their doing so now so that I have a good prospect as far as they are concerned, [.] I have also a very fine little pig, bought about a month or so ago, for two dollars, and about the usual amount of preserves, extra stock of Pickles, at least twenty bars of Soap, a good quantity of Lard, half a crock of Butter, Box of Honey (a present) and about five pair of new Linen Sheets, besides two new quilted patchwork comforters [.] My Wardrobe, I must confess does not share in the general prosperity, but as things when they come to the worst, mend, I suppose it will follow the general rule, the carpets too; are greatly the worse for wear [.] I do not see any prospect of renewing them, as what little I ever have left, I put by for future contingencies [.] However if pa sells his lots[21] I may claim a

PAGE 3

little as Dowery which will be very convenient.—Thomas last year, went into the Bacon Business and though he lost about at least eighty dollars by it, it was a useful business for me, as I got all my Lard free. his Bacon was most excellent, but many who bought, never paid, they were many of them acquaintances respectable but poor, and as they had nothing it was impossible to collect it [.] several were singers, and some of them his father's labourers, who felt they had a claim on his generosity ---- At any rate it was given up and after working on the farm a few months he said one day, he should go to Grandpa, and get some lessons [.][22] no sooner said than done, and at the same time, he said he should attend some Medicine Lectures,[23] which Grandpa said must be to his advantage, how long this will continue I cannot say, however it will be an unquestionable advantage to him the rest of his life for which he may be thankful --- papa has been at home for the last few days with some complaint in his chest [;] it seems to be rather easier today— Mr. Sugden[24] the organist at Yorkville Church,[25] came to tea this afternoon [.] he says he too is invited to the teacher's party tomorrow ---- Thomas has gone to Mr. Robinson's[26] tonight.

PAGE 4

January 7th pa seems rather better, he has taken a walk for while and intends going out this evening [.] The weather is astonishingly mild, snow, rain, and sleet, by turns, Patrick is selling hay, but we went sleighing, to get the wood from Maple Woods [.][27] The turnips are all sold, and we are at a standstill almost, for work for the horses—I owe six dollars and a half to Bethel[28] but as I paid, just that sum, and a quarter more for some fruit trees, and a rose bush last spring I do not consider myself in debt as they are worth the money, and will soon bring me in some. - - - - -

January 8 We went last night to the teacher's Meeting [.][29] Father made a few remarks—Thomas brought home a <u>Dagurretype</u>[30] of the students, himself included standing round a table on which is a subject for examination; it pleased me very much.—I have paid two dollars on Bethel's A[cc] [.] Today is the first sleighing of any account, we were able to send for wood; it was very cold,

January 10 This is the most intense cold day of the season, we have kept the stove burning in the back hall, as far as we could night and day, but the heat is scarcely perceptible [.] an apple was frozen about two feet from the

PAGE 5

fire, and word was brought form the City that the thermometer was thirty degrees below zero [.][31] My poor fowls seem to have suffered considerably although I took all the care I could of them, two of them laid yesterday cold as it was, but not one of them to day.—Thomas and his papa, have ventured to town to the Missionary meeting at Adelaide St. [.][32] A Farmer took tea with us, who had come with Cattle, he had found Law, to be a bad resource, having been engaged in a suit which had cost him nine hundred dollars, I have written to Orme[33] to night, sending him a new year's gift from Saml. while Papa & Thomas at Adelaide St. Missionary Meeting, the cold seems to be abating a little [.]

January 11th My fowls have scarcely recovered from the effects of yesterday though the weather is evidently moderating. no Eggs. the Little Chickadees are emboldened by the cold to come to the window for crumbs [.]

[*January*] *12th* The snow is very deep indeed but the air is decidily [decidedly] milder. Thomas went down to Father's as usual this morning, but returned as Father had gone to the Election of School Trustees[34]— Father had told him the day before, he should be engaged, but Thomas

PAGE 6

had forgotten it, about eleven o'clock Father came up to our house, very fatigued, but not complaining particularly, he said he enjoyed his dinner very much,—in the afternoon he said he must return home before the time for the evening Service[35] as he had some little matters to do, or words to that effect, I insisted on his not attempting to walk down and he went down in the market sleigh as Saml. had not come home, he was present at the Missionary Meeting[36] with Mother and still did not complain.

On Thursday [*January*] 13th Thomas said when he came home at noon, that father was very poorly indeed, that he had entirely lost his consciousness for a few minutes, and that Grandma,[37] had been crying when he got there, I said Father could not have been able to attend to you then my dear, he said yes that strange as it seemed, it appeared to relieve his mind, or at least to divert his mind but you must be sure and go down and see them,—when I arrived I found Mother in great distress, there was a neighbour there, and the Servant girl, no one else,

PAGE 7

she told me my dear Father had had a fit of some kind yesterday morning and that day, at about six o'clock, but as he had recovered himself, so rapidly, she did not like to alarm Thomas, or me, but after, Thomas had gone home, at noon, Father had lain down on the Sofa, gone to sleep and about two o'clock had had a recurrence of the fit, more violent and longer continued [.] she had sent a very kind neighbour the second time that day, he came in the morning for our brother John who came almost directly bringing Dr. Richardson[38] with him, Father was still on the Sofa [,] he asked me the time [.]

I said, (as near as I can recollect) ["] it is a quarter to three, [."]

he said he thought it was only nine in the morning, he looked very ill [.] by this time, Saml. had arrived but was so affected, with the illness of his father as to be incapable of seeing him, Arthur, John and I wept together [.] at last I ventured to ask the Dr.'s opinion,

I said ["] You don't think it is anything serious doctor, you hope not, [?"] I said, interrupting his answer, which I saw was being given, with great hesitation, and as if to prevent him, from telling me anything worse,

"no, I hope," he repeated, "there is

PAGE 8

no immediate danger, but I must say I think it is the breaking up of his constitution." This remark, strange to say caused a complete revulsion of my feelings, I did not believe it at all. I feel completely relieved, if he had tried to hide the danger I should have been almost crazy, because in the case of our dear Sister in law Anne Mary,[39] the doctor always said she was getting better till the night before she died, and as Dr. Scott[40] many years ago alarmed us very much about Father, by saying he could not say his disease might not prove fatal, his answer proved a mercy to me and am still in very great hopes my father will be raised up this time also ---- John returned in a very short time with the medicine, and we put Father's feet in hot water in which was dissolved strong mustard, Mr. Armstrong and Mother rubbed them well, and put him to bed. Father remarked he did not know when he had been so weak before [.] as soon as possible a mustard plaster was applied to the back, between his shoulders, Arthur's present wife

PAGE 9

came in about this time, and very kindly rendered all the assistance in her power for which may God reward her, Father seems to enjoy his rest now, said he felt very comfortable, but complained of the plaster, feeling cold to him [.] upon taking it off we found it had taken very good effect, and after swallowing a little tea and a morsel of toast, he had very refreshing night—Thomas called about seven o'clock while his papa and I returned home to arrange some matter's [sic] on our going back with our sleigh Saml. returned in it [.] Arthur [,] being very poorly, went home too. John came back, and arranged for Rusby to come, who called about eleven o'clock and Thomas again in five minutes after but as father was so much revived we thought it sufficient for Mr. A and I to remain [.] papa stopped till five in the morning and, I till, John came about nine, when I had to return home, the rain has been so incessant I have not been able to go back but Thomas would call there at one, and, I am expecting to hear every minute by Saml. for Mr. A, they have not yet come though it

PAGE 10

is four o'clock ----------
------------ Mother said that day he was first affected, that he asked her where he was? if he was at Beaconsfield? if his brother in law, Edward Taylor[41] was living? he asked her of his daughters, was his daughter Sarah dead? also who was at his house yesterday, [?] Upon Mother telling him Thomas Armstrong had been he said ["] Thomas Armstrong? I don't know such a person [."] ---

John told me this morning that when Mr Smith,[42] came for him, the second time, his heart beat so violently that he thought he should have fallen on the floor, it seemed to take his powers away all together; he

was so distressed at the idea that father might be taken from us without being able to speak to us --- he felt relieved unspeakably when
he found him so much better this morning and after conversing privately a short time once more with him felt more connected to the will
of God whatever that might be [.][43]

PAGE 11

Saturday [*January*] *15* Father seems much the same [.] Dr. Richardson
ordered him to take one new Laid Egg beaten up with milk and a
spoonful of spirits every morning as soon as he awakes, said he thought
there was defective circulation of the blood, and that he required much
nourishment [.] Arthur and Mary ann,[44] were there, with myself and others during the day ---- I have sent two letters to day, one to Orme
another to George,[45] I think Saml. is going to stop at Father's to night,
Father mentioned Sarah to me once or twice and something about
Orme writing and expressed a wish to hear from James and Jane [.][46]
I think his memory is not quite recovered yet though it rejoiced me very
much to see so well as he is [.]

Sunday [*January*] *16* I called to see Father this morning before Chapel [,]
thought him poorly [.] called again after Service, and found him better, staid during the evening, thought him very low spirited [.]

Monday [*January*] *17* Thomas went to Father's who once more instructed
him, but Mother thought it was more than Father was equal to and
advised, it should be given

PAGE 12

up for the present, Father & Mother then went to Arthur's to spend the
day, I thought Father very much better went I went [*sic*] down to spend
the evening with them [.] we did not stay the night, Mother thought
they could do without us [.]

Tuesday [*January*] *18* Went down in the Sleigh to fetch Father and Mother
up [.] they seemed to enjoy themselves very much but went back at
night, Went to hear Dr. Wilson lecture at the Temperance Hall on
Ancient Amusements,[47] said the Drama in those times, occupied the
place of our Newspaper's [*sic*], Magazines, &c, but was now worn out,
and use less ---
--- One Hen Laid to day, the first, for eight days ----
Saml. staid at Father's this night -----

Wednesday [*January*] *19* Robert's little Boy[48] went home to day, he has been staying with us, some time, he is one of the best children I ever knew, Father & Mother went to John's to day and father went to the Yorkville Church in the Evening, Saml. staid at night.

PAGE 13

Thursday [*January*] *20th* Very wet and sloppy. I went down to Father's and thought him still very poorly; my heart feels very heavy, I find so low spirited, he did not even ask after Thomas which he never fails to do when he is well; Oh my God! have Mercy on us all.

Friday [*January*] *21* Father is once more himself [.] when I went down this afternoon almost the first thing, Father mentioned something about Thomas, and seemed to take a general part in the conversation, well may we say "God is a God answering as well as a God hearing prayer"

January 22 Quite Winterly, Father continue's [*sic*] getting better.

January 23 Father was at Chapel this morning though the cold is very severe [.]

January 24th Through the Divine Goodness Father has been able once more to instruct Thomas, though he seemed rather fatigued ---- two hens Laid yesterday, one of the eggs so frozen, as to break [.]

January 25 Father kindly instructed Thomas as usual ---- The weather is unusually mild, we seem to have a regular gradation from Excessive Heat to Intense Cold, and vice-versa.—two eggs today [.]

PAGE 14

I went to town today with Mother to get the trimmings for my French Merino [.][49] in the afternoon, pa and I went in the gig,[50] to Woodhill,[51] it was not so pleasant as the time before (17th) when we took our Cutter[52] we did not get out, as we were in a hurry to return in time, for Professor Croft's Lecture on the Curiosities of Chemistry [.][53] it was very well attended [.] Hon. Mrs. De Blagguiere[54] was there with her daughters [.] she is of higher Rank than any other families at Yorkville or indeed at Toronto, her daughters sat, one on each side of her, they are very much like their Mother, Chestnut Hair and delicate complexions, which contrasted most admirably with the blue hemmings of their bonnets [.] they sat just behind us, and expressed great pleasure at the Meeting ----

January 26 Like a Spring day, warm and balmy, Thomas made me a present yesterday, of two dollars and a quarter [.] as I was very much in want of some change, it was doubly welcome and I hope when he is short of cash, I shall have some to spare, there is nothing like "reciprocity [.]" One Hen Laid today [.]

PAGE 15

January 27 I was delighted to see father once more at our house, he looked very well, brought two letters one from Sister Caruther's, the other from Mr Ebbs,[55] he went down in Thomas's buggy and Alick[56] brought Mary ann home from School, at the same time, I have been melting Lard to day, and feel very tired - - - - the weather is very stormy to night - - - - yesterday was like Spring, to night midwinter [.] we find the days very considerably Lengthened, Last Sunday we went to Chapel in the evening by daylight and Mother used to say "As the days Lengthen, the cold strengthens"- - - - One Hen Laid - - - -

[*January*] *28* We find it is one of the small pullets Rusby bought for us, that lays us an egg every day - - - The weather is very slushy - - - - Mrs. Hooper[57] has commenced taking Milk of us to day as her cow is going dry, it is an ill wind that blows no one any good—

Saturday [*January*] *29th* Cloudy and thawing. Thomas at the Lunatic Asylum and hospital,[58] saw several operations performed - - - -
At Market as usual, but suffering with Influenza, go to please myself, fancying I do some good [.]

PAGE 16

yesterday Bessy, a Scotch Girl, who lived with me last Summer, came to see me, and I hired her for the year, at six dollars and half a month, as I hope, if it so pleases God, to have three or four cows to milk—two eggs today [;] they are worth having now, as they fetch 32 cents a dzn [.]

Monday [*January*] *31* Still very poorly, though doing about I went out yesterday Morning, met Father & Mother at Chapel, but did not go in the evening. Mr Sugden was up, and practised some beautiful music [.] The words were something like these [:]
"Life is a soft and Silken thread"
Nor is it drawn too long [.]

Mr. Hooper's Man was here, before daylight to order some butter [,] he says their hens have been laying since Christmas Day, they have a great number, and keep them very warm [.] I must see if can get a better henhouse for mine next winter [.] They never succeed, they say, so well with their Cow, the milk and butter is always strong, though she seems to be a very good sort, and receives every attention [.] it is well for me that she is now nearly dry as I shall have their custom, Till April----

two eggs yesterday, three to day.

February 1st The weather continues quite open [.] went down town this morning, to get some Calico for Thomas's Shirts. Mother & Father came up to dinner --- am still very poorly, can scarcely steady my hand to write but thought the air might do me good—

only two eggs to day.

Feb[ruary] 2nd The weather is Cold, and the Snowbirds have paid us a visit hopping about in the woodshed, and pecking at the sides of the posts, for Insects, they put me in mind of the Woodpecker tapping the hollow Beechtree [.] I did not go to the Lecture[59] last night on account of my indisposition—I feel very restless, can neither work, write, or sit still long together, neither do I sleep well at night, though I have but little pain, and am not low spirited, I have managed to churn, make the bread, starch the Linen [.] Knit some at Father's Stockings cut out Thomas's Shirts and sewed at them, for an hour or so, which later caused me more satisfaction than anything I have done for the last week and yet I had the greatest disinclination to set about it --- three Eggs today [.]

Feb[ruary] 3rd A Thorough February day [.] Snowing since daylight—the pullets keep on laying, and one hen has slacked, they only lay every other day but the combs of the others, are brightening, so they will not be long, they generally say as soon as they come to vivid Crimson and never before,—though they sometimes continue to look bright, after they have quit laying, hence the disappointment sometimes experienced, on buying them because when they are Aged, you can not see, that they look poor, instead of plump and heavy, though some young pullets do appear slim when they begin laying [.]

Saml. has brought a Circular from Mr. Carter requesting Thomas to join them in getting up a concert for St. Geo's Society.[60]

Feb[ruary] 4th Feel a little better though a long way off being well [.] Slept better at night—Weather moderate, the snow is too light for sleighing though we have had another fall today—we, find the afternoons much longer, light till half past five now—The cows in the barn yard, keep in good condition [.]

PAGE 19

I think Shorthorns[61] appears to be springing, at least I fancied her teats looked larger and I have told the girl to leave off stripping her, The white cow daisy I intend to have milked till Summer [.] I omitted to put down the accounts of Lard Melted. 65$\underline{u}$ Leaf Lard made 47$\underline{u}$ good and about 6u rather inferior from being pressed out of the <u>scraps</u>, which we did not value [.]

65$\underline{u}$	Leaf Lard	at 5 [p]	1/7/1
47$\underline{u}$	Melted	at 7 [p] ÷	1/9/4 ÷
6$\underline{u}$	Inferior	at 6 [p]	0/3/0
			1/12/4 ÷

$$1/12/4 \div$$
$$- 1/7/1$$
$$\text{Profit} \quad - 0/5/3 \div$$

Profit 5/3 ÷ which I think good as it only took the girl and myself the morning, though I was exceedingly tired [.] I am not sure that I should have more than the six pound of lard for my trouble but I am well satisfied and think it a good days work[62] ----

--- The dear little Snow Birds paid a visit to the cookhouse window to peck a few crumbs, just before the Snow shower.

PAGE 20

Feb[*ruary*] *5* Cold—no sleighing—

[*February*] *6 Sunday* Good sleighing, to Chapel twice [.]

[*February*] *7 Monday* Cold with occasional showers of snow, which the Chickadees foretold [.] The hens have taken the advantage of the cold as an excuse for laying fewer eggs [.] I only obtained five the last three days [.] These are only the three pullets and one muffled hen laying the pullets are not more than six months old—Our two Canarys that Thomas raised summer before last, have sung the whole of this winter [.] Sometimes we can not hear ourselves speak [.] We keep them in the Kitchen all the time, and they amply repay us for our trouble, Patrick is able to go, for Wood.

Feb[*ruary*] *8 Tuesday,* One of Nature's Gala Days, the Sun is shining Gloriously [.] I have been to town with Mother, to bye some linen for Thos

Shirts, I left our house at a half past ten, and was home exactly at half past twelve, walking to and from Yorkville [.] The City Omnibuses are a very great accommodation at a very low rate, the two of us from Yorkville Post Office to town and back, for a york shilling[63]—My cold or Influenza, seems to be almost as bad

PAGE 21

now, as it was at first [.] one time I try stopping in, and then, I try going out it seems to have such an affection for me, that it can be neither, worked, or driven, away.—four eggs to day [.]

February 9th Snow fell in considerable quantity this morning but the sun soon came out beautifully and dispersed it [.] it is now commencing to freeze—I heard the Geese at our neighbours screaming loudly and thought it was a sign of rain, but Patrick, and the girl, say it is a sign of Spring [.] at any rate it sounded very pleasant in my ears—
Both Cows and poultry seemed happy [.] Alick had just taken out of the barn several bushels of Chaff from the oats they were thrashing yesterday and disposed it in heaps round the yard so that each of the four cows and the two horses had a share to themselves [.] the little heifer Shamrock and the two fat Cattle had to fight for theirs but there was more than enough for all if they could only think so—I did not go to the Lecture[64] last night but two Ladies who took tea with us, went down

PAGE 22

with Saml., (Miss Stonehouse & Charlton)[65] and Mary Ann went with Liddy.[66] Mr. A was there too, and enjoyed it very much it was a very popular subject, the <u>Moon</u> and so crowded that most of the gentlemen stood all the time --- I feel better to day, than I have yet done, through the mercy of God and hope soon to recover my usual health---
My Butter was a long time coming to day, instead of a pail of hot water to heat the churn before churning I found afterwards, my girl, had only put about a quart, which left the churn as cold after it was emptied out, as it was before it was put in, however though, it took me at least an hour longer, I had beautiful butter at last. To night it is very moonlight, cold and clear, the northern lights are very brilliant --- Tho[s] has not been to Father the last few days as he has so much to do with his Medicine Studies [.] he generally studies for one or two hours, say, from seven to nine then goes to the School[67] in Richmond St till a half past twelve [,] gets his dinner with

PAGE 23

Saml. [,] returns again to the School till about five [,] and home to tea [.] after that if he is not too tired he studies till ten or eleven--- Saml. is gone down to Mother's to night—I thought Mother might feel a little dull, as they generally come here on Wednesday, but were prevented to day, by the new fallen snow [.] Father has been to the market the last two days for a change [.] he seems tolerably well now, but we sometimes rejoice with fear, I feel my dear sister's absence very much especially as my mind is at rest about Thomas; it seems as if I would enjoy her society so much we do not expect her for sixteen long months,[68] but I have dreampt twice that she was back, The last time, I thought she told me that she had only come to see how we were, and that she must go back, and finish her Studies [.] Papa is gone to Chapel, Mary Ann to bed, Lydy[69] to the cookhouse, Thomas is sleeping soundly in the arm chair and I may be said to be alone, which is the reason for my writing so much, the fire is burning brightly [,] the copper preserving pan, the

PAGE 24

tea kettle and the bright tins, reflect the light the same as ever, but Oh how many? that once sat at different times around this very Table, have faded for ever from our eyes? Let me recollect a few of them [.] at this very table our poor Anne sat down with Robert and me the night they went down to Mr. Grassett[']s[70] to be married [.] It is nearly three years and a half since, she went to sleep[71] ---

----

---Poor dear child at three different times when she thought herself in danger did she make me Promise I would take her little girl to live with me, if any thing should happen to her [.] I recollect the last time, I told her I would do just the same for her, as I had done forself if that would satisfy her, she was too much affected to speak, but nodded her head and smiled through her Tears [.] I kissed her at the time as if to satisfy the promise, and she never afterwards seemed to feel any uneasiness about her children [.] I told her I could not promise about the little boy but she said she thought his Father would take care of him as he was always the favourite [.]

PAGE 25

Though to do Robert justice I believe he would have done his part to have taken care of both --- as it was as soon as I heard of her death her Father and I getting ready to go to chapel that Sunday Morning it was

I think the first Anniversary of Yorkville church, no; it must have been the second [.] [72] I saw Mr. Walker [73] come past the window, it was up, for it was a beautiful day in September (and Mr. Armstrong had gone to sit in the parlour till I was ready) that was a man that worked on the farm with Robert and I said to him [:]

["] Why Mr. Walker is anything the matter [?"]

he said ["] yes [,] matter enough [,] where is Mr. Armstrong? ["] I directed him to the front door which was open and gained the parlour first,

I said ["] Pa something is wrong for Walker is down from their farm, ["]

he said, ["] Come in Mr. Walker what is it [?"]

"Why Mrs. Pallet is dead"---

it seems they apprehended no danger till Saturday Night and before daylight she had left them—The doctor told her, she was dying, but she seemed to think not,

she said ["] Oh Dr. you should not tell me so, you know I am so nervous [."]

PAGE 26

however he sent for Robert out of the field and told him of her danger and called himself on the nurse that always waited on Anne when she was sick and sent her at once [.] a very intimate friend of hers was there two [too], but as she seemed to be easier, she requested them to retire which they did, leaving Robert sleeping on a bed in the same room, as the bedroom door opened into the sitting room [.] they thought they could hear if she moved at all, Robert had been holding her hand, rubbing it, to restore animation but it seemed to fatigue her, as did the application of hot flannels, and she drew it in, saying it would do no good and might give her cold, In answer to my enquiries they told me she had repeated that verse "Talk with me, lord [,] thy self reveal;" and said He is here [.] another expression of her's [sic] was "Oh how Unfaithful I have been [.] " but as she thought herself better, and Mrs Wilson [74] had seen her to all appearances worse before, and recover, they yielded to her request, but went to look at her as they thought every ten minutes [.]

PAGE 27

at first she did seem to doze a little, but the last time they went in, she just threw her arms up and drew her last breath [.] They awoke her husband instantly, but it was too late, she was gone ---

I believe he was as kind a husband as ever woman had, but I believe she inherited her mother's[75] complaint, though the doctors never knew what it was, and nothing on earth could stay her --- The two children did not know of her death, till I went in to the bedroom and lifted the covering from her poor dear face [.] Robert had not seen her since, either and we all wept Together, after staying some time we brought away Mary Ann but took her back the next day to the funeral—she was most beautifully laid out and looked remarkably well stouter than she had ever been when in health and literally covered with flowers [.] Father Mother and Arthur were there—the rain was falling fast as we laid her down to rest,

PAGE 28

at the closing of the day [.] but it was more sobering than if the bright beams of the sun, had looked down upon us, for it seemed, to sympathize with our sorrow whereas the daylight would only have mocked our grief - - - - -

- -

In consequence of her mother's bad health, little Mary Ann[76] had grown up anything but interesting [.] she had been taught her letters but had entirely forgotten them [.] she had been allowed to follow her father to the field, and also, to carry his lunch with her brother, as well as to pick up the fruit in the orchard, and one day, when I went out to see them with Mr. Armstrong, I was very much shocked to see her so untidy but the child looked up and said

"I have been feeding the pigs," she had nothing on her arms which were covered with coarse hair and her complexion was as dingy as you could conceive [.] if she had been a healthy child she would have looked at least fresh but Dr. Stratford[77]

PAGE 29

said she had been not been brought up but dragged up [.] I do not know who was to blame [.] they always paid a girl wages to attend to the children, and her poor mother could not bear to part with her, as long as she lived, for small as she was, her mother said she waited upon her better often than the girl when Robert was away, and the nurse [,] when there [,] was often, obliged to be out of the room. I measured her by the cupboard door, soon after I brought her home she just reached the top of the hinge and was as thin as it was <u>possible</u> for a child to be, in any kind of health at all, her little brother[78] seemed to thrive better, he had always a little rose colour in his cheeks and was altogether fairer;

but Mary Ann is very much improved now, she reads and writes very nicely and is almost twice the size of her Mother [.]

PAGE 30

[*Page left blank*]

PAGE 31

Feb[*ruary*] *10* I was very glad to see Mother to day [.] we had a very pleasant conversation. we talked of Sarah in England, Orme in the States, Geo. & Biddy,[79] John & Eliza [,] not forgetting our friends & neighbours, and last though not least, the troublesome qualities of servants [.] during this time, we stopped but once, that I remember, and that was to discuss the merits of a cup of tea, and some roast Beef and mashed potatoes, about this time, pa and Saml. came home from market [.] I recollected some house work required attention and mother began to look for her over shoes -----

February 11 Some fresh birds have arrived to break the monotony of the Winter [.] I did not see them but heard them screaming in the Orchard, Mr. A. thinks they must be blue Jays,—went up to Woodhill this afternoon, started in the Sleigh about half past four, returned by six [.] saw a pretty little Squirrel running along a fence by the Side of a barn --- Two more hens have been kind enough to favour me with a contribution [.] one a Black hen that Sarah raised [,] the other a light yellow one that

PAGE 32

had her comb so frozen that the crimson of it, seems to have a border of blueish white ---- I have an excellent opportunity for writing (but my eyes are so weakened by the Influenza I can see but very indistinctly) as Pa is at Singing Meeting,[80] Saml. & Thomas at a very <u>interesting</u> Lecture,[81] that no Ladies are to be admitted to, I should not have heard of the above clause, but Liddy was in such a hurry, and there was such a demand for blacking brushes and candles in the cookhouse and the hired boy's were clattering up and down to their bedroom, that I was informed they were going to follow their masters to the above entertainment, Liddy herself was under the obligation of paying a visit to a neighbour's, this very night, which employed the remaining boy, and I and mary ann have the house to ourselves [.]

PAGE 33

Saturday [*February*] *12* Went to Market as usual weather moderate, dined at Arthur's according to custom, enjoyed a pleasant chat, stopped an hour at Mother's and reached home about five, bought more needle-work, Calico for Shirts and pastellettes besides towelings. I think no one ever had a better appetite for plain sewing than I have, when I have a good stock on hand, I always seem to have some thread in store, but at dressmaking, I am but a poor hand [.] Papa is sleeping in the rocking chair to night, Saml. is not yet come from market, Thomas is gone to a party at a Mr. McCullum's [.][82] Mary ann is in bed and Liddy has been helping me get in the bedroom firewood [.] only two eggs to day, though I rec'd two shillings, three pence a doz for those I sold. --- The geese have been screaming all round, and Saml. says he has heard and seen the Crows, it would have delighted me, to have heard them so early—The Clock is striking nine there was some Rhubarb in Mar-ket to day but I think it must be from a hothouse [.]

PAGE 34

Monday [February] 14 Five Eggs yesterday, one from the Large Brown Hen [.] only two to day, it seems strange that of the three pullets in the one brood one should Lay and the others not – I suppose the ball at the Lunatic Asylum[83] will soon be commencing [.] The Students were all invited and the Omnibus was engaged for their convenience, but Thos' pa so strenuously opposed his going he had the good grace to give it up and is now sleeping soundly at my elbow, his head resting on his arm which is spread over his open back --- May God Almighty be pleased in his infinite Wisdom to grant to my dear child, the fulfil-ment of that promise that thy days may be long in the Land, which the Lord My God giveth thee ---

-----

I have been busy to day, churning, baking, and sewing [.] finished one of Thomas shirts, the weather continues open --- There is a great Talk, going on, about the removal

PAGE 35

of the Government to Quebec,[84] but it does not bother me, I expect there will always be people enough, to buy all the eggs and butter I have to spare, and if not we can eat them ourselves, the fields will look as green, the birds will sing as sweetly as ever and I shall not miss the passing of the Governor's Carriage — Pa is at Yorkville [.] Saml. is copy-ing music, for the practice of the St Geo Society, tomorrow night [.] Thomas is woke up, and studying hard at his dislocations, Mary ann is in bed [.] Liddy in the cookhouse [.] we have beautiful moonlight nights now ----

PAGE 36

February

Tuesday 15 Very sloppy, inclining to rain, Papa, Saml. and Thomas all away, at the practice for St Geo's Concert [.] this is the night for the Lecture at Yorkville, but the weather prevents Mary Ann and I going, one would almost expect to hear the frogs, the air is so mild [.] I have cut out two more Shirts for Thomas, and two pair of pantilettes, for Mary Ann which I hope to get made up, before the Spring -----
There is an instance shewing the disappointment often connected with property lately come to my knowledge [.] A Lady who is well known had a Wharve which brought her in one thousand pounds a year, Owing to the railroad coming into the full operation the Steamboats have nearly ceased running and this year she could not rent it for anything ---
I begin to feel myself, throwing off the Influenza though my eyes continue very weak.

PAGE 37

February

Wednesday [16] A beautiful sunshiny day [.] Mother came up to dinner [.] Father is attending the Market on account of the absence of John's clerk (Mr. Bishop) through illness, we had a fire in the parlour and I got on well with my sewing and so did mother with hers, but my sight continues dim, I am in hopes that when the fine spring season, brings back the flowers and I employ myself more out of doors, I may regain it; at any rate I think I have read as much in the last thirty years as I can inwardly digest in the years that are to come [.] I have long since adopted the advice contained in these words "Whatsoever thy hand findeth to do [,] do it with thy might" so that when I shall have finished the shirts (about a dozen) that I have begun I can very well afford to be idle for a little while, though I shall have to give up the principal pleasure of my life [.] Saml. and papa are at Mrs. Widder[']s[85] practising for a concert to be held for a new church [.] Thomas at a Lecture by Dr. Aiken[86] at eight o[']clock [.]

PAGE 38

February

Thursday 17 Rather overcast ---

Thomas attended a Lecture at the University by Dr. Croft [,][87] came home to dinner [,] went to the School in Richmond St. at two [,] attended an operation for cancer or rather I should say assisted [,] as Dr. Aiken sent for some of the students to come for that purpose and he went with two others, came home to tea and is now gone down with his pa to Mr. Carter's practise for St Geo's concert [.] Saml. thinks he must rest a little to night, and is now taking a nap, in the old arm chair [.] Mary ann is sleeping in her own corner and Liddy is reading the newspaper [.] The crickets are chirping, the fire is cracking and blazing, the puppy is stretched out on the hearth and the old grey cat is enjoying herself in the corner—The fire has a right to be noisy as Patrick as [sic] just brought a fresh Load of Wood from Maple Woods [,] White Oak which is well known for its sparking qualities—Five eggs today - - - - -

PAGE 39

February 18th 1859
Friday "My Birthday, what a different sound"
        "That word had in my youthful years [.]"

I have the honour of being born in the same year as our beloved Queen,[88] I was a bride, and a happy mother, two years before her, but she has stolen a mark upon me now, as she is a grandmother before me —
What a wonderful thing memory is! I can recollect since I was about two years old[89] or at least a very little more, and it seems to me but yesterday, it was at a house in Mount St [.][90] There was a front and back room on a floor, there was some company in the parlour, and Fanny a faithful servant, who was trying to keep the baby quiet, it was my brother George who was born two years after me and rocking with all her might, her chair came down on a guinea pig who ran in a corner and died, my two elder brothers and myself, did not make much noise after that, I question if we ever knew what death was before but I remember there was a silence in the kitchen then, such as had not been that evening before - - - - -

PAGE 40

it was a little after this, that another accident took place which might have been more serious. I was in the parlour while the girl was cleaning it up one morning, and seeing the baby cap on the table, which at been left there over night, I thought I would put it on, but having seen them hold the thing by the fire, before putting them on, I did the same, it soon began to smoke and the next minute was all in a blaze [.] Through the mercy of God I had sense to let it drop in the ashes; and I suppose my mother was so glad that I escaped she cared nothing about the cap ----

The next reminiscence is in another house, Mother had made me a little winter cloak, of Grey Cloth or rather pelisse[91] for it had a band of the same material that tied with Ribbon to match, the moment I saw this band, I said to Mother

["] what did you do with the ribbon you cut out when you put the cloth in, [?"]

["] I did not cut any out, ["] she said, I held my

PAGE 41

tongue it is true, but I firmly believed that sooner or later I should fall in with the piece of ribbons, for I could not conceive how the cloth could be put in, and not the ribbons taken out, about this time I remember I was required to sleep in a different bed and as a matter of course I refused but on account of a very simple matter I altered my mind, I thought it would be such a pleasure, to awake in the morning and look at the bunches of leaves and fruit which were depicted on the curtains of the best bed in my new sleeping room [.] though they thought I was a whimsical child, crying one minute and delighted the next — It was at this time I went to a most excellent school[92] kept by three sisters, who taught us by turns [.] I suppose by this time they are beyond reach of praise or reward and so their works do follow them, to the last day of my life [.] I shall have reason to bear their memory for they stored mine with the most precious truths [.] nor do I remember ever being reproved by

PAGE 42

either of them, what pleased me most was to recite after them, Mrs. Barboued[']s Hymn's [sic] in prose ----

I think I must have been a better child at School, than I was at home for coming in to my dinner one day I took the liberty of calling in a very haughty answer to the girl to enquire what we were going to have [.]

["] Leg of Mutton ["] she said, I immediately answered,

["] I hate Leg of Mutton, ["] though I am sure at that time, I could not distinguish one joint of meat from another [.] however my dear father, who was just within hearing saved me from such a disagreeable necessity, for cutting me a slice of bread from the table, which was just set [,] he very wisely ordered me up to my bedroom where I remained till the girl came for me to go to School [.]

I think the happiest memories of my childhood, are connected with Rosemary Branch Lane,[93] in some particulars it resembled this house on Rose hill but there was no prospect, in the least [,]

PAGE 43

it was very usual however, and very roomy, I do not think the plan of the house could be much improved [.] The little garden in front had a holly tree in it which was trimmed over the sitting room window [.] I seem to have a distinct recollection of its scarlet berries [,] the other parlour which had French windows was shaded with the clematis,[94] besides these two rooms on the same floor was a very large kitchen with old fashioned dressers where to my delight we not only heard the crickets but saw them, at the back of that was a bakehouse and after that a good sized washhouse [.]

PAGE 44

[*Page left blank*]

PAGE 45

February

Saturday 19 The weather continues open --- At Market as usual ----
Patrick came home in a great fright without his wood, one of the horses had been taken ill on the road. Fortunately pa was at home and after rubbing it with turpentine, gave him some Sugar tea, with onions steeped in it, which together, with bleeding seemed to relieve him [.] this horse had been subject to inflammation when young, but since we had him, for years had never had an attack ------
Thomas is gone to bed, papa sleeps just now, very comfortably in the armchair, Saml. is not yet come home, Mary Ann is but poorly, which makes me often afraid, she will follow her poor Mother, she grows very fast, but is always troubled with indigestion --- It is near ten o'clock [;] Saml. is come and is getting his supper, he says the water is running down the streets like the breaking up of winter, indeed it has the whole of this week [.] the

PAGE 46

February

Market was well supplied with all kinds of provisions [.] it reminded me of the last day of Lent, such an abundance of poultry both alive and dead, such a crackling of fowls [,] quacking of chicks as well as geese and turkey was never surpassed in the genial days of spring, I could have bought very nice hens at a quarter of a dollar each but my excheq-uer has had so many drains upon it, I was forced to forgo that pleas-ure --- my eggs fetched one and eight pence a dozen to day, but they do not lay very well yet [.]

Yesterday, Sunday 20, was a real March day blustering and cold but I en-joyed the walk to chapel very much, Arthur and Mary Ann were, there [.] Saml. went home with them to dinner [.] our Mary Ann is better [,] I took her down in the evening ----- The horse that Mr. A bled and doctored, got better in spite of all [.] It seems our horses will not die [.]

PAGE 47

February 21 I donot [*sic*] feel so well to day, perhaps because the weather is dull and cloudy, or else the churning and the baking is rather too much for me. Liddy is washing, as I expect for the last time, as her time is more than expired, but Bessy[95] has not yet made her appearance although Holme's [*sic*][96] has brought her box --- Papa and Saml. are away at Mrs. Widder's practise [.] Thomas is gone to bed whither I intend following him as I am so sleepy, I can hardly keep my eyes open, Mary Ann is already in the arms of Morpheaus[97] though sitting in her usual corner, Liddy is visiting as she thinks for the last time round here, and the fire is burning as brightly as ever [.]

February 22 A most delightful day [.] one seems to assure the cows their happiness in not losing one ray of the sun, I seemed to want to stay out in the barnyard with them they are so glad to see me for they always expect either salt or cabbage leaves, The fowls on

PAGE 48

February

the contrary, seem uneasy while I am watching them [.] they like to have the henhouse to themselves though they take the liberty of fol-lowing me about when they are not particularly engaged in hiding among the hay [.] There are a number of birds chirping in all direc-tions, but they cannot sing like our canarys --- I have just finished the second of Thoma's [*sic*] shirts, and am going to begin some aprons for the Market [.] Thomas is going to get some buns in town, to save me the trouble of cooking much dinner, as I am entirely without a girl [.] he will not return till night-----

---Twenty minutes past eight---- Bessy, has been up, to tell me she has a bad finger, which will keep her for a day, or so longer, --- I

have made the four aprons, part of the time I was amusing Mary Ann
with stories of Robbers which I thought might stimulate her to a greater
love for reading ----Thomas and his papa with

PAGE 49

Saml. have gone to a practise for the St Geo's Society [.] I began to feel
a little tired today of stopping home so many evenings by myself but
being busy, I soon forgot it and I shall be out, for two or three I expect
directly---Father keeps pretty well [.] Mother had gone to Arthur [']s
when I sent down to day to see about a girl---
five eggs yesterday, and four to day [.]

February 23 No signs of a girl ---
I was very glad when I saw the shadow of Mother come past the window
and soon after, Arthur's little boy came up with his nurse, which amused
Mary Ann greatly----

February 24 Mrs. Widder having sent her Compliments to me by Saml.
and expressed a wish I should be present at the last Rehearsal of the
concert, I sent Mary Ann down with mother to go to the Missionary
Meeting[98] while I went to town--- I had a great desire to be introduced to the arrangement of a great house [.][99] I wanted to judge

PAGE 50

for myself, where happiness was most likely to be found; I believe it is
most equally distributed—that notwithstanding the grandeur of the
Halls, and the number of the attendants, there is as much enjoyment
in the parties of the middle classes, and in many cases far less anxiety [.] I would not have missed the pleasure for any consideration. Mr.
and Mrs. Widder were both polite and kind [.] I saw a cornucopia from
Russia which was filled with artificial flowers, I had read of the superiority of their Floral Pastures and if they were an exact model of them
they certainly surpass ours [.] it was placed on a table in Mrs. W's
boudoir, which was about the size of our front parlour [,] but hardly
came up to my idea of one, The walls were hung with beautiful pictures,
but not with satin or velvet, and the refreshment table [,] though two
footmen were in waiting [,] was not covered

PAGE 51

with finer damask, than I often use myself, the bedrooms and dressing
rooms, were however beyond all praise, almost every room had bright
coal fire that gave them an air of Cosiness in spite of their Lofty
grandeur [.] in most of them there were two or three immense Mirrors

and in the dining room was an oil painting of Mr. W's sister the size of life which reminded me of one I saw in the Dueuish[100] Gallery of Mrs. Siddon's.[101]

The weather was very disagreeable [,] rain and mud were the order of the evening [,] which sadly annoyed those who had to walk [.]

February 25 Mother's girl came up this morning much to my delight for I was almost worn out with the work [.] The Hens are laying better [,] we have had seven, two days running [.]

February 26 At Market --- the weather changeable --- Snow, Sunshine and Rain by turns [.] Went to Mr. & Mrs. Baggeur,[102] spent Papa's four dollars, and received scarcely

PAGE 52

anything, the articles being charged three times their value but as I received a profusion of thanks, I suppose I had my reward [.] --- dined at Arthur's, called at Mother's, walked home, made bread, and cooked the supper, and finally dressed myself for the concert at St Lawrence Hall --- The music was delightful, the band of the Rifles Brigade, alone, was worth all the trouble of going down, In fancy I saw the rival armies alternately throwing out a challenge and bidding their enemies approach [.] I actually felt a desire to go to battle, not to hear the music but to gain a victory [.] I felt as if death would be glorious in such a cause --- We walked home in good time being Saturday night [.] Yesterday, Sunday --- At Chapel twice [.] Arthur's little boy[103] and mother there in the morning [.]

PAGE 53

February 28th Monday Churned, and baked [.] Had a woman to wash --- Bessy came to night, and Mother's girl went home — Last Saturday Patrick saw some very fine fowls in the market and brought them into the stall to shew me, I bought a pair of hens, one quite white, said to be a year old, and which appears to have been laying, the other grey, and white, about six months old, they are splendid fowls, and a bargain not often to be met with, as I paid only a quarter dollar each [.]

March 1st Went to the Lecture at the Temperance Hall -- heard Professor Meredith read some Dramatic performances [.][104] Saml. at St Geo's Concert — Thomas and his papa had attended the practices but the latter having taken offence at something declined signing and went with me to the Lecture, Thomas having been to the University[105] in the morning, and to the Medical School in the afternoon, felt too tired when he went home at six to go down again

PAGE 54

He therefore stayed home with Mary Ann - - - - - - -

March 2nd Wednesday Very glad to see Father and Mother came up to day [.] Father is but feeble, complained of his ancle [ankle], Mother is very uneasy about him [,] but he seemed to enjoy his dinner and supper and took a comfortable rest on the bed in the afternoon. - - - The weather is beautiful [.]

Thursday March 3rd Cold and rainy [.] I was much affected to think of the Unhappy Criminals that are to be executed tomorrow morning — Flemming [*sic*] has confessed his knowledge of the murder of the young man that was found dead in the street not long since and the other, O'Leary, seems to be a hardened wretch as he has made an assault upon two of his keepers [.][106]

Friday [*March*] *4th* This seems an awful morning, to think of a young man not yet eighteen, in consequence of bad company, being brought to such

PAGE 55

a dreadful end, I could scarcely think of anything else all the forenoon but when some of them, came home from the city, and told me of O'Leary[']s sister, going to the Dr. begging the body of her unfortunate brother my tears could not longer be restrained, she had come from Ireland only two years ago, and had never been able to find her brother, till she saw the trial, in the "Globe" and then she broke into the bitter exclamation [:]
    "Was it for this I crossed the Salt Sea?"
and though living in Service in a good family she thought nothing of her own character but immediately made her way to the prison - - - - - Out of her scanty earnings, she hired a hearse with white feathers which passed our house at three o[']clock this afternoon herself and few of her acquaintances following in two cabs and about five or six on foot [.]

PAGE 56

Saturday March 5th Early this morning, the crows were calling to one another, as they flew over my head, as I was feeding my fowls, every thing, looked like spring, but I had no time to spare, but made haste to market—returning, bought Thomas a book "Dunglison's Lexicon [.]"[107] called at Arthur's, and took dinner though there was no one but the servant at home, which disappointed me a little, came up to Mother's and went back with her, to Bloor St to look at a house [.] after going through all the rooms (still carrying the book) returned home, found everything all right—after tea, Thomas studied his new work, till he fell asleep [.] after mending a few things I enjoyed the paper exceedingly, and when at last I laid it down [,] I found Papa had preceded Thomas in going to bed, so I took the arm chair when I had set Saml. supper, on the table and enjoyed the fire by myself [.] Saml. came a little after ten

PAGE 57

by which time, I was ready to join him at the table and this ended my first week in March

Sunday March 6th Went to Chapel twice. Mr. Sugden and Mr. Sanderson[108] were up to tea [.]

Monday [March] 7th Churned and baked as usual ---- the hens do not lay very well [,] though I had ten eggs one day last week [,] the average is about six or seven [.]

Shrove Tuesday [March] 8th I expect a little calf this week, th'o Bessy says it cannot come for a fortnight at least, as the cow has no milk, but I think it may be owing to poor feed in the show yard, though she is in very good condition [.] I have a hen that wants to set but I think it is too early, --- I finished another of Tho[s] Shirts yesterday which makes three completed, and commenced another --- I have been helping the girl to wash this morning and by rising early [,] got all the best, on the line before

PAGE 58

eleven, Tho[s] has been studying the whole of this morning and is now getting ready to go to town, Mary Ann at School[109] --- The Weather is rather gloomey [,] something like fall, it rained all last night but is tolerably fair now [.] Patrick is gone for a load of hay to Woodhill, he says the gardener is getting his hotbeds ready, how anxious I shall be to go up, as soon as the spring comes, to look for snowdrops, Papa brought me some down, the first year we had it, and they kept in water a long while, but the plough turned up the roots and I must go further in the bush to look for them now [.] I long also to see if my Apple tree's [*sic*] are going to do well [.] I once planted some Peach Trees, at Maple-

woods [,] but they were destroyed by the Cattle [.] -- one I bought
and planted in this garden bore well the first year [,] but the severe frost
killed it soon after as it did all our neighbour's [.] I think there will be
less risk with Apples [.] .

PAGE 59

March 9th Ash Wednesday Thos who was studying his "back Medicine" had
just left off, to say Ma,

["] I do not think Grandma will be here now, ["]
it is near eleven when we saw her welcome shadow come past the window, Father came up just as we were sitting down to dinner [,] and
enjoyed the fried pork and onions with mashed potatoes, very much [.]
a cup of tea and a nice apple pudding with some good cheese concluded our meal and Mr. Robinson[110] coming in about supper time
helped us to dispatch it, with an additional jest as he and father, both
agreed in their political views which were to the effect that no matter,
how good a man was, before he went into parliament [,] he was as bad
as the rest when he got there --- Thos bought a new work this afternoon [,] a Dispensatory which I promised to pay for, as it was to be got
a bargain [.] it is almost new and a most useful book for reference [.]
the weather is unusually mild, but the hens do not lay very well [.] only
five to day, some want to set but it is too soon [.]

PAGE 60

March 1859

Thursday March 10th A Beautiful Day [.] The road just froze enough to
allow me to pay my daily visit to the barn yard without soiling my boots,
Crows flying in all directions [.] The ground is once more to be seen—
The brown earth, has thrown off, her becoming white mantle, and
resumed her working dress, she has no time to lose, the husbandman
is waiting with his horses, for her to say, she is ready, The peoneys have
looked out for her and the little birds, are sure now, of getting their
breakfast, the children are gathering tea berries and Hyacinth glasses,
brighten the windows, of the houses in town, we are walking on tiptoe,
we are holding our breath, to see the spring flowers, we shall soon
behold them, for already, ~~the leaves of the iris are encasing their buds~~ [.]

PAGE 61

March 1859

In the evening we went to Bond St. to drink tea with Mrs. Robinson and
enjoyed ourselves very much, Thos and Saml. played games, and I

rejoiced in an easy chair, while while [*sic*] papa assisted Mr. Baxter and
Miss Mary Jane with singing [.]

Friday [March] 11th The weather cloudy, rain fell in the evening very close,
and warm, I pulled carrots, which had been left in the ground for the
cows, they were as sound as need be desired. I must next Summer have
both pumpkins and Corn put away for them, if I can manage it any
way --- Cut out two more shirts [.]

Saturday [March] 12 I never felt more disposed to thank God, than to day,
the occasion was this; calling at Webb[']s[111] for Buns and Cheesecakes
I was requested to walk in the parlour for a minute [,] on doing so I
found it was to enquire if I thought there was any one up our way who
would be willing to take charge of an <u>Idiot Child</u>, one about the age of
ten, who did not know her own sisters, or Father, and would eat soup
as readily as Cheese [,] who could never be left night or day

PAGE 62

March 1859

and had his fits, sometimes three or four in a night -----

The weather is still like spring though the roads, are in an awful state [.]
I had some roses in my hand, to day with pinks and Geraniums ---
The market was quite brisk at least in our department, though poultry
was dear and Butter scarce at eighteen pence a pound [.] dined at
Arthur[']s, called at Mother's and reached home at half past four [.]
Mary Ann had discovered a small plant in blossom in the garden about
the size of thyme of a similar colour, small as it was we hailed it as a treas-
ure [.]

Sunday [March] 13 At Chapel twice, An acquaintance of Thoma's [*sic*] up
to tea—Arthur's little boy came with us from Chapel in the morning [.]

PAGE 63

March 1859

Monday [March] 14 Went to town to transact some business for pa at the
Registery Office, called at Mother's, going, and returning [.] started at
nine, got back at twenty minutes to twelve, Mother had heard the robin
for the first time, this spring and Thomas, the grey bird, ---
Papa is reading the newspaper, Saml. is writing, Thomas is studying
his last work on Medicine, Mary Ann is in bed and I have been enjoying myself in the Arm chair—

I churned this morning before going to town but only made, three and a half pounds of Butter [.] we have no bran or Cabbages for them and the hay is very dry [.]

Tuesday March 15 Helped Bessy with the washing in the morning [,] in the afternoon went down to Mother[']s and met Arthur & Mary Ann,[112] as papa and Saml., came too, I had no uneasiness as I knew Bessy would give Tho[s] his tea and I enjoyed the evening very much [.] Papa and Saml. went to the Lecture[113] and Mary Ann[114] and I had our needle-work [.]

PAGE 64

Wednesday March 16th I took a rest this day and got a good deal of sewing done [.]

Thursday [March] 17th St. Patrick's Day [.] Most delightful weather [.] I went as far as the back lot, to look at Shorthorns, who seemed to have got tired of company, she seemed pleased to see me, but did not follow me down-----
Father came up about ten, he is only poorly—Mother came about an hour after—We had a pleasant dinner together once more and afterward, when Father went to lay down, Mother and I went to see Mrs. Hooper, we had just got into her walk, in front of her house, when Tho[s] called over the fence,
["] Mama your Cow has a Calf, ["] and strange enough, Mrs. H's cow, that we noticed as we went to the house as looking very well [,] calved a few minutes after we were there—We had a good laugh, and a very pleasant chat for about an hour-----

PAGE 65

March 17th 1859
This day was more remarkable still, for it was that on which Rusby attained his Majority [.] I had met him in town on Monday and told him if he was not engaged on his birthday I should be happy to see him to tea, he promised to come and we spent a very pleasant evening.—He said he felt it to be a very serious thing to think his childhood and youth, were really passed, and he must now take upon him the serious responsibilitys of Manhood [.]

Friday [March] 18th Busy Ironing, Papa and Saml. went to practise, but there was none [.] Saml. staid the evening at Father's, he said he thought he was about as well as as [*sic*] usual [.] I am sometimes very uneasy about him --- I did not hear anything more about our sister Ebbs [,][115] she had been very ill, but Father had received a letter the next day saying that the Dr. thought her decidedly better [.] We heard the frogs very plainly tonight [.]

PAGE 66

March 19th 1859

Saturday Not at Market, much to my regret—when Bessy went down stairs this morning, she felt her feet in water and thought some one had carelessly left a tub standing in the way [,] but on groping with her hands she could not get hold of the handles [.] she waded to the hearth that had been newly laid and found water there too [.] she then came to our room in a great fright and said the water was up to her knees,— I dressed as quickly as possible and found it over our ankles, it was impossible to light the fire on the hearth [.] it seemed a cruel calamity, the dear old fire not to be kindled [.] I walked across on a plank, and found the bricks submerged, but on putting my hand on the ashes, I found some warmth [.] but pa who had by this time got up would not think of having it lit—so we took breakfast in the parlour but such was the force of habit, I could not enjoy it at all and it was

PAGE 67

March 19th 1859

not till the fire was once more kindled that I could settle to anything -----it had done some good however, for there were two cats drowned, or at least had come to an untimely death, in consequence of it, for they were dead on the floor [.] The Indian Rubbers[116] were sailing along the water, and Saml. Desk was filled with the same, spoiling all his envelopes ---The reason of all this was the Cistern was too full and ran over [.]

The little Calf is thriving amazingly and Bessy has just brought in about three quarts of Milk from her, the rain did not get into the stables or henhouse—seven eggs today [.]

Tho[s] brought home a specimen of his Anatomy to day [,] which certainly demonstrates his perseverance [.] it gave me great pleasure, to see his application and so it does, my dear Father,

Tho[s] wished me, to enter here, that --- [he] has bought a beautiful gold watch [.]

PAGE 68

March 19th 1859

it is certainly the most unique of its kind, it is a perfect gem of art engraved both back and face [.] on the latter is a church—query? does it lead to that, it has beside an exceedingly elegant, gentleman's chain, with a very superior

I have been fixing a shirt for Mary Ann and going on with shirts as usual [.]

It seems singular to think after all the signs of Spring [,] to see the ground covered with Snow, which is even freezing on the planks [.]

Sunday [*March*] *20* At Chapel twice [.] Arthur[']s baby[117] was there— Mother said she was going home with him to dinner but he said he wanted to go to the Armstrongs, I love the little fellow dearly, he sleeps on my arm the whole of the sermon and does not distrust my attention at all [.]

PAGE 69

March 1859

Monday 21st Went down to town, as soon as I had churned (4$\underline{u}$ Butter) to get some Dry goods that I had ordered the week before and also to get my pass book from Mason[118] – met Father at the post office and called at their house – was very sorry to hear so little encouragement from <u>Paris</u> [.][119] Sister seems to be in a very critical state, if she does not get better, I must contrive to go up to see her [.]

Tuesday [*March*] *22* Washing—in the afternoon baking and sewing—finished another of the Shirts,—made two bolster cases yesterday [,] strong twill, Most beautiful weather [.] Mr Armstrong & Sam at the Lecture [.] Mr Hodgens[120] read a paper on the Cities of Antiquity [.]

Wednesday [*March*] *23* Father came up quite early this morning, and Mother soon after [.] Weather beautiful, birds signing indoors and out, set one of the hens; after baking in the morning [,] had the day pretty much for sewing,—no word from Paris which must be a good sign—glad to hear from Sarah—and to receive a blossom of wallflowers which is an especial

PAGE 70

March 1859

favourite of mine Tho[s] said if he was an old Englishman it would bring tears to his eyes—he must inherit his sensibility from his mother for I don't think his relations on the other side feel much, though they accomplish a great deal [.][121]

Thursday [March] 24th Heavy Rain in the night accompanied with thunder and lightning --- the frosts that we have at nights too, are rather severe, on the flower buds but the sun is shining now, in all its glory -- --- we have three additional hands, employed in making the Road, for the building lots [.] Mr. Passmore the surveyor has been up to lay them out—I rather regret it ----- I have had a very severe cold, this spring, and general debillity [*sic*] but I hope with a little care, to get better, as with Bessie I am more at ease, and take a little rest [.]

PAGE 71

March 24 1859

Papa has gone to an agricultural meeting.[122] Thos took lunch at eleven, to go to the hospital [.] Saml. is not yet come from Market [.] Mary ann at School as usual [.] I have been busy this morning, starching, and ironing but having got through early, I have made some progress with my sewing --- we get more milk now from the cows which is as useful to me, as a ship coming home to a Merchant [.]

Friday, March 25 The Pidgeons have been flying over yesterday, although the weather is not so warm to day [.]

Thos brought home a Photograph of the Medical Students [.] His own Likeness is uncommonly good [.]

My cold is certainly increasing, I can hardly speak, so as to be heard [.]

PAGE 72

March 26 1859

Saturday This has been, through the blessing of God, one of the most prosperous days, Thos gave me, some of the bacon and Ham and they brought me thirteen dollars and twenty five cents [.] I also had four dollars and 63 Cents Credited to me for Interest ---

It is past six o'clock, and getting dusk but I wish to keep in mind that my cold seemed to be better for sitting in the Market without a fire for since I dined at Arthur[']s to day I feel very much better, perhaps the good news I heard of Jane's partial recovery put it out of my head --- Mother—Father seemed / very well [.]

PAGE 73

Monday March 28 Churned 5/4$\underline{u}$ Butter [.] In the afternoon went to town to buy my [*sic*] the silk Dress, with Tho[s] present chose a very pretty, delicate, Lilack, shaded with white [.] Mother was pleased with the colour because it so much resembled my Wedding Dress [.] it cost exactly fifteen dollars for the thirteen yards --- came home to tea [.] Tho[s] went down to Father at <u>seven o[']clock this morning</u> [.]

Tuesday [*March*] *29* Washing—Just as we had got through, one of Bessie's brother's [*sic*] came and she had to go to town with him, leaving me the Supper to get for the boys [.]

Wednesday [*March*] *30* Feel very much fatigued from the work yesterday but intend resting myself this day—Father and Mother came up and we had a very pleasant time sewing in the afternoon [.] the Weather is cold and quite like March [.]

Thursday [*March*] *31* Ironing day—Cold with Snow Showers [.]

PAGE 74

April 1st 1859

Enjoyed myself very much, with reading and sewing ---

Tho[s] goes to Father regularly every morning at seven, comes home between ten and eleven, gets his dinner, and attends the hospital, in the afternoon, besides going to the school in Richmond St, returning at six [.]

April 2nd At Market as usual ---

Went to Arthur's but they were away [.] Called at Father's and stopped an hour [.]

April 3 At Chapel twice—I always take Mary Ann with me [.]

April 4th Went down to Mother's <u>and took my sewing</u> for the first time since Mother came to Yorkville—Saml. undertook to see after the house being at home writing [.]

Tuesday [*April*] *5th* Washing Day—I was exceedingly tired, but as I had promised Mary Ann to go to the Lecture,[123] I went [.] Saml. also and Thomas were there—Rusby came up to tea, but declined going [.]

PAGE 75

Wednesday [*April*] *6th* Mother and Father came up to day [,] which made it very pleasant [.] it was the ploughing Match[124] and Mr Robinson on returning, staid and took tea, papa did not get home till late—I sent a letter to Orme wishing him to come over[125] at once instead of waiting for a year or so as he proposed [,] and [I] have commenced taking Books from the Library at Yorkville.[126] The weather has been so cold that we seem to be further from spring now, than when we first heard the frogs [.]

Friday April 8 I have had an exemplification of that truth, a painful one too [:]

"He builds too low"

"who builds below the Skies"

I thought Bessie, was going to be a treasure to me this Summer, but she is not like the same girl she was, when she lied with me before ----- five months passed in taverns, have altogether spoilt her [.] she does nothing but quarrel the whole time, about nothing which almost worries the life out of me [.]

PAGE 76

April 8th 1859

but I must look to the Strong for help, who has said,

["] As thy days, so shall thy strength be [."]

I pray God to give me faith in his promises, for I have need of them, and especially in that one,—

"Whatever ye shall ask the Father in my name, he will give it you"

On Lord God I ask for Jesus Christ[']s sake convert my dear child, and make him a living epistle, known and end of all men --------

Saturday [April] 9th At Market as usual, Dined at Arthur's, came home soon to let Bessie go to town, she came home about eleven o[']clock with a Black Felt Hat, with Black Feathers [.]

Sunday [April] 10th At Chapel twice, Mother & Father there also, Mrs Taylor's Funeral Sermon[127] preached in the evening, I think I never heard anything more exalting, than the Latter part of the Dying Christian:

"Oh Death where is thy Victory [?] "

I felt that we were more than Conquerors, through Christ who loved us [.] Tho[s] sat with us in our seat, as he had not practised

PAGE 77

with them. --------

Monday [April] 11 Father came up to teach Thomas and staid to dinner [.]

Tuesday [April] 12 I took Mary Ann to town for a change, as she was not
very well and also to hear a Temperance Lecture by Mr Sinclair[128] in the
Yorkville Church. One of his illustrations was very well worth remembering, it was about a Pickaxe, which had on one end this Motto: ["] <u>If
there is a way, into the earth; I'll find it;</u> ["] and on the other; ["]<u>If there
is no way I'll make one.</u> ["] - - -

Wednesday [April] 13 Mother & Father came up and we had a very pleasant time though it was too Cold to look about as much, the Spring
seems quite as far off now, as it did the 10th of March and even more
so [.] we have no cause to complain, however [,] for it will be safest,
when it comes [.] The little Calf went to Market to day [,] I expect to
receive four dollars for it [.]

PAGE 78

April 1859
    which I shall hand over to Mr. Mason[129] as soon as I go to town. - - -

Thursday [April] 14 Pleasantly employed sewing [.] I want to get all my
needlework done, before the fine weather sets in, and then I have
promised my self to look round me a little [.] - - - I begin to think, that
as half of my probable stay upon earth has now been spent in unceasing efforts to keep a tidy house and every thing mended up and made
the very most of, it is now time, that I should enjoy the fruit of my
labour, - - - I think my mind upon the whole has enjoyed more peace,
the last three months <u>than at any former period of my life</u>, this is partly
owing, to Thos having commenced his Studies which occupies all his
time and partly to a resolution, which I formed the beginning of the
year, not to worry myself over things of which I had no control but to
trust in God who has said,
    "I will never leave thee nor forsake Thee" and the promise is to you

PAGE 79

and <u>your children</u>. - - - -

Friday [April] 15th Papa is at home to day working in the Garden, but the
day is to [*sic*] cold, to allow of my being out much at least to walk
about [,] though it is is [*sic*] not so stormy as yesterday. — I have eight
little chickens hatched last Tuesday, but the weather is almost too cold
for them, they have not come out of the barn yet - - - I get about ten
eggs daily but as they are cheap, we use them for puddings [,] as I do

not know any thing I can buy cheaper and fresh eggs are so handy to provide a meal with; When Papa kept the house, we did not expect so many dainties, and if we had, we should not have got them and I was glad to see all I could, to make a little money, which I should have the pleasure of spending, and very useful things, I bought too, which I have never regretted, especially the Melodian;[130] which has been a source of endless amusement to us all.

PAGE 80

April 15th 1859

When Tho[s] came home to day, he said Grandpa had been poorly again but as Mother had not spoken to Tho[s] about it, I am in hopes, it was only a slight attack, at the same time I think it long, till tomorrow comes; and I go down to enquire more particularly about it [.] Father had spoken, about being delirious; and his having been up about three o[']clock in the morning, but as he was able to instruct Tho[s] as usual, and had gone to Arthur[']s, I must rest quietly till the time comes ----- I miss my Sister Sarah very much, I think she has been gone eight months now,[131] so the time must be running on towards her return. —I often think she will come back, before they expect her, I know if she once makes up her mind, to return, nothing will stop her, and I heartily wish she would [.]

Saturday [*April*] *16* At Market, took dinner at Mr. Sugden[']s [,] called at Arthur's, found they were going to spend Easter at Mr. Buckam's[132] at Paris as they think Sister Ebbs would

PAGE 81

April 1858 [*sic*]

be sufficiently recovered to entertain company.

Sunday [*April*] *17th* At Chapel twice. Mother went to Arthur's to dinner.

Tuesday [*April*] *19th* Pa, Saml., Tho[s], and I, went to the Tea party at the Temperance Hall Complimentary to Mr. Sinclair the Temperance Lecturer. Malcolm Cameron[133] in the Chair, he is an excellent speaker, Colonel Playfair[134] and some others addressed the Meeting but the principal attraction was the music, Vocal & Instrumental [.] Mr. Sugden surpassed himself in the variations and Briscoe[135] sang the Irish Emigrant's Lament with so much feeling that it drew forth unbound admiration & an Encore that fairly made the hall resound again.—Pa was so kind as to treat Tho[s] and me not only to our Tickets but the Omnibus beside [.]

Wednesday

April 20 Father and Mother came up early and brought a letter from
Sarah containing an English daisy double Violet and Primrose [.] it
contained the welcome also that she might probably come home in
the fall—I quite expect her [.]

PAGE 82

April 20th 1859

To day the Mezereon[136] is out in all its beauty, and also one blossom of
the Polyanthus[137] --- Mother & I enjoyed ourselves sitting by the fire
sewing, which is a great help to me [.] we finished a dress this week for
me to wear in the house [.]

Good Friday April 22nd This day I am almost tempted to say, "friends of my
youth, where are ye?" so late as six years ago we three sisters met and
were happy [,] now one is in England and the other in Paris (C.W.) [.]
however by the mercy of God we still have our Parents to visit us and
in this respect we are the most favoured of all their children. Mr. &
Mrs. Sugden came up to dinner, Rusby too, but Saml. missed him on
the road and took dinner at John's [,] he came up directly afterwards
and we had some beautiful singing. -----

Saturday April 23rd St Geo[s] Day At Market as usual but the weather was
very cold indeed it snowed and rained nearly all day [.] I enjoyed it very
much in spite of all --- I took

PAGE 83

dinner at Isaac Robinson's who were very glad to see me, and we went
to the Cathedral[138] to hear, the Choral Services of the Day performed,
we sat in the same seat or nearly so that we had before in the Gallery,
and had the pleasure to see Thomas come in with a student and occupy
one on the opposite side so that we sat facing each other [.] There
were three voices that could be distinguished above all the rest, and one
of those was our own Organist [.][139] I enjoyed it exceedingly [.] Perhaps
I ought to mention the other two Mr. Baxter and Mrs. Kemp [.][140] I
certainly never heard either of their voices to such advantage before.
Another remark I will make is this [,] that I feel as much spirituallity
of Divine things, during the reading of the Liturgy and as much fervour
of devotion during the prayers as I ever remember to have felt in our
own Church at Yorkville [.] The Cathedral itself seemed to inspire me
with holy feelings, and the Articles of my belief [,] which I had been

taught to rehearse by a worthy Governess when I was under six years of age [,] seemed to stir the inmost recesses

PAGE 84

of my head. -----

Sunday [April] At Chapel twice, two very good Sermons, on the Ascension, being Easter Sunday. Mother was there, Father had gone to town. ---

Easter Monday [April] 25 Tho.ˢ brought word when he came from Father's that they heard from Orme, but he would not come to Toronto, till the fall -----

----

I have just rec'd a very polite note from John & Eliza inviting us to the Baptism of their twins,[141] which I shall find great pleasure in accepting, as it contains invitations also for Saml. and Tho.ˢ [.] I hope Arthur and Maryann will be home in time, for I should like so much to be altogether ---

I wonder if the Old Kent Road is as much crowded today as ever [.] I hope Sarah will remember Greenwich Fair for though we never went to it, we took great pleasure in looking at the holiday folk & I have a great fancy for old memorys [.][142]

PAGE 85

Tuesday [April] 26 Took Mary Ann to the City for a treat,—we called for Mother going down and went as far as King St, Mother bought Mary Ann a very pretty toy—a little figure dressed as a baby, sitting up in a tiny Carriage and looking the very picture of happy Innocence with its little chubby arms spread over its dainty blue covering—Even Saml. admired it --- Mother came home to dinner with us, but went home to tea [.]

Wednesday [April 27] Went down to the Baptism. was consulted about the name's [*sic*], held the little girl in my arm's [*sic*] during Mr. Ellerby's[143] address, was in introduced to a young Lady, who did not come quite up to my idea of elegance --- was Complimented by the company (particularly by Mrs. Ellerby & Mrs. Lillie)[144] on the fine looking young man who stood behind my chair during the Ceremony and returned home just before Papa came from the fair at Scarboro—I trust I feel truly grateful to God, for all of his kindness to me, particularly for this evening's enjoyment [.]

PAGE 86

April 28 1858 [*sic*]
Thursday
~~Wednesday~~ [*April*] *28* Soirriee [*sic*] at Yorkville [.][145] Mother, Father, Mr. A,
    Saml., Tho[s], and myself were there [.] I enjoyed it exceedingly especially
    the patriotic Songs each one of which was worth the price of the enter-
    tainment [.] —Mr. Sugden was most rapturously encored but my feel-
    ings were wrought up to the highest pitch by a song of Mr. Roches[146]
        "I'm an Englishman"
        "Deny it who can?"
    I felt that nothing could so effectually raise the Loyalty of a people as
    heart stiring Music set to such sentiments [.]
        ---A Stranger might have thought we were exclusive for we all sat
    together at one table, Father near the head then Mr. A, I came next with
    Tho[s] at my left hand then Mother & Saml., just opposite sat Mr. Ash[147]
    our Minister, one of the most enthusiastic of men [,] young, and not
    long from Merrie England and not the less excited, from having his
    intended by his side,—he ought to have gone on the dais, erected for
    the Guests, as he had been one of the Lecturers and was frequently

PAGE 87

    requested to do so, but he preferred staying where he could be free
    from restraint and I verily believe, pa and he, tried who could cheer
    most, in which they were joined by an Irishman, who said he agreed with
    their Sentiments, because they were against the Yankees, holding the
    Creed it seemed, that if we loved one, we must hate another, and was
    not far astray neither, for certainly in choosing our Leaders, we would
    infinitely prefer an Aristocracy to a Mobocracy [.]

Friday [*April*] *29th* Mary Ann having had Eliza Jane Wickson[148] to spend
    yesterday with her, they arranged to go to tea at Mother's to day [.] I
    was not destined to have the house to myself however for three of
    John's boys came to tea beside Mr. Wadsworth from Weston,[149] I missed
    Mary Ann very much in getting tea ready [.] I did some sewing, finished
    one of Papa's Shirts.

Saturday [*April 30*] At Market as usual [.] Dined at Arthur's and had some
    pleasant conversation with her[150] on the

PAGE 88

1859
    subject of death, which she said had never been a trouble to her. -----

Sunday [May 1] May Day This might have been an English one, in regard
to the weather, the sun shone so brightly, too; bright, I might say, for
as it streamed in at the Kitchen windows, as we sat at breakfast I saw to
my surprise, for the very first time, that our dear Pa's whisker's were
turning Gray, now I like to see white hair above every thing, on an old
gentleman, but when I knew Pa was not quite fifty, I thought Time had
taken a great Liberty [.] the upper part of them it is true, still retained
its sunny brown hue, which I so much admire in Tho[s], which always
seems to me to denote, a pure Saxon Descent [,] but all the rest were
changing, to a dark Iron Gray [.] his beautiful curly Brown hair is still
untouched [.] I mean to get one good lock to keep if it is possible but
he is so much averse to keepsakes, that I shall have to steal

PAGE 89

May 1st 1859

It [.]—The Opening of A New Church[151] was attended with invitations
for us to four different familys [,] but as we could not all attend (for the
distance would not admit of walking, and Tho[s] buggy required some
attention) that I preferred staying home with him and a very pleasant
Sunday afternoon we spent [.] Tho[s] read some of Jay's Exer[c][152] aloud
and then I read some sublime views on immortallity [.] Pa [,] Saml. &
Mr. Sugden came home to tea and we all went to Chapel in the
Evening [.] We noticed as we sat at the parlour windows that the Horse
Chestnut leaves were expanding [.]

Monday May 2nd Alick is very busy this morning whitewashing the pretty
light fence, that bounds our garden on the South --- Papa is planting
potatoes, in the back lot; this afternoon Patrick has been ploughing at
Woodhill [.] --- Tho[s] at the hospital as usual, Mary Ann is amusing
herself in the Orchard, Saml. writing in

PAGE 90

the parlour, and myself making a new Jacket for Mary Ann [.] The Polyanthus and the Iris's [*sic*] are to be seen [.]

Tuesday May 3rd I am rather anxious this morning; Tho[s] has gone to
Dr. Aiken's to see about the removal of a small tumour on his neck [.]
If it pleases God I shall be glad to have it away but I am always for letting every thing alone [.] it is only a very slight inconvenience to him
but I have confidence in Dr. Aiken's not allowing the operation, if
attended with any danger [.]

The Painters have commenced at the front of the house, my heart
beats a little, at the proposed sale of Lots; It seems worse, than cutting

down, the few noble pines, that crowned the small hill, at the bottom, of the orchard: but I comfort myself with the thought that they <u>are not sold yet</u> [.]

PAGE 91

Papa is sowing Oats at Woodhill to day [.] --- The gardener that we employ there, only cultivating as much of the Land as is wanted for fruits and vegetables. —I wish Thos home, it is near eleven; I am <u>very anxious</u> [.]

Soon after writing the above to my great relief, I saw Thos come past the window [.] I went to the door, but he was rather longer coming round the corner than usual [.] he looked tired but was smiling as if he was making believe, I could scarcely contain myself for joy when I found he had actually undergone the operation [.] he said he felt rather faint, but as soon as I got him some tea, he seemed better [.] I could hardly keep from crying, I felt so excited [.] he offered me a paper but I shut my eyes for I saw something almost the size of a pullet[']s egg covered with blood [.] if ever I thanked God in my heart of hearts it was then [.]

PAGE 92

Wednesday May 4th Thos seems to be doing well (through the goodness of God) he complains only of stiffness [.] he went down to Dr. Aiken this morning, and had it dressed --- Father & Mother came up soon after and we had a very pleasant time [.] Papa was planting Potatoes and so was able to dine at home [.] after dinner, Pa set off to go to Jesse Thomson's Sale, but he was too late for his Father Thomson Sen had brought the property in. Papa thinks there may not be many at our Sale tomorrow, but he says he will go through with the Sale, as it has been announced [.][153]

Arthur & Mary Ann came up in the afternoon, and still further increased our pleasure [.] There are quite a number of flowers in blossom now, Hyacinths, Pholx, Iris's [*sic*] &, &, and the Willows are already waving there [*sic*] green sprays [.] Yesterday Papa & Saml., took some pasture for their Cattle, I am allowed to send Calves [.]

PAGE 93

Thursday May 5th We are prepared for the <u>Sale</u> at last [.]

We have a splendid round of Beef cooked and the day is fine as could be desired, I do not seem to care much about it; but <u>I do wish it was over</u> [.]

I think it must be past the time and there are not more than a Dozen or so on the ground. Rose Hill will yet go down to my descendants unmutilated [.]

Tho³ is gone to the hospital for the first time since Monday, he did not want to see the Auctioneer on this beautiful estate [.] it is surely soon enough, to part with one's property when it can no longer be kept [.]

The Quietness in the immediate vicinity of the house is delightful—it is very warm—but some robins in some trees close by are signing most sweetly—now I hear our own Canarys—there is the Railroad Whistle, now the Carriage on the road [.] —I am sitting in my dear little bedroom with the window up but the Green blinds closed—I can see all

PAGE 94

May 5th 1859

without being seen, just now, some one asked if Mrs. Armstrong was at home, the girl said she was somewhere about, if she was wanted [.]

The answer was "not particularly," so I remain in my desired seclusion - - - - -

I have just put some Lunch in the parlour for seven or eight, the rest have left - - -

Pa is calling out for more water [,] one Loaf the girl says has disappeared [.] I am glad they are enjoying themselves after their walk [.] I am so thankful to them for leaving me Rose hill to myself [.] It will be all over before Tho⁵ & Saml. return. I am glad of it [.]

[*Two horizontal lines of looping squiggles drawn in here, as an elaborate break*]

This is a delightful summer evening - - - Saml. & Tho⁵ are in their own rooms, Tho⁵ lying on the bed, Saml. talking to the boy's outside, doubtless something alluding to the prowess of their dogs; as he had them away at the pasture this afternoon [.] I can hear his voice plainly [,] and also that of Tho⁵ who (though he enjoyed the gossip) kept calling out for

PAGE 95

Mischief,

["] Sam, come away to your writing - - - ["]

here in the parlour with the window's open I catch also the Music at the Brick house over the way; <u>that</u> Brick house, what changes have taken place there, since we came up here—it was the first time I had heard the piano there this Summer and it struck strangely on my ear --- The first time I ever went over death was in the house—the property belonged to a Mr. Rose[154]—it was a brother of his who was then Laid out [.] there was a widow, but no children [.] Mr. Rose came up from town while I was there, he did not seem to have a particle of affection in his bosom, as a proof of it, he asked me if one of our men, could go round with the funeral notices, as he thought their men were all work- ing on the farm, his Sister in law told him the men were all at leisure as they did not feel like working, when a death had taken place [.]

PAGE 96

he moved up from town, and took possession, but, his heart told him it mattered little where he came he could not silence the voice of re- morse --- he knew of children that wanted a mother's nursing and though he had married a daughter (for his third wife) of Major Bain's [,][155] and though worldly friends said The Royal Rose, would revive, when blessed by gentle rains [,] it was all in vain [.] his remorse embittered his peace, and the wine he drank to drown it, only inflamed his anger till wife and child avoided him, as they would a reptile, and passers by would declare that all hours of the night he might be seen, out on the Veranda trying to cool the fever of his soul [.]

    --- It was not long, before the same room, was once more dark- ne'd [sic]—and what mattered it though the Coffin was more costly [,] there were even less signs of grief-----
The secret that he had so carefully

PAGE 97

smothered down, soon came to light [.] little did his poor wife think that even his death was to be a source of annoyance to her, she knew drunken wretch as he was, the Land still remaining and though twice married before, there were no children by either marriage and there- fore she would be at least comfortably provided for [.]
no such thing—when the will was read, there were no less than three children to be provided for—was this the reward for all her patience? she had long since given up all hopes of being a happy wife, she did expect the property for her Child, no wonder that when the Will was read, she fainted, but there was no need of anxiety for him [.] God had given his angel permission to transplant him to a happier world had he not said

    "the Seed of evil doer's should never be removed" on this earth at any rate [.]

PAGE 98

[*Page left blank*]

PAGE 99

Saturday May 7 I enjoyed the ride to Market in the Omnibus exceedingly, it starts from Yorkville at eight, and the air at that time of the morning was refreshing [.] the gardens were just beginning to look pretty and I always think there is a charm in the spring that we look for in vain when the hot weather has once set in—Coming home I met Mother and returned with her to look at the shops, having made our purchase's [*sic*] [,] Mother went home and I staid at Arthur[']s [*sic*] [.] I like to talk with his wife about the time I used to live next door and to set at their window and think of my old home before Thomas was born.[156] I can see the lane I used to carry him up and down in, and where, before that, I used to walk with my little step daughter[157] and let her repeat verses after me or at other time's [*sic*] let her bring me as many different shaped leaves as she could find, to amuse her, well do I recollect chasing a Squirrel in that very lane and catching it too; but after keeping it a day or two it left me as most pets do [.] what a story it would have to relate when it got back to its mates in the garden [.] how it was fed with

PAGE 100

the choicest dainties and rewarded me by tearing up for its nest, some needlework that I set my mind upon—it is more than one and twenty years since that now and yet it seems but yesterday [.] I believe this is one of the reasons I enjoy so much to go and see Mary Ann,[158] and in so many ways she reminds me of myself [.] we each of us married a Widower, with one child, we came home to the same spot, at nearly the same time of the year, we each, were eldest daughters and had each a happy home, full of brother's [*sic*] and Sisters almost as young as our step children, what could we have more in common even in our <u>personal experience</u> we are precisely the same.

Sunday [*May 8*] At Chapel twice [.] Arthur's little boy[159] was there in the morning, and Mother was so kind as to invite Mary Ann to go to their house with him [.] The little fellow is very good at Chapel [,] better I must confess than Tho[s] was at his age or Mary Ann either [,] he always does exactly what I wish him and it is a source of great pleasure to me to have him there [.] how pleased my dear Sister will be to see him [.] how I wish she would come back.

PAGE 101

Monday May 9th Through the mercy of God I have the comfort of know-
ing that Tho[s] has again set about his studies in good earnest [.] May it
please him to Grant that he may continue in well doing, Mary Ann has
gone to school as usual—she is growing very tall, but does not look
healthy [.]

My Cows are increasing in milk on account of the good pasture, and
my hens lay well, but as mary ann grows older, my expenses seem to
increase, or it may be Tho'[s] being out of business, I do not know why,
but I find it more difficult to keep house than I did, I seem to be as ecco-
nomical [*sic*] as possible, and yet even my money that I get for my rum-
mets[160] has to go for the housekeeping [,] or at least it has this week [.]

Wednesday May 11th Mother & Father came up to day [.] The weather is
rather cooler [.] we made a fire in the parlour where we sat to sew [,]
Mother helped me a great deal with my needlework to day [.] but I feel
very poorly [.] Pa is Ploughing and is very cross [,] which affects me
good deal; though I always mean, not to mind

PAGE 102

May 12 1859

it [.] his temper like old Wine gains strength from age, but unlike Old
Wine does not improve by it [.] I have no doubt he is sorry for it at times
for he says it is very hard that no one will speak about anything but
him, for it makes him a perfect Bully, but I never knew him to be
pleased with anything or think anything right but what he did himself [.] so we must just let it pass [.] I always try to put the pretty garden
and the beautiful orchard in the foreground and sometimes succeed
in keeping it there [.] Tho[s] came home from the hospital about three
but going to study in his own room fell asleep --- Saml. went for a ride
to Forest Hill with John[161]—Our little Lilly[162] (as we always call her)
found a pretty little colt in the pasture to day [;] Alick went over to see
her, he says it is a dark gray and quite livly [*sic*]—After Father and
Mother had gone I went with some salt to my cows [,] what a pleasure
it is to me [.] Tho[s] having had a good sleep went down to the bible
Meeting [.] I was awake till he came and was glad to hear him say they
had an excellent, meeting [.] he was in the choir.

PAGE 103

May 1859

Thursday 13th The grass is brightened with the gay dandelions and though it may be treason I hail their coming as much, as I used, the buttercups in the rich pasture grounds of Old England [.] The Sumachs have unfolded their leaves and the blossoms are shewing their white petals on the Plum trees [,] while the buds on the apple trees are a Vivid rose colour

Saturday May 14 A Cold Morning [.] Went down in time to call at Father's [.]

Wednesday May 18 Mother & Father came up, a very pleasant day—went to Captain Dick[']s,[163] to see the new house, across the road, Mother was very delighted with the prospect. Papa's countenance has once more cleared up a little, I think the clouds generally disperse about the third or fourth day [.] Tho[s] seems to be in a studious mood notwithstanding the allurements of the fine weather [.] The Lilacks are not fully blown but the yellow flowering currant is in its glory [.]

Saturday May 21 At Market, we had some very heavy showers, for which we were very thankful

PAGE 104

1859

as the garden was suffering from the dry weather, I walked home after dining at Arthur[']s and found everything right [.]

Sunday [May] 22nd Cold after the rain, in the afternoon we (S.S. M A)[164] all sat once more round the fire, in which pa joined when he came home from the Sunday School [.]

Monday May 23rd Saml. set off this morning early to spend his holiday at Lyons,[165] he has fine weather and I hope will enjoy himself though he was but poorly, when he started. --- After churning, I went down to Mother's and we went to town, in the Omnibus, I got home at a quarter to one, and felt much better for the change [.]

My cows are milking well now, I make about ten pound of Butter a week, and have plenty of milk, for my two pig's [.]

Tuesday May 24 Queen's Birthday All up in good time, I bid my dear Thomas goodby before seven [.] he thought he would go down to the boats and if he saw any one he knew going to the falls[166] he would take a trip too [.] Mr Armstrong went to the Market for an

PAGE 105

hour or so as it would be too early for him to start for Richmond Hill, whither he intends going to attend a fair [.][167]—Saml. is I hope enjoy-

ing himself at Lyons [.] —Mother was here about ten, Mary Ann had
prepared to go and meet her but being too late went to yorkville by herself and spent her coppers [.] Mother brought up a very welcome letter from our Sister Caruthers[168] in which she expresses her desire to
return about July and which afforded us much pleasure [.] Father
came up in time for dinner and soon after John called in his gig[169]
and left his little girl to play with mary ann, they went out fishing, and
gathering flowers [.] Mother and I walked through the Orchard and
admired the blossoms of the Apple trees very much [.] the grass too is
very luxuriant, and owing to the late rain, of the brightest green ---
there are no end of carriages of every description passing on the road
all bound in quest of pleasure [.] many throng the sidewalks in town
but what is there compared to the country in spring [.] the two children
have just

PAGE 106

brought in some pretty wreaths of wild flowers and though tea time [,]
they have run out to make another—I have had a very happy rest to
day [,] but after all, I must confess work has its charms,—I am afraid the
wind is rising, my thoughts are on the lake, I hope Thomas is on his way
home, though it is not more than half past five, he said he missed Saml.
very much last night, I am glad two days of his visit are expired [;] it
seems odd to set down to tea without either of them and papa away
too—Mother & Father had to return to Yorkville as a young minister had
engaged to call on them [.] they would have gladly had our company
but I could not leave the dear old home to the care of a stranger (Bessie
being away, and another in her place for this day) [.] I miss the music
beyond every thing for we always had some tunes

PAGE 107

when the boys are at home. Mr. Sugden was engaged for this night at
the St Lawrence Hall[170] and Mr. B[171] is engaged now all the time as his
wife who has delicate health has a baby and being poor, they are not
able to keep a girl just now, does it not seem strange that talent is so little benefit to a man and does it not seem wonderful that we should ever
despise work, when it is so remunerative, I speak of myself now more
particularly as I sometimes feel so very tired and though I do not complain, feel so much like it, sometimes, when I see my neighbours apparently doing nothing ---
After tea Mrs. Palmer and daughter came in for an hour, and tasted the
honey from our Bee's [sic]—the painter called in to leave his brushes

and to say he would finish the street door tomorrow—the house is very quiet now, I hear nothing but the ticking of the two clocks, one upstairs and one in the kitchen, out of doors in the direction of Yorkville, you would think bedlam had blasted loose [.]

❋

DIARY OF MARY ARMSTRONG

✳

1869

PAGE 1

John Likens [*probably the publisher of the formatted diary*]
Diary for 1861 [*sic*]
Toronto C.W. [*These lines are from the formatted diary's title page.*]

January 1st, 1869 Friday New Years Day
Thank God we are all in good health and I never was happier in my life
than today, sitting down in the kitchen mending socks—outside it is
dreadfully stormy [,] blowing

PAGE 2

in every direction—Papa went to town but soon came back and has
just taken his dinner he is now sitting in the parlour reading the bible,
one of the hired men has gone up to my dear son's to haul wood for
him [;] the other man, has been feeding the Cattle, & is now chop-
ping wood [.] we have three fires in the house and one outside [.]
~~Walton Street~~   ~~Taking grade~~   ~~making plan~~

Last Christmas Day we had a very pleasant gathering it was a beautiful
day and so it continued till this morning but old winter is fairly set in
now at all events [.]

PAGE 3

Perhaps one reason I feel in good spirits is because "All the bunkers are
filled"[1] that is to say we did everything in the way of work, that it was
possible to do before the New Year came in and so now we can breathe
freely. I posted a letter last night to William Orme—I have my subscription to the Chapel Fund[2] ready & though I have not received my
bill from Mrs Heward[3] I have the money at hand—so I owe no one
anything [.]

Monday [January] 4th

The weather for the last three days has been a perfect thaw—the hens have commenced to lay & but for the snow we might fancy it was spring—any amount of soft water [.]

My dear son & his wife[4] took tea with us yesterday [.] They went up the street to chapel[5] and I went to see my Father in the evening [.]

PAGE 4

Tuesday [January] 5th

Mary Ann Pallett & a Miss Watson[6] came to pay a visit—we went to Yorkville together & called on Mother on Wednes[day.]
Mary Ann & Miss Watson went to the City on Thursday—staid home Friday [.] Saturday we went to town together [.]

Sunday we went to SS[7] at nine staid to chapel in the morning went to SS at two—to Mother's to tea [,] chapel again at night—Monday we all went to my dear son's to tea & at night they went home [.][8] Mary Ann cried a good deal at going away but I felt I was not equal to the task of letting her stay here more especially as her Grandpa[9] did not express any wish to that effect—I told her however if she could not make herself comfortable at her Father[']s perhaps she could come back in a week [.]

Wednesday [January] 13

My dear son came down and drove me as far as Father[']s, where I staid till he came back [.] I had received a letter from Orme & mother was very glad to hear about him [.] - - - - -

I am not quite well enough to walk after washing and churning—so it is a great benefit to me to have my son so near for I feel certain, I shall not be able to walk about as I have done [.]

PAGE 5

Thursday [January] 14

My Girl, Mary Ann Shields,[10] gets up without any trouble in the morning and gets the men their breakfast which is a great blessing to me then she starts out to milk and I get papa's breakfast and my own ready then we feed the calf & fowls [.] I set the upstairs in order and she clears up below, then we both hurry the dinner as we get our's [*sic*] at half past eleven so it can be removed for the men at twelve—I can truly say I am as happy as the day is long [.] - - - - - - - - -

Friday [January] 15th

My dear son & daughter in law came to see us & staid to tea—the weather is most splended [*sic*] not one cold day since New Year's [.]

Saturday [January] 16

I went down to Father[']s in the afternoon, but felt very poorly; at night I found my finger very painful and began poulticing [.]

[Sunday January 17]

On Sunday morning it seemed rather better but towards night, got very bad [.]

PAGE 6

Monday [January] 18

Hardly a wink of sleep last night the pain was so great—being my right hand I was quite helpless could neither comb my hair or fasten my clothes let alone sewing writing or knitting could not even put on my spectacles and had not even the desire to open the paper—sent for some of Holloway[']s Ointment[11] but it made it worse [.]

Tuesday [January] 19th

Last night the pain was intolerate and when I got some cold water the heat of my poor hand fairly made it steam but on this day my dear son came in and lanced it at once the relief was wonderful he also left me some powder's [*sic*] to procure sleep and ordered me medicine to be taken the next day [.]

Wednesday [January] 20

Through God[']s blessing on the means used I slept the first part of last night but could do nothing at all [,] all day [.]

PAGE 7

Thursday [January] 21

I sat in the arm chair in the kitchen all this day too—directing the girl as well as I could but it is easier to do a Thing than to learn [.] Mary Ann Shields I thought while I was [*entry stops here mid-page*]

Friday [January] 22

My finger was much the same [.]

Saturday [January] 23

This day I felt very tired of being in the house, without being able to sew, knit, wash, or churn,

PAGE 8

Monday [January] 25

Not able to dress myself properly yet but was determined to go to the City because papa gave me the money to pay Gibson & Dodgson & Shields their quarterly bills—I enjoyed the fresh air amazingly though this was the first hard frost since New Year[']s Day—I paid a small amount due Mrs Heward[12] on her November bill for Dry Goods & then went to Father[']s & staid about half an hour—I also bought a small account book for ninepence at Piddingtons[13]—papa had started for Barrie before I came home [.]

Tuesday [January] 26

To day was rather gloomy—I should be very dull if it was not for the Cows and Fowls—both of which are doing remarkably well indeed I think I never had the fowls lay so well in January before, but there is no demand for butter round here just now people have mostly laid in a winter supply [.] Gibson of course would take it but I prefer selling it at the house & I think the price may go up [.]

PAGE 9

Wednesday [January] 27th

My dear son called & took dinner then we drove down in his buggy to the City and I enjoyed the ride very much—I was able to churn this morning & made about eight pounds of butter—sent the girl with it to Gibson[']s to help pay for the fowls feed [.] —This day was very mild, but I hear the lake roaring tonight & suppose we shall have the snow before long [.]

January Friday 29 [Printed format "February, Friday, 1" crossed out and redated]

Weather still mild but cloudy. Churned pretty early this morning and drove up to Woodhill with papa [,] came home to dinner at twelve and had the last roast of our Christmas Beef and tonight a good mince pie, but we are not nearly at the end of our mince meat—Papa went to the City this Afternoon for some new tools & is gone down again to night to an Agricultural M [.][14] ----- It has rained some to night [.]

Saturday [January] 30th

Another beautiful day—Did our washing today instead of waiting till Monday [.] Felt very tired in the afternoon & so staid home [.] Papa was in town all day [.]

Donald, went down with wood [;] Hall, with turnips [.][15]

PAGE 10

February 1st Monday

 Still beautiful weather [.] Our white Cow Dolly took it into her head to go back to Brougham[16] last night but got tired on the road & turned back [.] Hall was taking a load of Pea Straw to our dear son's York Mills[17] this morning & met her returning. we should have missed her sadly as she gives more milk than any other cow & I am just beginning to get good sale for it [.]

Tuesday [February] 2nd

 To day old Father Winter is resuming his sway—the wind roars—the skies look threatening, our hands ache with the cold, while feeding the fowls:—but indoors everything looks bright there is an abundance of fire wood piled under the stairs a good fire in the parlour & the same in the kitchen where I am sitting—Papa has gone to the City on agricultural business [.] Donald has gone to the City with wood [.] Hall is bringing wood out of the bush we have no boy at present an out-door hand is threshing the pease in the barn [.]

Wednesday [February] 3rd Had quite a fall of snow last night [.] sleighing good today.

PAGE 11

 I find a leaf of this book has been torn out but I still think I will make it do, as a new one would cost me half a dollar & this time of the year I have less coming in [.] My dear son & the three little boys[18] (one a lovely baby) & their Mama came to see me today I went down with the Dr to get Braithwaite's Retrospect[19] & bought two little toys for the children - - - -

 To night papa is gone to the social at Yorkville—I was too tired to walk [.]

Thursday the fourth, was a bitter cold day out, on account of the storm but we did not find it so in the house [.] - - - - - The fowls however made it an excuse for not laying as usual—the cows too only gave about half the quantity of milk as it was too stormy to get out their turnips [.]

Friday [February 5] I went up as far as York Mills but did not stay any [.] Today is very pleasant again—went down to the city in the doctor[']s cutter and brought papa back with us [.]—Our man Donald has been seriously ill to day—seems to be better for my dear son's treatment - - - - -

PAGE 12

Monday [February] 8

Donald was very ill all day on Sunday [.] I only went out in the morning [.] Papa staid home with me in the evening [.]
The weather keeps very mild [.]

Tuesday [February] 9

Donald was much the same [.] The Doctor[20] (my dear son) said there seemed a great tendency to run into Typhoid Fever—but fortunately I had not the slightest fear of taking it so I continued to wait upon him [.]

Wednesday [February] 10

Donald seemed a great deal easier to day though no sleep could be obtained in spite of all narcotics but to night when I took him in some refreshment he seemed to have been dozing [.]—The girl has gone down to the Druggist[']s with a prescription [.] Papa is sleeping soundly on the sofa—one man has brought a load of oats from Maplewoods[21] the other is staying out there till tomorrow [.]

PAGE 13

Thursday [February] 11th

Donald keeps much the same [.]—The snow has nearly disappeared— Our two men had great difficulty in bringing home the oats from Maplewoods—Willie Pallet brought a load too [.] He is a very good boy in every particular [and] seems to be really unselfish as well as industrious [.]

Friday [February] 12

Donald seems to be getting better, but I should like to know what keeps my dear son away yesterday & to-day [.] Papa brought in a branch of palm today just bursting out—six weeks before palm Sunday & sometimes we could hardly get any then [.]   '

Saturday [February] 13th

My dear son came down today they were all well through the goodness of God—he had been very much engaged with patients [.] I went out for a ride to the City [.]

PAGE 14

Monday [February] 15

Yesterday & today it looks more like Winter snowing & raining [,] thawing & freezing [.] this afternoon is decidedly milder [.]—On the opposite side of the road men are at work digging out the foundation for a house—just now the sun is shining [.]

Mr Simmers['] men are making a road on the hillside just opposite so Rosehill will change its appearance this summer [.][22]

PAGE 15

Thursday [February] 18

My Birthday—Washed & Churned in the forenoon—went out with papa in the afternoon for a sleighride papa offered to buy me some oranges or anything else in that line but I declined, I want to save every copper I can get for my dear & only son and I thought papa would take a note that he laid out nothing for me & put that to my account—Bro Saml. & our son were here to tea [.] Beautiful Weather [.]

Saturday [February] 20th

Weather, I must own rather severe [.] went to the city for a sleighride Papa was in town before us—He saw Mary Ann & Willie Pallet just starting for home they were both well

PAGE 16

February Monday 22nd [Printed format "March, Monday, 4" crossed out and re-dated]

We had a very heavy fall of snow yesterday but the sun is shining gloriously to day, and the snow is melting fast—Mr Simmer's [*sic*] men are still working with vigour, they got water in the well on Saturday [.] He is a seedsman but for some reason he is not popular as a Neighbour though I think he will keep his grounds in good order [.] Papa has gone to town—I have been Churning—The Hen's [*sic*] are laying well, but the cows are on the decrease well, "the nearer the spokes of the wheel are to the ground; the sooner they will go up again [.] "

PAGE 17

February 23rd Tuesday

To day the snow is knee deep and the wind very cold [.] it is almost impossible to move about our yard [.] I think the folks will beleive [*sic*] now the winter is not all over [.]

Thursday [February] 25

Yesterday & to-day are regular old fashioned Winter days [.] The Snow is very deep on the ground & the air is cold though not intensely—Papa & the men are threshing Wheat at Woodhill—they are not yet

home though it is past eight [.] The girl & I have <u>had to look after the</u>
<u>Cows</u> [.]

Friday [February 26] & Saturday [February 27] Papa & the men were still
away at Woodhill [.] Papa sent the Wheat to the Humber the weather
is very cold [.]

PAGE 18

March 1st Monday
Still cold & snowey, I might also say dull & gloomy for we have not seen
the sun out fully these ten days [.] I am well off, however through God's
Goodness—abundance of dry Cordwood—good expectation of calves—
hens laying well & plenty of feed for them & all of us in the enjoyment
of good, though not robust, health [.]

Tuesday [March] 2nd
The men started off at five to day to go to Woodhill for two loads of straw
which they will take to Market [.] Papa has gone to town, I am going
to make Cakes for little Philip's birthday,[23]—yesterday I had a good
rest, though we washed in the morning I knitted the rest of the day as
they were all at Woodhill [.]

PAGE 19

March 3rd Wednesday
We went up to York Mills to keep little Philip's Birthday—The weather
was delightful—as it was the day he first made his appearance on this
beautiful earth—

Thursday [March] 4th [and] Friday [March] 5th
<u>The weather is extremely cold</u> [.] The two little boys are both learning
their letters but with Philip as it was with his dear papa, it is all uphill
work [;] with dear little Norman however the case is very different
though only three years old last December he learns with great quick-
ness indeed he has already almost all his learnt, [*sic*] but They are both
lovely children and have (especially Philip) the most unbounded affection for their infant brother [.][24]

PAGE 20

Monday [March] 8th
Last Saturday & Yesterday were quite winterly but to-day though the
ground is still covered with snow it does seem a little Springlike—Hall &
Cooney[25] are gone to Woodhill for Hay and Chaff [.]

Tuesday [March] 9th

A beautiful day—Washed & churned in the morning & went out for a sleighride in the afternoon—The doctor[26] drove me past the Governor's Residence[27] which is now building [.]

Wednesday [March] 10th

Old Father Winter resumed his sway, it snowed from morning till night, and the wind howled [.]—It was the day appointed for the Eglinton SS[28] going out sleighing but some of them did not get further than our house [.]

PAGE 21

There was to be a party at Yorkmills but papa & I had promised to go to a social at Yorkville[29] but it was impossible to walk anywhere so we had to enjoy our own fireside, & no bad thing either - - - - -

Thursday [March] 11th

This morning papa had to go to the Mill[30] to see about getting some wheat ground so that we might have the bran for the Cows [.] I went with him though the cold was intense going north but it was near our son's, and I staid there while papa went; afterward we both took lunch off a cold Ham which cut up splendidly & a good cup of tea so we did not feel the cold at all coming back—Their company had come in spite of the storm (those that lived near) & the children were in high spirits as a little Uncle & Aunt had stopped all night—Papa went to the Station[31] to start to Barrie but was too late [,] I was very glad to see him come back [.]

PAGE 22

Friday [March] 12th

Papa started again this morning for Barrie [;] it was tolerably fine then but has turned out very stormy [.] I thank God with all my heart for the abundance of good fire wood that we have; all sawed the right size, every thing that we can desire in the way of provisions and no anticipations of sorrow—and more than all, we have an express command to take no thought for the morrow, for the morrow shall take thought for the things of itself [.]

- - - - - I have been out to the henhouse to feed them and the girl has taken the Cows to water—one man went to the Mill & brought home a load of Flour, Shorts, & Bran—the other man took a load of Wood to market, & brought home the money [.] they are both hauling out manure to the Hazel Dell Fields[32] this afternoon—The snow is so fine there will likely be a great fall of it but it cannot lay very long now [.]

PAGE 23

Saturday [March] 13th

Was a nice fine day—My dear son & Mrs Armstrong came down to dinner & we had a very pleasant sleighride to the City—we called at Grandpa Wickson[33] coming back [.]

[Monday] March 15th

Monday was very fine so we washed & churned, in the afternoon I sent a letter to the post for my sister at Ottawa[34]—The two men went up to Woodhill for two loads of Hay—one load sold coming down for sixteen dollars, & saved tolls & fees [.]

Tuesday [March] 16th Our two men started early for two more loads of hay—sold in good time—Papa has been to town

Wednesday March 17th St Patricks Day

the last two days which will be a good change for him—I have been busy at Shirtmaking which is a good rest for me—Housework will soon increase [.]

PAGE 24

March Monday 22 [Printed format "April, Monday, 1" crossed out and redated]
Was a very cold day —dreadful

Tuesday [March 23] was very fine like Spring -----

Wednesday [March 24] was fine too; I went to Yorkville to see my Father when I came home Princess had calved.

Good Friday 26 March

Very Gloomy [.] The snow is so deep I cannot get out about the barnyard, but I am having a good rest, which is perhaps better, yesterday we cleaned up the house for Easter [.] I let my girl go to Church to day [.] I am cooking roast Beef & plum pudding for the sake of old times [.] There is a good fire in the parlour & Papa is enjoying his paper [.] I think perhaps Sam will come up to dinner [;] my dear son could hardly get away so soon as there will be a tea party at the primitive Church which we have

PAGE 25

March 26 Good Friday [*sic*]

partly provided, which we think they will come down to [.]—The rain has ceased for the present, but no signs of my favourite, the Sun [,] peeping out never mind it will soon be April [.]

March 27th Saturday

My dear son & Mrs Armstrong came to the Social last night & Mrs A sang[35] Eve's Lamentation very sweetly but the doctors mind was on his patients so they hurried back—

Eggs and Butter are a great price to day but I did not charge more [.] March 27th 30 C Butter [,] Eggs 35 C [.]

Today the Sun is shining splendidly and I enjoyed myself by getting the churning & washing done in advance [.] I intend to go to town this afternoon but my dear son did not come down [.]

PAGE 26

March 30th Tuesday

Thank God we see some signs of Spring [.] The weather though rather gloomey has moderated, it rained all day yesterday and all last night but the crows are calling to each other, the cocks are crowing and the earth is looking brown again [.] Papa & I went to Mr Mathieson's Sale[36] yesterday & bought a quantity of good furniture but before the goods could be removed the Sheriff put in an appearance [.] but if we do not get out bargains we shall save our money [.] I do not see how it was for the Auctioneer said at the commencement it was a Bailiff[']s Sale [.][37]—Word was brought afterwards we could get them but Papa thought it was too wet to go then so we got them the next day Wednesday [.]

[*A long division calculation appears beside this entry*]

PAGE 27

[*Page left blank except for some addition, multiplication, and division calculations*]

PAGE 28

Thursday 1st [*April*]

I feel a little fatigued today from arranging the new furniture there is one splended [*sic*] Bookcase which I promised to pay papa for, in the full; forty eight dollars [.] The rest papa bought on his own account [:]

one Toilette Stand with Mirror cost about nine dollars & a half (it would cost thirty new) [;] a large Black Walnut Cupboard for the breakfast room, seven dollars [;] a two set Black W Washstand two dollars & a half; six volumes of Hume[']s History [of] England[38] well bound two dollars & forty cents, [;] five other books about one dollar concluding with a common table to stand on for thirty five cents [.]

PAGE 29

[April] 1st
— Papa is getting his hot beds ready but the weather feels very chilly to me yet & the ground is very damp—there has been as usual a great rush of water [,] it carried one of the supports of the Hazel Dell Bridge away [.]

Saturday [April] 3rd
Mr Matheson called to-day & I asked him if he had any objection to tell me what he paid for the bookcase he said seventy five dollars but he bought several other pieces of furniture at the same time or he should have had to pay more for it [.]

Sunday April 4th was very cold but towards evening it got milder [.] Mr Dunbar[39] came over in the afternoon to tell us our black cow had calved at the Hazel Dell barn [.] I thought it very kind of him [.]

PAGE 30

Friday [April] 9th
This had been the first week of spring weather [.] —The robins are come & I saw yesterday the first flight of wild pidgeons [.] —The snow is almost gone [.]

April 16th Friday
Was a beautiful day I went up with papa to the back lot to see George[40] starting to plough it—Afterwards went with Miss Seagram[41] to the Hazel Dell Barn for a walk, -- enjoyed it very much [.]

Saturday [April] 17th
Been busy today—Churning & Ironing [,] April weather, [.] Papa has gone to town now, but was very hard at work all the morning—I think I could not live without work (in more senses than one) but I do really like it [.]

PAGE 31

Tuesday [April] 20th

We have had some very heavy showers with Thunder and Lightning [.]
Heard the Frogs for the first time plainly, last night [.] The Tulips &
Hyacinths are up pretty high [.] Papa & the men are raking the grass-
plots in front—the ground is too wet to plough [.]—My dear son Dr Armstrong was down and took dinner with us [.] I am very glad he has
come to York Mills as I generally go to town with him once a week & I
am getting too tired now to walk [;] indeed my health is very far from
being what it once was [.]

PAGE 32

April 21st Thursday

I must confess to feeling very disheartened today for some robbers
broke into my fowl house and stole at least a dozen of my best hens—
yesterday I got twenty three eggs in—the day before the same and today at four o[']clock I could only find six [.] I know it might have
been worse & if I get a calf from "Queen's Own" to night I hope I shall
forget it—I am sure I bear no malice to the thieves, whoever they are &
that is one comfort to me.—I must try & buy some more to make up my
loss & the sooner I forget all about it the better [.]

PAGE 33

[May] 3rd Monday

Last Saturday was very cold & so was yesterday raining most of the
time—this morning the sun was out and bright but we require two fires
in the house still—I have churned & washed to-day as usual, but I get
very fatigued over it & so I think I should if I did nothing but I am very
glad we had the rain to make the grass grow for my cows—Queen's
Own calved a week ago & I think I shall go ahead now [.] The grass-plots
which ten days ago were to all appearances entirely dead, are as green
as it is possible for them to be [.] The brick house building across the
road is nearly finished and forms a very pretty object to our view [.]

PAGE 34

Queen's Birthday [Monday May] 24th

One of the brightest of the season—My dear son & wife were to go out
to Brougham[42] to a church opening yesterday which deprived us of
their company today, but Samuel came up for a walk, & sat in the gar-

den chair reading after dinner, the birds were singing all round & the children shouting with delight, our hill was never so lively before [.]

PAGE 35

July 1st [Thursday] Dominion Day

This is a beautiful cool day & indeed we have had very little else this summer—I am entirely alone—sitting in the front hall but there are innumerable sweet sounds all around; the chirping of the grasshoppers, the whirring of the other insects, the whistle of the robin [,] the shrill crowing of the cocks, the sound of the workmen across the road saw-ing & hammering as they put the last touches on Mr Simmers['] new brick house interest me [.] as I write this I hear endless exclamations of delight too, from the holiday folks passing as they catch the first view of our pretty garden [;] a group all standing up in their carriage

PAGE 36

July 1st Thursday

crying out simultaneously,

"isn[']t it lovely, did you ever see anything like that, look at the roses, [."] and one girl walking a little ahead called to the rest of her party [:] "we didn[']t know it was summer, did we, till we got up here—[."] My dear son & Mrs Armstrong are at a picnic at Eglinton [,] we were invited, but we could hardly leave our grounds unwatched as a temta-tion [*sic*] to strollers so Papa & I took our lamb & green pease with a plum pudding quietly alone—one man went down to the city with a load of clover [,] another was ploughing [,] the other two I think were hoe-ing [.]—The first

PAGE 37

July 1st

two were at a merrymaking last night so I suppose they work today to make up for it—I have allowed my girl to go to the Island this afternoon as we did most of our work yesterday and papa will go to the horticul-tural Gardens[43]—he has gone across to the Hazel Dell fields just now to sow some turnip seed and gather a few early pease for market [.]—Brother Sam has gone up to Eglinton too; the band of the Queen's Own passed up about noon—Sam came up here & took tea [;] he had not felt well enough to go to the picnic but went down with papa to the Garden's [*sic*] [.]

PAGE 38

July 7th Wednesday

Was my party day,[44] and we had a capital time—my dear daught[er]-in law [,] Mrs Armstrong, came in the morning & we were all ready, to receive our guests at five—We certainly had the best table laid out I ever saw in a private house [.] The roses were splended [*sic*] & the bride cake excellent "the red ripe straw berries" contrasted beautifully with the snowey blancmonges [.]

PAGE 39

[Saturday] July 10th

Papa has just brought in a basket of strawberries off our own vines first fruits thank God almost as large as those we bought for our party and a beautiful flavour [.]

PAGE 40

August 1869 [Tuesday] 3rd

My dearly beloved Father died at nine o[']clock in the evening of this day - - - - -
My brother Samuel came up for me between nine & ten in the morning & I staid by his[45] bedside till five when I came home (with Eliza)[46] for a few minutes [.] we swallowed a cup of tea & went back immediately [,] the moment I went into the room I found his

PAGE 41

breathing was more difficult but I had the sweet consolation of watching by him till the last and giving him the last refreshment he ever took [;] he had been very restless but about a quarter to nine for

PAGE 42

[*Printed format entry spaces for June 3, 4, 5. Page left blank.*]

PAGE 43

1869 [*Printed format header "Cash Account—January" crossed out except for month.*]

Needlework
Mended all the Sacks
Made a fancy Apron
"   a Grey Calico Waist
"   a pr Scarlet Flannel Drawers

"   a Striped Calico Waist
        Mending in general

February
    Made a new Scarlet Flannel Petticoat
    Finished the first, of a pair of white Socks
    Made two Grey Calico C—
    Made a new White Shirt for Papa
        Mending in general

March (The Blood Stone, Courage)
    Made a new Grey Calico Waist
    Finished Knitting the White Socks
    Made the second of Papa's White Shirts
    "   a new coloured Petticoat

April (The Sapphire (Repentance & Innocence)
    Made a new white Shirt—third
    Mended Coat & Waistcoat
    Fixed up my Drab Dress
    Made the skirt of a new cotton dress

PAGE 44

1869 [*Printed format header "Cash Account—February" crossed out except for month.*]

Needlework done in May
    Finished another of Papa's White Shirts (fourth)
    Made a grey calico sheet
    Hemed a new tablecloth
    Fixed four pair of worn stockings
    Made a new coarse apron
    "   a Tea Towel
    Finished two waists with edging

Needlework in June
    Made another of the White Shirts but too busy to do ay more at present [.] Papa has at least nine or ten white shirts on hand now, which will last till I feel inclined to start making again [.]

PAGE 45

[*Printed format header "Cash Account—March" not crossed out.*]

Dec *31st 1869*

This night concludes this year let think what more was done [.]

Peiced [*sic*] a very pretty quilt Star pattern

Peiced [*sic*] a pretty buff & White Cradle quilt

Knitted two pair of Scarlet Stockings

"   One pair Grey Socks

Made a new woollen shirt

Mending in general

PAGE 46

[*Printed format header "Cash Account—April" not crossed out.*]

1870 Jan'y

Made the first of a set of Grey Cotton C—

Finished the first of a set of Grey Cotton Drawer's [*sic*]

One of the new Aprons Brown H

Mended a number of the Sacks

PAGE 47

[*Printed format header "Bills Payable — January"; "Receivable" at middle of page. Page left blank.*]

PAGE 48

[*Printed format header "Bills Payable— February."*]

1869

~~Mrs Heward's Bill for Dry Goods~~   Paid

Mr Gibson's for Small Wheat   Paid

[*Printed format "Receivable" at middle of page.*]

PAGE 49

[*Most of this page torn out here, a small piece remains close to the binding. Other pages may also have been torn out.*]

W Lawson [*Written vertically close to the binding.*]

PAGE 50

[*Unlined pages at back of diary begin here.*]

First Class Entrys [47]

Paid	Dougal McLean	3rd	York	$4.00
	1st Class			
Paid	James King		York	4.00
Paid	Pimpson Hewitt	2nd	Scarboro	4.00
Paid	Andrew Hood	4th	Scarboro	4.00
Paid	James McLean	1st	Vaughan	4.00
Paid	George Morgan		Scarboro	4.00
Paid	Thomas Davidson		York	4.00
Paid	Seth Haycock	5th	King	4.00
Paid	Benjamin Hollinshead	6th	King	4.00
Paid	Duncan McLean		York	4.00
				40.00

PAGE 51

2nd Class

Paid	Mr James Newton		King	$3.00
Paid	George Smith		Whitchurch	3.00
Paid	William Milliken	Prize	Markham	3.00
Paid	Robert Webster		Scarboro	3.00
Paid	William Patton	6th	Markham	3.00
Paid	William Bayes		Etobicoke	3.00
Paid	William Coxworth		Markham	3.00
Paid	Donald Cummins		Toronto	3.00
Paid	Alan McLean		West-York	3.00
Paid	John Coleman		York	3.00
Paid	James Stewart		York	3.00
Paid	James McLean	4th	York	3.00
Paid	James Patterson	5th	Scarboro	3.00
				39.00

PAGE 52

3rd Class Patent Ploughs

Paid	Mr James McKay		West-Gwilliambury	$2.00
	42	3rd	P.O. Bradford	

	43	2nd	P.O. Gormleys Markham	
Paid	William Smith		Whitchurch	2.00

Paid	39 William Armstrong	1st	Scarboro	2.00
Paid	George Anderson no prize		Markham	2.00
Paid	John McLean		York	2.00

~~Prizes in the Second Class~~

No 20 1st Prize   39   ~~39~~
—26   48   ~~43~~
                  42   ~~42~~
                  4¹   4¹

PAGE 53

4th Class Boys

Paid	6 Jonathan Ackrow		Etobicoke	$1.00
Paid	10 Thomas Dickson	4th	Scarboro	1.00
Paid	8 Adam Hood	1st	Scarboro	1.00
Paid	13 Reuben Phillips		Markham	1.00
Paid	9 William Russell		Markham	1.00
Paid	11 James Wylie		Markham	1.00
Paid	5 David Mason	5th	Scarboro	1.00
Paid	7 Milton Cummer		York	1.00
Paid	14 Andrew Annow	2nd	West York	1.00
Paid	12 Thomas Brown	3rd	Toronto	1.00

❊

LIST OF INDIVIDUALS

*

Individuals Mentioned in the 1859 Diary

Family

Mary (Wickson) Armstrong—author of the diary

Philip Armstrong—Mary's husband (Mary refers to him as "Pa," "Papa," "Mr. Armstrong," or "Mr. A")

Thomas Armstrong—son of Philip Armstrong and Mary Wickson

Robert Pallett—son-in-law of Philip Armstrong

Anne (Armstrong) Pallett—daughter of Philip Armstrong and Mary Calvert

Mary Ann Pallett—daughter of Robert Pallett and Anne Armstrong

William Pallett—son of Robert Pallett and Anne Armstrong

James Wickson—Mary's father (Mary refers to him as "Father")

Jane (Tuesman) Wickson—Mary's mother (Mary refers to her as "Mother")

Samuel Wickson—Mary's brother

Rev. Arthur Wickson—Mary's brother

Mary Ann (Thomas) Wickson—second wife of Arthur Wickson

Paul Giovanni Wickson—son of Arthur Wickson

Sarah (Wickson) Carruthers—Mary's sister (in England during 1859)

Jane (Wickson) Ebbs—Mary's sister in Paris, C.W.

Rev. Edward Ebbs—husband of Jane Wickson in Paris, C.W.

William Orme Wickson—Mary's brother (perhaps in England or New York during 1859)

George Guest Wickson—Mary's brother (perhaps in Lyons, New York, during 1859)

Biddy—perhaps a nickname for George Wickson's wife, Catherine Ray, or his daughter Eliza Jane

John Wickson—Mary's brother
Eliza (Chilver) Wickson—wife of John Wickson
Eliza Jane Wickson—daughter of John and Eliza Wickson
Rusby—John Rusby Wickson, son of John and Eliza Wickson
Emma—Emma Wickson, daughter of John and Eliza Wickson
Alfred George Wickson—infant son of John and Eliza Wickson
Agnes Rebecca Wickson—infant daughter of John and Eliza Wickson
Edward Taylor—Mary's uncle, husband of her aunt Hannah Wickson, in England

Household Staff
Patrick—a farmhand
Alick—a farmhand, whitewashing fence
Bessy—a hired "help" girl
Liddy—a hired "help" girl
Holmes—perhaps a cabman

Ministers and Their Wives
Mr. Ellerby—Rev. T.S. Ellerby, pastor of the First Congregational Church on John Street
Mrs. Lillie—wife of Rev. Adam Lillie, a Congregational minister
Mr. Grassett—Rev. H.J. Grasett, M.A., Rector of St. James' Cathedral
Mr. Ash—Rev J.C. Ash, the Armstrongs' minister at the Yorkville Church

Doctors, Professors, and Lecturers
Mr. Hodgens—perhaps J. George Hodgins, M.A., deputy superintendent of education for Upper Canada
Mr. Sinclair—temperance lecturer from Edinburgh, Scotland
Malcolm Cameron—businessman, politician, and temperance advocate, chair of one of Sinclair's temperance lectures
Colonel Playfair—temperance lecturer
Dr. Aiken—W.T. Aikins, Thomas's medical instructor at Toronto School of Medicine
Dr. Richardson—probably Dr. J.H. Richardson of Toronto School of Medicine
Dr. Scott—perhaps Dr. W.J. Scott
Dr. Stratford—perhaps Dr. S.J. Stratford
Dr. Wilson—Professor Daniel Wilson, instructor in English and History at University College at the University of Toronto

Professor Croft—Professor Henry Holmes Croft, instructor in
   Chemistry at University College at the University of Toronto and on
   the faculty of the Toronto School of Medicine
Professor Meredith—perhaps Edward A. Meredith, who lived on the
   east side of Yonge Street in Rosedale

Neighbours and Friends
Mr. Sugden—a singer and vocal instructor
Mr. Sanderson—Rev. R.S.G.R. Sanderson of the Wesleyan Methodist
   Book Room on King Street East; his residence was on Bloor Street in
   Yorkville
MacKenzie—perhaps Walter MacKenzie, a barrister living in Yorkville
Edward Hooper—owned land to the north of Armstrongs; built
   "Farnham Lodge"
Mrs. Hooper—wife of Edward Hooper
Mr. Rose—neighbour across Yonge Street; his name was given to Rose
   Hill
Mrs. Taylor—Margaret Bowes Taylor, widow of Samuel E. Taylor,
   merchant
Mr. Ross—perhaps husband of Mrs. Ross of New Kent Road, a widow in
   1868
Hausman—perhaps Francis Hauman, a combmaker on Sydenham
   Street in Yorkville
Isaac Robinson—a family friend
Misses Robinson—probably Isaac Robinson's daughters
Miss Givens—perhaps the daughter of Dr. H.H. Givens
Mr. Smith—a family friend
Mr. Walker—probably a neighbour
Mr. Buckam—a friend in Paris, C.W.
Mr. Wadsworth—uncertain, "from Weston"
Mrs. Palmer—a neighbour

Other
Mr. Passmore—a surveyor
Mr. & Mrs. Widder—members of the colonial elite; Frederick Widder
   was a commissioner of the Canada Company
Major Bain—uncertain
Hon. Peter Boyle de Blaquière & Mrs. de Blaquière—members of
   colonial elite; Peter Boyle de Blaquière was a member of the
   legislative council

Mr. Mason—uncertain, something to do with a "pass book"
Lilly—uncertain, perhaps a nickname for Mary Ann or a dog
Bethel—perhaps a neighbour or shopkeeper
Briscoe—William Briscoe, a vocalist for the St. George's Society
Mr. Baxter—a vocalist for the St George's Society
Mr. Carter—music professor and conductor for the St. George's Society
Mrs. Kemp—"Miss" Kemp in the *Globe*, a vocalist for the St. George's Society
Mrs. Siddon—perhaps the wife of Silvanus Sedon of Richmond Street
Mr. & Mrs. Baggeur—uncertain
Mr. Bishop—John Wickson's clerk

Individuals Mentioned in the 1869 Diary, but not in the 1859 Diary

Family
Fidelia Jane (Maughan) Armstrong—wife of Thomas Armstrong
Philip Maughan Armstrong—son of Thomas and Fidelia
Thomas Norman Armstrong—son of Thomas and Fidelia
Albert Eugene Armstrong—son of Thomas and Fidelia

Household Staff
Mary Ann Shields—a hired "help" girl
Donald—a farm hand
Hall—a farm hand
Cooney—a farm hand
George—a farm hand

Friends and Neighbours
Mr. Simmers—Joseph A. Simmers, the Armstrongs' new neighbour
Miss Watson—a friend of Mary Ann Pallett
Mr. Dunbar—a neighbour to the south at the Hazel Dell property
Miss Seagram—a friend

Other
Mrs. Heward, Gibson, Dogson, Shields—probably shopkeepers
Piddingtons—a store in Toronto
Mr. Mathieson—held a bankruptcy sale

Property Mentioned in Either Diary

Rose Hill—Yonge Street and Farnham Avenue, at the toll bar

Maple Woods—probably south of Mount Pleasant Cemetery, along Heath Street East

Hazel Dell Fields—south of St. Clair Avenue, west of Inglewood Drive, east of ravine

Woodhill—perhaps at Dufferin Street and Eglinton Avenue

NOTES

�֎

Notes to Introduction

PART I

A Canadian's Story

1   For a discussion of how families made the decision to emigrate, see B. Maas, *Helpmates of Man: Middle Class Women and Gender Ideology in Nineteenth-Century Ontario* (Bochum: N. Brockmeyer, 1990), 22, 78.

2   H.J. Dyos, *Victorian Suburb: A Study of the Growth of Camberwell* (London: Leicester University Press, 1961), 33, 37, 50. See also J.S. Dearden, *John Ruskin's Camberwell* (St. Albans: Brentham Press, 1990).

3   Mary's grandfather, James Wickson, who died in 1815. This James married a woman named Sarah. They lived at 7 Baker's Row and had three children: James junior (born c.1794), Hannah, and Sarah. All three married and produced children of their own. See AAFP: Wickson folder.

4   The family was living at 20 Alfred Place, Newington Causeway, in 1826-27, and in 1832-34 they lived at Aylesbury Place, on Old Kent Road, where they seem to have been since at least 1829. See AAFP: Wickson folder; WFP: transcript of indenture between James Wickson, Edward Taylor, and William Maidlow, 21 August 1829. See also *Holden's Triennial Directory for 1805, 1806, 1807*, 4th ed., vol. 2 (London: sold by the proprietor, Messrs. Richardsons & H.D. Symonds, printed by W. Glendinning et al., 1807), page unnumbered, see entry under Wickson; *Holden's Triennial Directory for 1809, 1810, 1811*, 5th ed., vol. 2 (London: sold by the proprietor, printed by J. Davenport et al., 1811), page unnumbered, see entry under Wickson; *Pigot and Co.'s London and Provincial New Commercial Directory for 1826-27*, 3rd ed. (London: J. Pigot, 1826), 132; *Pigot and Co.'s National London and Provincial Commercial Directory for 1832-33-34* (London: J. Pigot, 1834), 329, 341. The directories listed above are held at the London Metropolitan Archive, the Southwark Local Studies Library, and the British Library. I am grateful to Alexander Baron for locating them for me.

5   On his father's death in 1815, James the coal merchant inherited a sixty-eight-year lease, dating from 1809, for property on Mount Street in Walworth. See WFP: transcript of indenture between James Wickson, Edward Taylor, and William Maidlow, 21 August 1829; GAFP: birth certificate of Mary Wickson, dated 6 July 1825. See also 1859 diary, entries for 18 February and 25 April.

6   The Wicksons were married on 28 November. Jane Tuesman, the daughter of John Tuesman and Mary Hardwidge, was from Reigate parish in Surrey. Reigate is about

twenty-five kilometres south of Camberwell. See AAFP: Wickson folder; TNA: baptism register of Mansion House Chapel (Independent), Camberwell, PRO Cat. No. RG 4/4381, 5-10; R.A. Ford, *Camberwell Green Congregational Church, 1774-1966* (Broadstairs, Kent: Westwood Press, 1967), 5-13. I am grateful to Alexander Baron for locating this publication.

7   The chapel hosted a debate on this issue in August 1832. See S. Isaacson, *A Vindication of the West-India Proprietors* (London: James Fraser, 1832); for a discussion of the abolition debate, see L. Colley, *Britons: Forging the Nation 1707-1837* (New Haven: Yale University Press, 1992), 350-59. Abolition was one of several volatile public issues around which the evangelical churches (such as the Congregationalists) and the Anglican Church co-operated, from the 1820s to the 1840s, to promote order, stability, and peaceable Christian behaviour. See L. Davidoff and C. Hall, *Family Fortunes: Men and Women of the English Middle Class* (Chicago: University of Chicago Press, 1987), 92-95.

8   Colley, *Britons*, 321-24. See also Davidoff and Hall, *Family Fortunes*, 92-95; Maas, *Helpmates*, 15, 83.

9   This melee took place in St. Peter's Fields and became known, sardonically, as "Peterloo."

10 Colley, *Britons*, 264, 321-24; D.G. Wright, *Popular Radicalism: The Working Class Experience, 1780-1880* (London: Longman, 1988), 86-91; C. Harvie and C. Matthew, *Nineteenth-Century Britain* (Oxford: Oxford University Press, 2000), 31-38; H.I. Cowan, *British Emigration to British North America* (Toronto: University of Toronto Library, 1961), 18-39.

11 Colley, *Britons*, 321-24; D.G. Burley, *A Particular Condition in Life: Self-Employment and Social Mobility in Mid-Victorian Brantford, Ontario* (Montreal: McGill-Queen's University Press, 1994), 63-64; N. Macdonald, *Canada 1763-1841, Immigration and Settlement* (London: Longman, 1939), 10-31; Cowan, *British Emigration*, 179-82; Maas, *Helpmates*, 15 n. 41; P. Russell, *Attitudes to Social Structure and Mobility in Upper Canada, 1815-40* (Lewiston, New York: E. Mellen Press, 1990), 88-91. See also C. Gray, *Sisters in the Wilderness: The Lives of Susanna Moodie and Catharine Parr Traill* (Toronto: Penguin, 1999), 40-41; *The Emigrant's Informant, or A Guide to Upper Canada* (London: G. Cowie, 1834); S. Butler, *The Emigrant's Complete Guide to Canada* (London: N.H. Cotes, 1843).

12 D. McCalla, *Planting the Province: The Economic History of Upper Canada* (Toronto: University of Toronto Press, 1993), 180; Cowan, *British Emigration*, 185-86.

13 WFP: transcript of indenture between James Wickson, Edward Taylor, and William Maidlow, 21 August 1829; Cowan, *British Emigration*, 189.

14 James married Bridget Rusby and John married Eliza Chilver. See AAFP: Wickson folder. See also the short biography of James Wickson in C.P. Mulvaney and A.G. Mercer, *History of Toronto and County of York, Ontario*, vol. 2 (Toronto: C.B. Robinson, 1885), 171-72.

15 GAFP: marriage certificate of Philip Armstrong and Mary Wickson, 1837; J.R. Robertson, *History of the Brantford Congregational Church, 1820 to 1920*, comp. S. Wright (Brantford, Ontario: Renfrew Mercury Print, 1920; reprint, Brant County Branch, Ontario Genealogical Society, 1990), 40-41.

16 See 1859 diary, entry for 27 April. See also "A Diarist's World" at pages 56, 61-62.

17 CRO: Wetheral Parish Registers, baptisms, 1790-1813, 1813-1837.

18 W. Parson and W. White, eds., *History, Directory, and Gazeteer of the Counties of Cumberland and Westmorland* (Leeds: W. White, 1829), 46-47, 387-88. See also W. Rollinson, *A History of Cumberland and Westmorland* (London: Phillimore, 1978), 85. St. Martin's Day, or Martinmas, is November 11. Henry Howard's father, Philip Howard, Esq., died in 1810, and Philip Armstrong's mother, Dorothy Armstrong, seems to have given her youngest son his name. The Howards were descended from Lord William

Howard, also known as "Belted Will," a younger son of the Duke of Norfolk who had received his Cumberland estate in the early seventeenth century. The senior line of his descendants were (and still are) the Howards of Naworth, Earls of Carlisle, whose seat is Naworth Castle, to the north of Great Corby. A junior line settled in Corby manor and became known as the Howards of Corby. The Armstrong surname was and is frequently found on both sides of the western border between Scotland and England. The Armstrong family name, with some notorious sixteenth-century members, dates to the thirteenth century in this part of Britain.

19 Two days after his death, John Armstrong was buried in the parish cemetery across the river in the churchyard of the Church of the Holy Trinity and St. Constantine. John had married Dorothy Kelly on the Isle of Man in 1787. They had one child in 1789, named John, and they moved sixty-three kilometres across the Irish Sea to Cumberland and settled in Great Corby, where they had seven other children, including Thomas and Philip. See CRO: Wetheral Parish Registers, burials, 1796–1812; Wetheral Churchyard headstone transcripts 1964, no. 115; Wetheral Parish Registers, baptisms, 1790–1813, 1813–1837; Manx National Heritage Library: Braddan Parish Registers, marriages and baptisms, 1787, 1789.

20 F. Collier, *The Family Economy of the Working Classes in the Cotton Industry, 1784–1833* (Manchester: Manchester University Press, 1964), 5–9.

21 Collier, *Family Economy*, 9.

22 At the time of John Armstrong's death, while she was pregnant with Philip, Dorothy's children were John (turning 19), Christopher (16), Robert (13), Elizabeth (turning 11), Jane Christian (7), Dorothy (4), and Thomas (1). The 1810 militia returns for Cumberland County (Eskdale Ward, Corby Lordship) list Christopher Armstrong, age 21, gardener, as exempt from service, as he was a member of the local volunteer force called the Cumberland Rangers. The Rangers consisted of seven infantry companies under the command of Lieutenant Colonel Henry Howard of Corby Castle. The militia returns for 1813 list Christopher Armstrong, age 22, gardener, and Robert Armstrong, age 19, joiner, as liable for service. It is very likely that these two individuals (despite the age disparity for Christopher, which may have been inaccurate or falsified) were Philip's brothers: Christopher, baptized 28 August 1791, and Robert, baptized 13 April 1794. See CRO: H. Cunningham, *Historical Research Service Report Number C08/00/235;* Militia records CQ/Mil/1810, Eskdale Ward, Corby Lordship Return, and CQ/Mil/1813 Eskdale Ward, Corby Lordship Return; Wetheral Parish Registers, baptisms, 1790–1813.

23 CRO: Cunningham, *Historical Research Service Report Number C08/00/235.*

24 H. Lonsdale, *The Worthies of Cumberland: The Rt. Hon. Sir J.R.G. Graham, Bart. of Netherby* (London: George Routledge & Sons, 1868), 57–58.

25 CRO: Wetheral Parish Registers, burials, 1813–1834.

26 She was buried in Potter's Field Cemetery, located at the intersection of present-day Bloor and Yonge Streets. It closed in 1875 and has now been built over. See E. Hancocks, *Potter's Field Cemetery, 1826–1855* (Agincourt, Ontario: Generation Press, 1983), 3.

27 To work as a clerk anywhere Philip would have had to receive an education, but no record of his attending any local Cumberland schools can be found. Unfortunately, no records of the bishops' staff or accounts remain, as most incoming bishops simply made room for their own paperwork by burning that of their predecessors. No trace of Philip has been found in the Farnham parish registers.

28 LAC: Robert Pallett household, 1851 Census York Twp. (Part 1), York Co., Canada West, enumeration district no. 1, p. 9, line 47; LAC microfilm C-11760. See the short biography of Philip Armstrong in Mulvaney and Mercer, *History of Toronto and County of York*, vol. 2, 211–12.

29 Hancocks, *Potter's Field Cemetery*, 3.

30 E.J. Errington, *Wives and Mothers, School Mistresses, and Scullery Maids: Working Women in Upper Canada, 1790-1840* (Montreal: McGill-Queen's University Press, 1995), 194. See also Davidoff and Hall, *Family Fortunes*, 325.

31 *1833 Directory*, 48, 72; *1837 Directory*, 2.

32 Douglas McCalla points out that new settlers might have needed or preferred to rent land or even work initially for someone else before seeking land of their own. See McCalla, *Planting the Province*, 68.

33 Leonore Davidoff and Catherine Hall have shown that business alliances between families could be cemented with marriage. See Davidoff and Hall, *Family Fortunes*, 209, 217-18. See also discussion of business partnerships in "A Diarist's World" at pages 52-53.

34 The movement towards rebellion was fuelled by economic discontent, failed attempts at minor political reform, and antagonistic relations with Lieutenant-Governor Sir Francis Bond Head. In the autumn of 1837 frustrations in Upper and Lower Canada came to a head and the provinces moved towards armed internal conflict. See C. Read, *The Rebellion of 1837 in Upper Canada*, Historical Booklet No. 46 (Ottawa: Canadian Historical Association, 1988), 7-19; G.M. Craig, *Upper Canada: The Formative Years, 1784-1841* (Toronto: McClelland & Stewart, 1963), 232-49; F.H. Armstrong, "The York Riots of March 23, 1832," *OH* 55, no. 2 (1963), 61-72.

35 Robert Baldwin (1804-1858) was a leader in colonial politics who, with Louis-Hippolyte Lafontaine, formed the government in 1842-43 and 1848-51. Philip became "identified with the Conservative Party" in his later years. See Mulvaney and Mercer, *History of Toronto and County of York*, vol. 2, 211-12.

36 Craig, *Upper Canada*, 252-59.

37 Thomas seems to have been named after Philip's older brother. See GAFP: birth certificate of Thomas Armstrong, dated 4 September 1838. He was born on 11 August. At this time Philip and Mary lived beside 393 Yonge Street, probably near Gerrard Street, the address where Arthur Wickson lived in 1859. See 1859 diary, entry for 7 May. Dr. Robert Hornby (1813-1869) delivered Thomas. Hornby, who was a graduate of the University of Edinburgh and practised in Cleveland and Toronto, was charged with unprofessional actions in 1839. See C.M. Godfrey, *Medicine for Ontario: A History* (Belleville: Mika Publishing, 1979), 223, 277. Dr. Robert Hornby had given a lecture at the Mechanics Institute on 5 April 1838, and on 7 June 1838 had himself fathered a son. See *British Colonist*, 5 April 1838, 3, and 7 June 1838, 3.

38 The doctor's fee for the birth alone would have been about £1 5s. No midwives were recorded at the birth. See Errington, *Wives and Mothers*, 62-63; J. Duffin, *Langstaff: A Nineteenth Century Medical Life* (Toronto: University of Toronto Press, 1993), 47, 178-217.

39 Craig, *Upper Canada*, 227-28; Cowan, *British Emigration*, 185-86, 195.

40 This land is on the south side of where Farnham Avenue is now located. What is now Bloor Street was the second concession line. See AAFP: Armstrong folder.

41 In 1831 Elmsley had purchased 64-¼ acres of the surrounding land from Thomas Shepperd Smyth for £657 10s. In 1849 he would sell another six acres of the property to a Thomas Whitten, who paid £300. From these transactions land values for the area can be gauged: in 1831 land sold for roughly £10 an acre; in 1839 it went for £33 an acre; and ten years later the value had risen to £50 an acre. Philip's purchase from Elmsley is a problematic reference, as no deed has been located in the AO. Armstrong family papers make reference to the purchase, but do not include an original or copy of the deed. See AAFP: Armstrong folder. For Elmsley's purchase, see AO: Yorkville and Rosedale deeds 1799-1868, Copybooks of Instruments and Deeds, Toronto Boroughs and York South/Toronto Land Registry Office, Series RG 61-64, Microfilm GS 6390, deed no. 8150, 25 August 1831, pp. 16-17; for sale to Whitten, see pp. 48-49.

42 *1846-47 Directory*, 79, 116.

43 *1850-51 Directory*, 4, 135.

44 See 1859 diary, entry for 5 May. See also L.B. Martyn, *Aristocratic Toronto: 19th Century Grandeur* (Toronto: Gage, 1980), 65-66.

45 J.M.S. Careless, *The Union of the Canadas: The Growth of Canadian Institutes, 1841-1857* (Toronto: McClelland & Stewart, 1967), 1-13, 20, 27-28, 36, 47, 225 n. 26. For a discussion of the legal status of women in the nineteenth century, see C. Backhouse, *Petticoats and Prejudice: Women and Law in Nineteenth-Century Canada* (Toronto: Women's Press, 1991). See also discussion of women's legal status in "A Diarist's World" at page 37.

46 Careless, *Union*, 1-13, 27-28, 36, 47, 255 n. 26.

47 Cowan, *British Emigration*, 185.

48 GAFP: marriage certificate of Robert Pallett and Anne Armstrong, 1848.

49 LAC: Robert Pallett household, 1851 Census York Twp. (Part 1), York. Co., Canada West, enumeration district no. 1, p. 9, line 47; LAC microfilm C-11760.

50 See 1859 diary, entry for 9 February.

51 D.H. Akenson, *The Irish in Ontario: A Study in Rural History* (Montreal: McGill-Queen's University Press, 1984), 28-34. See also R.D. Fair, "Gentlemen, Farmers, and Gentlemen Half-Farmers: The Development of Agricultural Societies in Upper Canada, 1792-1846" (Ph.D. diss., Queen's University, 1998), 199 n.4.

52 Akenson, *Irish in Ontario*, 28-34, newspaper quote from 21 August 1847, 241; Careless, *Union*, 113.

53 "Death of the Roman Catholic Bishop of Toronto," *Globe*, 9 October 1847; Careless, *Union*, 113; Akenson, *Irish in Ontario*, 241.

54 Hazel Dell Fields, which Philip bought in the 1860s, was a twenty-three-acre plot of land from the Rose Estate just to the east of Rose Hill. Maple Woods and Woodhill have not been located by name in land records, but Mary refers to them in both diaries. Maple Woods was probably a plot of land that Philip owned, located immediately south of what is now Mount Pleasant Cemetery. As of 1860, and perhaps earlier, Philip also owned a plot of land just north of the intersection of Dufferin Street and Eglinton Avenue, which may have been Woodhill. See AO: *G.R. Tremaine's Map of the City of Toronto* (1860), A-10; *Illustrated Historical Atlas of the County of York* (Toronto: Miles, 1878), 19, 35, atlas 79. See also below note 68.

55 See discussion of agricultural societies in "A Diarist's World" at pages 66-67.

56 See reference to the bacon business in 1859 diary, entry for 6 January. See B.D. Palmer, *Working-Class Experience: Rethinking the History of Canadian Labour, 1800-1991* (Toronto: McClelland & Stewart, 1992), 65; Burley, *Particular Condition*, 114; A.C. Holman, *A Sense of Their Duty: Middle Class Formation in Victorian Ontario Towns* (Montreal: McGill-Queen's University Press, 2000), 35. See discussion of Thomas's career in "A Diarist's World" at pages 51-52.

57 The ceremony took place on 21 May 1863. The minister who performed the ceremony was Mary Armstrong's brother-in-law Edward Ebbs. Arthur Wickson, Mary's brother, assisted in the service.

  Fidelia's father, Nicholas Maughan (c.1822-1900), had come with his parents from Northumberland, England, to Canada in 1832. In 1843 he married Sophia Riley (1823-1892). They lived in the village of Eglinton and, from 1869, in Toronto. Nicholas was a carpenter, builder, and contractor, and in 1877 he was appointed assessment commissioner for the city of Toronto. His daughter Fidelia married Thomas in the "Brick Methodist Church" in Eglinton (also known as the Wesleyan Methodist Church), of which Nicholas Maughan was secretary treasurer. See GAFP: marriage certificate of Thomas Armstrong and Fidelia Maughan, 1863; declaration of Samuel Wickson under the Canada Evidence Act, 6 March 1908, "In the matter of the marriage of Thomas Armstrong with Fidelia Jane Maughan"; UCCA: Yonge Street (South)

Methodist Circuit (Toronto, ON) fonds, trustee book: 1855-1877, fonds no. 2528, location no. 77.725L, microfilm reel 1, trustee meeting minutes, 1870 February 22; Mulvaney and Mercer, *History of Toronto and County of York*, vol. 2, 108. See also "A Diarist's World" at page 56.

58   See discussion of business partnerships in "A Diarist's World" at pages 52-53.

59   See 1859 diary, entry for 6 January. The omnibus, operated by Henry B. Williams, ran between 8 a.m. and 8 p.m. and the fare was five cents. See also E.C. Guillet, "Toronto Street Railway Started with a Push," in his weekly column, "Old Times in Ontario," *Toronto Daily Star,* 9 September 1961, 18; *1859-60 Directory,* 295; *1866 Directory,* 425; AO: *Illustrated Historical Atlas of the County of York,* xiii, atlas 79. For a full discussion of these topics, see the section on social networks, community, and local identity in "A Diarist's World" at pages 60-68.

60   See Careless, *Union,* 132-35, 138; G.S. Kealey, *Toronto Workers Respond to Industrial Capitalism, 1867-1892* (Toronto: University of Toronto Press, 1980), 4-5, 18; G.S. Kealey, *Workers and Canadian History* (Montreal: McGill-Queen's University Press, 1995), 105-107.

61   Palmer, *Working-Class Experience,* 65. An excellent visual display of Toronto in the 1850s is preserved in the panoramic photographs of the city taken by William Armstrong (no relation to Mary), published in N. Matheson, "A Toronto Portrait, 1857," *The Beaver,* June/July 1990, 27-37.

62   From 1855 Toronto had been the capital of the united Canadas under the rotating system that had been put into effect after the Montreal riots of 1849 in protest of the Rebellion Losses Bill. See W.L. Morton, *The Critical Years: The Union of British North America, 1857-1873* (Toronto: McClelland & Stewart, 1964), 13, 71. See 1859 diary, entry for 14 February.

63   G.F.G. Stanley, *Canada's Soldiers: The Military History of an Unmilitary People* (Toronto: Macmillan, 1960), 211-13.

64   F.H. Armstrong, "The rebuilding of Toronto after the great fire of 1849," *OH* 53, no. 4 (1961): 233-50.

65   Morton, *Critical Years,* 13, 71; Careless, *Union,* 122-26, 150-65.

66   See discussion of health in life writing in "A Diarist's World" at pages 22-23.

67   *1864-65 Directory,* 328; *1867-68 Directory,* 174, 368.

68   The Rose estate, composed of the land held by Walter Rose in his lifetime, was known as lot 16 in the second concession from the bay. Philip purchased sub-lots 20 (10 acres) and 14 (23 acres). This property is south of modern-day St. Clair Avenue, between Inglewood Drive and the ravine to its west (lot 14), and then a few blocks along Inglewood and on the south side (lot 20). Lot 14 seems to have been cleared, but lot 20 was heavily wooded. The price paid is a guess based on the markings on the documents of the sale. See GAFP: "Plan of the Rose Estate," Dennis and Gossage Provincial Land Surveyors, document dated 18 October 1864; "York Instrument Number 88196, Memorial of Indenture, Hon. J.C. Morrison to Philip Armstrong," recorded 23 June 1865; "Chancery Sale of Valuable Freehold Property, Near Toronto, known as the Rose Estate," document dated 22 October 1864.

69   See discussion of social mobility in "A Diarist's World" at pages 42-43.

70   See 1869 diary, entries for 4, 16 April, and 1 July.

71   See discussion of household size in "A Diarist's World" at pages 48-49.

72   For example, see 1859 diary, entry for 6 January.

73   In 1862 a horse-drawn railcar extended service to the St. Lawrence Hall. Williams, the railcar proprietor, competed with the railway but soon was out of business. In 1892 the first electric cars replaced the horse-drawn system. See Guillet, "Toronto Street Railway." See also *1859-60 Directory,* 295.

74   Quote from 1859 diary, entry for 8 February. See discussion of social activities in "A Diarist's World" at pages 46-47.

75 Family tradition is the source of this story. Thomas was asked to serve when he graduated from medical school. His great-grandson Andrew Armstrong was asked by the
Americans to serve in Vietnam after he had graduated in medicine from the University of Toronto in 1971. Andrew also declined.

76 The possibility of ending the Rush-Bagot agreement, which banned naval ships in the
Great Lakes, and the lingering issue of Confederate cruisers being built in neutral
British ports were sources of tension. See Morton, *Critical Years*, 185-86.

77 Stanley, *Canada's Soldiers*, 222-29.

78 Morton, *Critical Years*, 223-24.

79 See discussion of politics in life writing in "A Diarist's World" at page 21, and discussion of social network and community at pages 67-68.

80 Mount Pleasant Cemetery, Toronto, Ontario: Interment Register no. 1, Interment
number 429; death notice, *Globe*, 24 March 1879; *1866 Directory*, 284; *1871 Directory*,
67.

81 Ostensibly, this name was chosen because both Philip and the former owner of the
property to the north, Edward Hooper, had roots in the town of Farnham in Surrey,
England. Hooper had named his house "Farnham Lodge" after his hometown, and
this name was carried to the street itself. See Martyn, *Aristocratic Toronto*, 104-109. See
above at page 6.

82 Mount Pleasant Cemetery, Toronto, Ontario: Interment Register no. 1, Interment
number 926.
     See also Interment numbers 68 and 188 for Mary's grandchildren, who died in 1877.
See "A Diarist's World" at pages 57 and 62.

Notes to Introduction
PART II
A Diarist's World

1 Maas, *Helpmates*, 8. For examples of published Canadian life writing, see below, notes
6 and 478.

2 W. Matthews, *British Diaries: An Annotated Bibliography of British Diaries Written between
1442 and 1942* (Berkeley: University of California Press, 1950), xv. Felicity Nussbaum
describes diaries as a form of "serial autobiographical narrative." See F. Nussbaum,
The Autobiographical Subject (Baltimore: Johns Hopkins University Press, 1989), 23.

3 H. Blodgett, *Centuries of Female Days: English Women's Private Diaries* (London: Rutgers
University Press, 1988), 6-7 n. 12; R. Fothergill, *Private Chronicles: A Study of English
Diaries* (Oxford: Oxford University Press, 1974), 3; M. Culley, ed., *A Day at a Time* (New
York: Feminist Press, 1985), xii-xiii; K. Carter, ed., *The Small Details of Life: Twenty
Diaries by Women in Canada, 1830-1996* (Toronto: University of Toronto Press, 2002),
5-6.

4 M. Kadar, ed., *Essays on Life Writing: From Genre to Critical Practice* (Toronto: University
of Toronto Press, 1992), 152. Donald A. Stauffer coined the phrase "life writing"; see
his *The Art of Biography in Eighteenth-Century England* (Princeton: Princeton University
Press, 1941), 10. For different "classes" of diaries, see Fothergill, *Private Chronicles*,
14-19.

5 For a discussion of the literary concerns of diaries, see Culley, *A Day at a Time*, 10-12.
See also Fothergill, *Private Chronicles*, esp. 32-33; C. Huff, *British Women's Diaries* (New
York: AMS Press, 1985); Blodgett, *Centuries;* Nussbaum, *Autobiographical Subject*.

6 Huff, *British Women's Diaries*, x. For a sample of historical and literary scholarship on Canadian women's life writing, see F. Hoffman and R. Taylor, *Much to Be Done: Private Life in Ontario from Victorian Diaries* (Toronto: Natural Heritage/Natural History, 1996); Carter, *Small Details;* K. Carter, "An Economy of Words: Emma Chadwick Stretch's Account Book Diary, 1859–1860," *Acadiensis* 29, no. 1 (Autumn 1999): 43–56; H. Buss, *Mapping Our Selves: Canadian Women's Autobiography* (Montreal: McGill-Queen's University Press, 1993); M. Conrad, "'Sundays Always Make Me Think of Home': Time and Place in Canadian Women's History," in *Not Just Pin Money: Selected Essays on the History of Women's Work in British Columbia*, ed. B.K. Latham and R.J. Pazdro (Victoria: Camosun College, 1984), 1–16; M. Conrad, T. Laidlaw, and D. Smyth, ed., *No Place Like Home: The Diaries of Nova Scotia Women, 1771–1938* (Halifax: Formac, 1988); K.M.J. McKenna, *A Life of Propriety: Anne Murray Powell and Her Family, 1755–1849* (Montreal: McGill-Queen's University Press, 1994); J.I. Little, ed., *Love Strong as Death: Lucy Peel's Canadian Journal, 1833–1836* (Waterloo: Wilfrid Laurier University Press, 2001); H.H. Langton, ed., *A Gentlewoman in Upper Canada: The Journals of Anne Langton* (Toronto: Clarke Irwin, 1950); B. Powell, "The Diaries of the Crease Family Women," *BC Studies* nos. 105–106 (Spring/Summer 1995): 45–58; V. Strong-Boag, ed., *A Woman with a Purpose: The Diaries of Elizabeth Smith, 1872–1884* (Toronto: University of Toronto Press, 1980); A.S. Miller, ed., *The Journals of Mary O'Brien: 1828–1838* (Toronto: Macmillan, 1968).

7 Davidoff and Hall, *Family Fortunes*, 162. See also M.F. Motz, "Folk Expression of Time and Place: Nineteenth-Century Midwestern Rural Diaries," *Journal of American Folklore* 100, no. 396 (1987): 131–47; Culley, *A Day at a Time*, 4; Fothergill, *Private Chronicles*, 34; Nussbaum, *Autobiographical Subject*, 19–29, 154–73, 201. On spiritual biography see R.M. Payne, *The Self and the Sacred: Conversion and Autobiography in Early American Protestantism* (Knoxville: University of Tennessee Press, 1998). The owners of late medieval and sixteenth-century books of hours, who were largely women, made personal entries on the fly pages and calendars of these texts, noting family births and deaths, political events, and even domestic details like the contents of their linen closets. See E. Duffy, "In the Margins: Medieval Prayer Books and Their Users" (Leonard Boyle Memorial Lecture presented at University of Toronto, 20 March 2003); E. Duffy, *The Stripping of the Altars: Traditional Religion in England, c.1400–1580* (New Haven: Yale University Press, 1992).

8 Huff, *British Women's Diaries*, xx–xxvi.

9 Blodgett, *Centuries*, 4, 67–68; Huff, *British Women's Diaries*, xx–xxvi; Maas, *Helpmates*, 142.

10 See 1869 diary, entry for 25 January.

11 Huff, *British Women's Diaries*, xxv; Culley, *A Day at a Time*, 4; Powell, "Crease Family Women," 51–52; Blodgett, *Centuries*, 34–38.

12 Blodgett, *Centuries*, 32–34; Culley, *A Day at a Time*, 3.

13 Huff, *British Women's Diaries*, xvii–xviii; Culley, *A Day at a Time*, 4–7; Powell, "Crease Family Women," 57.

14 See 1859 diary, entry for 19 March.

15 Some male diarists also justified their writing in this way. See Blodgett, *Centuries*, 16, 65–72; Powell, "Crease Family Women," 50–51; Fothergill, *Private Chronicles*, 66.

16 Huff, *British Women's Diaries*, xxvi; Culley, *A Day at a Time*, xi, 8; Fothergill, *Private Chronicles*, 69, 71–72.

17 Motz, "Folk Expression," 145–46.

18 See 1869 diary, entry for 21 April.

19 See 1859 diary, entries for 14 March, 4 April, and 2, 3, 5 May.

20 See 1859 diary, entry for 18 February; quote from 25 April.

21 See 1859 diary, entry for 9 February (contains quote). See also 1859 diary, entry for 11 February; 1869 diary, entry for 1 July.

22 Maas, *Helpmates*, 132–33; Blodgett, *Centuries*, 83; Strong-Boag, *Woman with a Purpose*, viii.

23 Blodgett, *Centuries*, 61–62, 203, 205–211, quote from 194.

24 See 1859 diary, entry for 9 February; Blodgett, *Centuries*, 22.

25 See 1859 diary, entry for 27 April.

26 Blodgett, *Centuries*, 119–23; C. Smith-Rosenberg, "The Female World of Love and Ritual: Relations between Women in Nineteenth-Century America," *Signs: Journal of Women in Culture and Society* 1 (1975): 1–30, esp. 14, 20. See discussion of personal deportment at page 47.

27 J.I. Little, "Death in the Lower St. John River Valley: The Diary of Alexander Machum, Jr., 1845–1849," *Acadiensis* 22, no. 1 (Autumn 1992): 125–26.

28 See 1859 diary, entry for 5 May.

29 Culley, *A Day at a Time*, 4, 8.

30 Blodgett, *Centuries*, 219–23.

31 On economy, see 1859 diary, entries for 19 February and 9 May; 1869 diary, entry for 3 February. On industry, see 1859 diary, entries for 2, 4, 16 February.

32 See, for example, 1859 diary, entry for 18 February.

33 Blodgett, *Centuries*, 148, 219–30; Nussbaum, *Autobiographical Subject*, 212–13; Huff, *British Women's Diaries*, xxxiii.

34 Blodgett, *Centuries*, 4, 197, 223. Some eighteenth-century diarists questioned their gender roles. See Nussbaum, *Autobiographical Subject*, 220. See also discussion of female networks at page 30.

35 For instance, in her entry for Tuesday, 30 March 1869, Mary recorded what she did on Wednesday, which would indicate that while writing her next entry on Thursday, she had gone back and added to her previous entry. Mary also crossed out certain phrases that she had written. See 1869 diary, entry for 1 January. On rereading and editing, see Huff, *British Women's Diaries*, xix; Blodgett, *Centuries*, 74; Culley, *A Day at a Time*, 13; Nussbaum, *Autobiographical Subject*, 202–203; Fothergill, *Private Chronicles*, 73, 89.

36 Nussbaum, *Autobiographical Subject*, xi, 8; Fothergill, *Private Chronicles*, 43–44, 64–65, 70, 74, quote from 43.

37 Culley, *A Day at a Time*, 3; Blodgett, *Centuries*, 65–72. Some male diarists made similar apologies. See Fothergill, *Private Chronicles*, 66.

38 Huff, *British Women's Diaries*, xvi–xvii, xxiv; Powell, "Crease Family Women," 51; Blodgett, *Centuries*, 156, 216; Conrad, "Sundays," 8; Culley, *A Day at a Time*, 20.

39 See 1859 diary, entry for 18 February. Motz argues that rural diaries tended to look outwards to the world, not inwards to the self. See Motz, "Folk Expression," 146.

40 Blodgett, *Centuries*, 78–85; Nussbaum, *Autobiographical Subject*, 221; Culley, *A Day at a Time*, 13; Fothergill, *Private Chronicles*, 66, 73, 88–89, 92.

41 Culley, *A Day at a Time*, 19.

42 See 1859 diary, entry for 3 May.

43 See "happy," 1869 diary, entries for 1, 14 January; "peace of mind," 1859 diary, entry for 14 April; "gladness," 1859 diary, entries for 23 February, 24 May; "joy," 1859 diary, entry for 10 March; "enjoying herself," 1859 diary, entries for 20, 23 April, and 1869 diary, entry for 27 March; "comfort," 1859 diary, entries for 9, 3 May.

44 See "uneasiness," 1859 diary, entry for 18 March; "not feeling well," 1859 diary, entry for 21 February; "feeling poorly," 1869 diary, entry for 16 January; "fatigued," 1869 diary, entries for 1 April, 3 May; "restless and indisposed," 1859 diary, entry for 2 February; "much affected," 1859 diary, entry for 3 March; "very heavy," 1859 diary, entry for 20 January; "revulsion," 1859 diary, entry for 13 January.

45 See 1859 diary, entry for 11 May. See discussion of Mary and Philip's marriage at pages 26–27.

46 See 1869 diary, entry for 26 January.

47 See 1859 diary, entries for 9, 3 May.

48 See 1869 diary, entry for 21 April; 1859 diary, entry for 23 May.

49 Middle age was frequently a problematic time, as women lost their identity as young women in a society that prized female youthfulness. See Blodgett, *Centuries*, 75, 211–17; Maas, *Helpmates*, 132–33, 153; Powell, "Crease Family Women," 50; C. Smith-Rosenberg, "The Hysterical Woman: Sex Roles and Role Conflict in Nineteenth-Century America," *Social Research* 39 (1972): 652–78.

50 See 1859 diary, entry for 5 May; announcement of sale in the *Globe*, 27 April 1859 and 4 May 1859. See discussion of home and garden at page 48.

51 Blodgett, *Centuries*, 40, 57–60; Culley, *A Day at a Time*, 12, 23; Fothergill, *Private Chronicles*, 83; Powell, "Crease Family Women," 49, 54. See discussion of diaries as family documents at page 16.

52 Maas, *Helpmates*, 53, 139; Blodgett, *Centuries*, 41–45.

53 Blodgett, *Centuries*, 48, 54–56, 61; Powell, "Crease Family Women," 56.

54 See 1859 diary, entry for 9 February. See section on family relationships at pages 25–32.

55 Culley, *A Day at a Time*, 6; Huff, *British Women's Diaries*, xxxi–xxxii; Maas, *Helpmates*, 144; A.S. Saunders, "Yonge Street Politics, 1828 to 1832," *OH* 62, no. 2 (1970): 101–118; Motz, "Folk Expression," 145.

56 See 1859 diary, entry for 14 February. See "A Canadian's Story" at page 11.

57 See 1859 diary, entries for 3, 4 March. See also "The Wellington-Street and Georgina Murders," *Globe*, 5 March 1859, 2; E.C. Kyte, *Old Toronto: A Selection of Excerpts from Landmarks of Toronto by John Ross Robertson* (Toronto: Macmillan, 1954), 188.

58 See 1859 diary, entries for 9 February and 24, 25, 26 March; 1869 diary, entries for 18, 19 January and 20 April.

59 See 1859 diary, entry for 3 May.

60 See 1859 diary, entries for 19 February and 9 May.

61 Maas, *Helpmates*, 102, 142; Blodgett, *Centuries*, 185–86; Davidoff and Hall, *Family Fortunes*, 340–41; Powell, "Crease Family Women," 50, 52.

62 Powell, "Crease Family Women," 49, 52.

63 Jacalyn Duffin points out that physicians may have decided to keep bad news from patients for fear that psychological depression might impair physical recovery. Of course, as in the case Mary cites, it is always possible that the doctor himself simply did not know the truth. See 1859 diary, entry for 13 January; Duffin, *Langstaff*, 89–90.

64 See 1859 diary, entry for 13 January.

65 See 1859 diary, entry for 3 May.

66 Duffin points out that many nineteenth-century patients had a fear of doctors. See Duffin, *Langstaff*, 83.

67 Davidoff and Hall, *Family Fortunes*, 339–40.

68 Nussbaum, *Autobiographical Subject*, 214–15; Duffin, *Langstaff*, 89–90.

69 See 1859 diary, entry for 14 April. Thomas certainly was busy. As a medical student, Mary reported that his typical day involved studying from 7 a.m. to 9 a.m., when he often visited his grandfather for tutoring. He would then go to the Richmond Street school till 12:30 p.m., take a break for "dinner," and return to school or attend operations at the hospital until 5 p.m. In the evenings he would come home for "tea" and then study till 10 or 11 p.m., often drifting off to sleep in a chair while reading his textbooks.

70 For a discussion of nineteenth-century medicine, see Duffin, *Langstaff*; Godfrey, *Medicine for Ontario*. See discussion of middle-class professionals at pages 51–52.

71 Younger female diarists were often preoccupied with courtship and marriage. See M. Ryan, *Cradle of the Middle Class: The Family in Oneida County, New York, 1790–1865* (Cambridge: Cambridge University Press, 1981), 219–22; Nussbaum, *Autobiographical Subject*, 219; Huff, *British Women's Diaries*, xxvi, xxxiv.

72 Davidoff and Hall, *Family Fortunes*, 339; Blodgett, *Centuries*, 171–73.

73 Little, "Death in the Valley," 124–27.

74 See 1859 diary, entry for 13 January.

75 See 1859 diary, entry for 9 February.

76 Huff, *British Women's Diaries*, xix.

77 See 1859 diary, entry for 18 February.

78 See 1859 diary, entry for 4 March.

79 See 1859 diary, entry for 26 February. On the imagery of warfare in evangelical thought, see P. Greven, *The Protestant Temperament: Patterns of Child-Rearing, Religious Experience and the Self in Early America* (Chicago: University of Chicago Press, 1977), 115.

80 See 1859 diary, entries for 30 April and 1 May.

81 Huff, *British Women's Diaries*, xxxiv.

82 In this sense the word "cult" is used to denote the popular veneration of a principle and not, as is more common today, to denote an extremist religious sect. See B. Welter, "The Cult of True Womanhood," *American Quarterly* 18 (1966): 151–74; N.F. Cott, *The Bonds of Womanhood* (New Haven: Yale University Press, 1977); M.J. Peterson, *Family, Love and Work in the Lives of Victorian Gentlewomen* (Bloomington: Indiana University Press, 1989); D. Gorham, *The Victorian Girl and the Feminine Ideal* (Bloomington: Indiana University Press, 1982); J.N. Burstyn, *Victorian Education and the Ideal of Womanhood* (London: Croom Helm, 1980); L. Davidoff, *The Best Circles: Society, Etiquette and the Season* (London: Croom Helm, 1973); McKenna, *A Life of Propriety;* N. Christie, ed., *Households of Faith: Family, Gender, and Community in Canada, 1760–1969* (Montreal: McGill-Queen's University Press, 2002); Ryan, *Cradle*, 146–54, 189; Davidoff and Hall, *Family Fortunes*, 117; Holman, *Duty*, 152; Errington, *Wives and Mothers*, 21–23.

83 Davidoff and Hall, *Family Fortunes*, 116, 359; Ryan, *Cradle*, 146–54; McKenna, *A Life of Propriety*, 60; Cott, *Bonds of Womanhood;* A. Clark, *Women's Silence, Men's Violence: Sexual Assault in England, 1770–1845* (London: Pandora, 1987), 3, 117. See discussion of cultivation at page 47.

84 Ryan, *Cradle*, 192; Conrad, Laidlaw, and Smyth, *No Place Like Home*, 302–304; Conrad, "Sundays," 4.

85 Davidoff and Hall, *Family Fortunes*, 117–18, quote from 118.

86 See, for example, Coventry Patmore, *The Angel in the House* (London: John W. Parker & Son, 1854).

87 Holman, *Duty*, 152.

88 Davidoff and Hall, *Family Fortunes*, 115, 117, 286, 329–31; Holman, *Duty*, 153; Maas, *Helpmates*, 44–46.

89 Maas, *Helpmates*, 47–49.

90 See section on women's work and household management at pages 32–39.

91 See 1859 diary, entry for 17 March.

92 See discussion of household size at pages 43–49, and discussion of female education at page 46.

93 See 1869 diary, entries for 5 January and 20 February.

94 Blodgett, *Centuries*, 157–63; Maas, *Helpmates*, 101; Smith-Rosenberg, "Female World," 28.

95 Blodgett, *Centuries*, 108–109. Cynthia Huff, however, notes that some women began using familiar names for their spouses on their wedding day. See Huff, *British Women's Diaries*, xxix.

96 Rev. James Reid commonly referred to his wife as "Mrs. Reid." See M.E. Reisner, ed., *Diary of a Country Clergyman, 1848–51* (Montreal: McGill-Queen's University Press, 2000).

97 Holman, *Duty*, 157.

98 Davidoff and Hall, *Family Fortunes*, 327–28; Ryan, *Cradle*, 196.

99   Errington, *Wives and Mothers*, 26, 37–39, 51, 78; Maas, *Helpmates*, 101–105, 135; A. Mac-
     farlane, *Marriage and Love in England: Modes of Reproduction, 1300–1840* (Oxford:
     Blackwell, 1986), 331–34.

100 Blodgett, *Centuries*, 82, 165–68; Huff, *British Women's Diaries*, xxvii–xxviii; Maas, *Help-
     mates*, 102. See discussion of silences in life writing at pages 20–21.

101 See 1859 diary, entry for 11 May.

102 See 1859 diary, entry for 18 May.

103 See 1859 diary, entry for 19 April; 1869 diary, entry for 18 February.

104 Davidoff and Hall, *Family Fortunes*, 335; A. Prentice, *The School Promoters: Education and
     Social Class in Mid-Nineteenth-Century Upper Canada* (Toronto: McClelland & Stewart,
     1977), 110.

105 Maas, *Helpmates*, 62; Ryan, *Cradle*, 230; Davidoff and Hall, *Family Fortunes*, 107, 335–42.
     See discussion of motherhood and status at page 46, and section on faith and religious
     practice at pages 55–60.

106 M. Van Die, *An Evangelical Mind: Nathanael Burwash and the Methodist Tradition in
     Canada, 1839–1918* (Montreal: McGill-Queen's University Press, 1989), 15, 19, 22, 24–
     25; Davidoff and Hall, *Family Fortunes*, 91. See also L. Marks, *Revivals and Roller Rinks:
     Religion, Leisure, and Identity in Late-Nineteenth-Century Small Town Ontario* (Toronto: Uni-
     versity of Toronto Press, 1996), 31, 35. See discussion of motherhood and status at page
     46.

107 Greven, *Protestant Temperament*, 32, 290; J.I. Little, "The Fireside Kingdom: A Mid-Nine-
     teenth-Century Anglican Perspective on Marriage and Parenthood," in *Households of
     Faith*, ed. N. Christie, esp. 78, 89–92.

108 See exploration of the relationship between Mary and Mary Ann Pallett from the
     perspective of middle-class motherhood at page 46.

109 Maas, *Helpmates*, 31, 115; Davidoff and Hall, *Family Fortunes*, 224, 335. See discussion
     of family size at page 49.

110 See 1859 diary, entry for 18 February.

111 Davidoff and Hall, *Family Fortunes*, 342; Blodgett, *Centuries*, 169, 181–82.

112 See 1859 dairy, entry for 25 March.

113 Davidoff and Hall, *Family Fortunes*, 356.

114 M. Katz, *The People of Hamilton, Canada West: Family and Class in a Mid-Nineteenth-Cen-
     tury City* (Cambridge: Harvard University Press, 1975), 256–83. See also Davidoff and
     Hall, *Family Fortunes*, 219.

115 Thomas and Fidelia were married on 21 May 1863. See "A Canadian's Story" at page
     10. The majority of men in Hamilton were not married until age twenty-seven. See Katz,
     People of Hamilton, 262–64; Davidoff and Hall, *Family Fortunes*, 323, 333. See also
     Ryan, *Cradle*, 167.

116 Katz, *People of Hamilton*, 274–76.

117 Holman, *Duty*, 158; Ryan, *Cradle*, 175–76; Davidoff and Hall, *Family Fortunes*, 329–35.

118 Recent skeptics of the doctrine of the spheres include: J. Tosh, *A Man's Place: Masculin-
     ity and the Middle-Class Home in Victorian England* (New Haven: Yale University Press,
     1999) and A. Vickery, "Golden Age to Separate Spheres? A Review of the Categories
     and Chronology of English Women's History," *Historical Journal* 36 (1993): 383–414.

119 On Peel, see Little, *Love Strong as Death;* on Child, see J.I. Little, *The Child Letters: Pub-
     lic and Private Life in a Canadian Merchant-Politician's Family, 1841–1845* (Montreal:
     McGill-Queen's University Press, 1995); on Reid, see Little, "The Fireside Kingdom,"
     esp. 92.

120 Quote from Little, "The Fireside Kingdom," 86.

121 Davidoff and Hall, *Family Fortunes*, 329–34.

122 Katz, *People of Hamilton*, 295; Burley, *Particular Condition*, 95–96, 176. See "A Canadian's
     Story" at page 10. See also section on occupation and trade at pages 50–55.

123 See page 30, and discussion of Thomas's medical education at page 51–52.

124 See 1859 diary, entry for 14 February.

125 AO: Estate file for Philip Armstrong, probated 31 March 1879, York Co. Surrogate Court estate files, RG 22-305, file #2963, microfilm GS 1, reel 982.

126 In 1859 Mary's parents, James and Jane Wickson, lived on William Street (now Yorkville Avenue), and they were still at that address in 1865. James Wickson, Mary's father, died on 3 August 1869, aged seventy-six. Jane Wickson, Mary's mother, died six years later on 21 August 1875 in Paris, Ontario. See AAFP: Wickson folder.

127 See 1859 diary, entry for 10 February. See also discussion of conversation at page 48.

128 Maas, *Helpmates*, 106–115; Ryan, *Cradle*, 196–97; Conrad, "Sundays," 12; Conrad, Laidlaw, and Smyth, *No Place Like Home*, 302–305; Nussbaum, *Autobiographical Subject*, 217; Strong-Boag, *Woman with a Purpose*, ix–x, xiii; Culley, *A Day at a Time*, 7.

129 Maas, *Helpmates*, 138–39, Ryan, *Cradle*, 193; quote from Smith-Rosenberg, "Female World," 15.

130 Blodgett, *Centuries*, 223–30; Powell, "Crease Family Women," 49, 50, 53.

131 Davidoff and Hall, *Family Fortunes*, 341–42.

132 Davidoff and Hall, *Family Fortunes*, 354.

133 For example, see 1859 diary, entry for 6 January.

134 WFP: Calendar "100th Anniversary of the founding of the business John H. Wickson" (c.1934). See discussion of status and education at page 42, and discussion of Thomas's medical career at pages 51–52.

135 See 1869 diary, entries for 3 February and 2, 3 March.

136 Davidoff and Hall, *Family Fortunes*, 217–18, 348–52. See discussion of business partnerships at pages 52–53.

137 Katz, *People of Hamilton*, 36.

138 Davidoff and Hall, *Family Fortunes*, 335.

139 See 1859 diary, entry for 5 May.

140 CTA: John Wickson entry, Village of Yorkville Assessment Roll, 1865, p. 20, line 350, Series 746, Files 2 and 3; *1859–60 Directory*, 204.

141 See 1859 diary, entry for 7 May.

142 See 1869 diary, entries for 18 February, 26 March, 24 May, 1 July, and 3 August.

143 Sarah and Norman married in 1865. It is unknown when her first husband, Carruthers, died. See AAFP: Wickson folder; 1859 diary, entry for 26 March. For a discussion of early postal services and networks, see McCalla, *Planting the Province*, 134–35. For a background on Norman Hamilton, see AAFP: Wickson folder: M. Deans, Wickson-Hamilton family history file and genealogical table (2003).

144 See 1859 diary, entry for 22 April.

145 Smith-Rosenberg, "Female World," 9–12. See also Conrad, "Sundays," 13; Davidoff and Hall, *Family Fortunes*, 341.

146 On Sarah as an artist, see 1859 diary, note 68. See also Maas, *Helpmates*, 121. Family tradition holds that Philip and Mary also made a trip to Europe in the 1860s or 1870s, when they attended a major international exhibition, perhaps in London or Paris. Philip purchased a pair of binoculars in Paris while on this trip, which are still in the family.

147 See 1859 diary, entries for 9 February and 15 April.

148 See discussion of social network and community at page 61.

149 Holman, *Duty*, 152–53; quote from Davidoff and Hall, *Family Fortunes*, 114. See discussion of gender ideology at page 25.

150 Ryan, *Cradle*, 207; quote from Holman, *Duty*, 153. Differences were apparent in how domestic labour was perceived in England and North America. See discussion of servants and help girls at page 34.

151 Maas, *Helpmates*, 26 (contains quote). See the discussion of the new middle class at page 40.

152 L. Johnson, "The Political Economy of Ontario Women in the Nineteenth Century," in *Women at Work: Ontario, 1850-1930*, ed. J. Acton, P. Goldsmith, and B. Shepard (Toronto: Canadian Women's Educational Press, 1974), 14, 22, 23, 28.

153 Errington, *Wives and Mothers*, 90-102; Ryan, *Cradle*, 198-207. See also M.G. Cohen, *Women's Work, Markets and Economic Development in Nineteenth-Century Ontario* (Toronto: University of Toronto Press, 1988), 67-68, 88, 95, 99, 102. See discussion of surplus household produce at page 38.

154 See 1859 dairy, entry for 15 March. See also Ryan, *Cradle*, 162.

155 See 1859 diary, entries for 20 April and 11 May.

156 See 1859 diary, entry for 22 February.

157 See 1869 diary, entries for 25, 26 January and 21 February.

158 See diary for 1869, entries for 30 January and 15, 27 March. Mondays and Tuesday were typically laundry days in Upper Canada. See Errington, *Wives and Mothers*, 98.

159 For example, see 1859 diary, entries for 29 January and 12, 19, 26 February; quote from 12 February.

160 Conrad, "Sundays," 6-7.

161 See 1869 diary, entries for 17 January and 4 March.

162 Errington, *Wives and Mothers*, 119.

163 See 1859 diary, entry for 29 January.

164 Katz, *People of Hamilton*, 222-24.

165 Errington, *Wives and Mothers*, 113.

166 See 1859 diary, entry for 29 January.

167 Errington, *Wives and Mothers*, 115. See also Miller, *Journals of Mary O'Brien*, 238-39.

168 See 1869 diary, entry for 14 January.

169 See 1859 diary, entry for 22 February.

170 See 1859 diary, entry for 25 February.

171 See 1859 diary, entries for 19 March and 24 May.

172 Marks, *Revivals*, 29.

173 Maas, *Helpmates*, 61. Cf. the management of household servants by middle-class women in England in Davidoff and Hall, *Family Fortunes*, 387-93. See discussion of household at pages 48-49.

174 See 1859 diary, entry for 8 April. See discussion of temperance reform at page 64.

175 See 1859 diary, entry for 11 February; 1869 diary, entries for 25 February and 1 July.

176 Errington, *Wives and Mothers*, 97.

177 See 1859 diary, entry for 10 March; 1869 diary, entry for 9 April.

178 Conrad, "Sundays," 6.

179 See 1859 diary, entry for 16 February.

180 See 1859 diary, entry for 14 April.

181 Davidoff and Hall, *Family Fortunes*, 342; Maas, *Helpmates*, chapters 4 and 5.

182 See 1859 diary, entry for 16 February.

183 Maas, *Helpmates*, 95-96, 143.

184 See 1859 diary, entry for 2 February.

185 See 1859 diary, entry for 14 April.

186 See 1859 diary, entry for 17 March.

187 See discussion of self-affirmation at pages 18-19.

188 See 1859 diary, entries for 6 January and 22 February; 1869 diary, entry for 21 April.

189 Backhouse, *Petticoats and Prejudice*, 177-78; C. Pateman, *The Sexual Contract* (Cambridge: Polity, 1988); Davidoff and Hall, *Family Fortunes*, 200. Legislation was passed in 1872 that allowed married women to hold and dispose of property and to enter into contracts as if they were unmarried. See Maas, *Helpmates*, 34-35.

190 Davidoff and Hall, *Family Fortunes*, 209-10.

191 See 1859 diary, entry for 6 January.

192 Some married couples had quite liberal financial arrangements, but the law allowed that these were entirely at the discretion of the husband. See Maas, *Helpmates,* 136. See also discussion of Mary and Philip's marital relationship at page 27.

193 See 1859 diary, entry for 19 February.

194 See 1869 diary, entries for 27 March and 1 April.

195 See 1859 diary, entry for 19 April.

196 Maas, *Helpmates,* 102, 136.

197 Maas, *Helpmates,* 56, 60–61, 172–73. See discussion of status maintenance at page 46.

198 Errington, *Wives and Mothers,* 90–102. See also Cohen, *Women's Work,* 67–68, 88, 95, 99, 102; Conrad, "Sundays," 6–7.

199 See, for example, 1859 diary, entry for 4 February.

200 Burley, *Particular Condition,* 101–102.

201 See discussion of respectability at page 45ff.

202 See 1859 diary, entry for 29 January; 1869 diary, entry for 27 March.

203 See 1869 diary, entry for 26 January.

204 See 1869 diary, entry for 27 January.

205 Quote from 1859 diary, entry for 9 May. See also entry for 7 January, and 1869 diary, entry for 1 January.

206 See 1859 diary, entry for 29 January. See also payment of help girl mentioned above at page 34.

207 See 1859 diary, entry for 24 February.

208 Maas, *Helpmates,* 25

209 Kealey, *Toronto Workers,* 18. Burley defines self-employment as owning one's own means of producing or distributing goods and services. See Burley, *Particular Condition,* 6, 65–66, 85.

210 Holman, *Duty,* 7.

211 Russell argues that a map of colonial social structure existed in the minds of Upper Canadians. See Russell, *Attitudes,* esp. 9, 81, 188.

212 Kealey, *Toronto Workers,* 4–5.

213 Russell, *Attitudes,* 195, 199.

214 Russell, *Attitudes,* 199–200.

215 B. D. Palmer, *A Culture in Conflict: Skilled Workers and Industrial Capitalism in Hamilton, Ontario, 1860–1914* (Montreal: McGill-Queen's University Press, 1979), 12; Palmer, *Working-Class Experience,* 65–69. See also Burley, *Particular Condition,* 33, 114.

216 Kealey, *Toronto Workers,* 18.

217 Burley, *Particular Condition,* 6, 61, 102, 196, 236–37.

218 Careless, *Union,* 28–29.

219 Holman, *Duty,* 9–17.

220 Holman, *Duty,* 6–7, 16–18, 21–27; Burley, *Particular Condition,* 9. This process was related to the decline of a "producer ideology" that had linked the interests of small manufacturers and their workers and had allowed the working class to participate, to a certain degree, in the development of industrial capitalism from mid-century. By the 1870s producerism had faltered, and the working class came into its own in the struggle to survive economic change. See Kealey, *Workers and Canadian History,* 107; Kealey, *Toronto Workers,* 126, 291; Palmer, *Culture in Conflict,* 98–122.

221 Prentice, *School Promoters,* 67, 89.

222 Marks, *Revivals;* Maas, *Helpmates,* esp. 21, 119ff. Maas uses the vaguer term "middle classes" in her study and extends her definition of this group to include those whom others might consider to be members of the Upper Canadian elite and the capitalist class of Canada West, or Ontario.

223 Burley, *Particular Condition.* Burley chooses not to focus on culture, family, or education in his research. He also uses the term "bourgeoisie," which I avoid because of its ambiguity.

224 Holman, *Duty,* 6–7, 9–10.

225 Ryan, *Cradle;* Davidoff and Hall, *Family Fortunes.*

226 Holman, *Duty.*

227 Prentice, *School Promoters,* 83–95; Katz, *People of Hamilton,* 94–176; Burley, *Particular Condition,* 173ff; Russell, *Attitudes,* 101–202.

228 See 1859 diary, entries for 25 January and 24 February.

229 Prentice, *School Promoters,* 91.

230 Maas, *Helpmates,* 66; Russell, *Attitudes,* 106, 162–63. See discussion of gender ideology at page 25, and discussion of social networks at page 67.

231 See "A Canadian's Story" above at pages 2–4. See also Russell, *Attitudes,* 9, 23, 81, 94–100.

232 Samuel attended UCC in 1843, William from 1842 to 1844, and Arthur from 1839 to 1844. See A.H. Young, ed., *The Roll of Pupils of Upper Canada College, Toronto: January 1830 to June 1916* (Kingston: Hanson, Crozier, & Edgar, 1917), 624. See also W.S. Wallace, "U.C.'s First Registrar," *University of Toronto Monthly* 47 (1946–47): 224.

233 Though school fees at that time were relatively moderate, the real expense was that the boys were not available for household chores, and help had to be hired. Tuition at Upper Canada College in the 1830s was £2 5s quarterly, including pen and ink expenses but excluding the cost of books and materials. Boarding fees were £25 per annum. I am grateful to Marian Spence of the UCC archives for this information and for directing me to Young's *Roll of Pupils.*

234 See discussion of land purchase in "A Canadian's Story" at page 7. On land investment, see Russell, *Attitudes,* 22–23; Burley, *Particular Condition,* 21. Russell argues that a degree of ambiguity as to one's degree of respectability is the distinguishing mark of the "marginal-respectable" stratum. While Philip and Mary were not as respectable as the elite Elmsleys from whom they purchased this land, they were certainly no longer merely independent. See Russell, *Attitudes,* 74.

235 Prentice, *School Promoters,* 83, 95.

236 Katz, *People of Hamilton,* 137–38, 149. See also Burley, *Particular Condition,* 174.

237 Burley, *Particular Condition,* 173–74.

238 See discussion of butcher trade at pages 52–55.

239 See discussion of property in "A Canadian's Story" at pages 10, and 12–13.

240 Burley, *Particular Condition,* 140, 159. Katz has also discussed land as a medium of speculation and source of rental income. See Katz, *People of Hamilton,* 78–79, 87.

241 See discussion of this sale of lots at page 20.

242 See discussion of signs of increased affluence in "A Canadian's Story" at page 13.

243 Burley, *Particular Condition,* 181.

244 *1866 Directory,* 284.

245 *1864–45 Directory, 328; 1867–68 Directory,* 174, 368. See discussion of partnerships at pages 52–53.

246 See discussion of agricultural societies at pages 66–67.

247 Holman, *Duty,* 105, 116–120. See also a similar argument for the amelioration of gentlemanly status in the pre–1846 period in Fair, "Gentlemen," 207.

248 *1871 Directory,* 67; Prentice, *School Promoters,* 92, 106. At mid-century, even gentlemen could find themselves involved in manual labour pursuits such as farming. See Prentice, *School Promoters,* 90. Six years earlier in an assessment roll, Mary's father, James Wickson (who died in 1869), was also described as a "gentleman." See CTA: James Wickson entry, Village of Yorkville Assessment Roll, 1865, p. 21, line 240, Series 746, Files 2 and 3.

249 Davidoff and Hall, *Family Fortunes,* 362.

250 Holman, *Duty,* 21.

251 Frederick Widder appears in the 1851 city directory as living on Front Street, near Brock Avenue. The Canada Company had been chartered in the 1820s as a land-company

to manage and develop the Crown Reserves and a portion of the Clergy Reserves as surveyed in 1824. In 1862 Widder is also listed as a director of the Toronto Horticultural Society, of which Philip Armstrong was a member. See *1850–51 Directory*, 136; *Annual Report of the Managing Committee of the Toronto Horticultural Society for 1861* (Toronto: Rowsell & Ellis, 1862); Craig, *Upper Canada*, 135–38.

252 See 1859 diary, entry for 24 February.

253 See 1859 diary, entry for 25 January. Mary's statement about rank was not entirely accurate, as all members of the upper house were entitled to adopt the style "Honourable," though she may have been referring to finer grades of rank, such as the de Blaquières' relations in Britain. From 1837, executive councillors took precedence over all others. See Russell, *Attitudes*, 105.

254 Holman, *Duty;* Davidoff and Hall, *Family Fortunes;* Ryan, *Cradle;* Prentice, *School Promoters;* W. Westfall, *Two Worlds: The Protestant Culture of Nineteenth-Century Ontario* (Montreal: McGill-Queen's University Press, 1989).

255 Prentice, *School Promoters*, 68; Westfall, *Two Worlds*, 69–70.

256 For a discussion of moral character and status before 1840, see Russell, *Attitudes*, 144–53.

257 Errington, *Wives and Mothers*, 19.

258 See 1859 diary, entry for 6 January.

259 Holman, *Duty*, 110.

260 According to Mary, Thomas's bacon business folded because he overextended credit to his customers.

261 See discussion of motherhood and family relationships at pages 25–28, and discussion of domestic work and finances at page 37 ff.

262 Holman, *Duty*, 98; Davidoff and Hall, *Family Fortunes*, 195, 359; Maas, *Helpmates*, 8.

263 On women deriving their status from male family members, see page 41. See also Maas, *Helpmates*, 66; Russell, *Attitudes*, 106, 162–63. On women's influence in the private sphere, see Holman, *Duty*, x, 150ff; Ryan, *Cradle*, 190–91; Maas, *Helpmates*, 171–72.

264 Ryan, *Cradle*, 158ff, 175–76; Maas, *Helpmates*, 171. See discussion of motherhood and family relationships at pages 27–28.

265 Ryan, *Cradle*, 197; Davidoff and Hall, *Family Fortunes*, 338.

266 See 1859 diary, entries for 27 January; 9, 22, 24 February; 15 March; and 3 April.

267 See 1859 diary, entry for 9 February. See discussion of Mary Ann at page 28. See also B. Bradbury, "Gender at Work at Home: Family Decisions, the Labour Market, and Girls' Contributions to the Family Economy," in *Canadian Family History: Selected Readings*, ed. B. Bradbury (Toronto: Copp Clark Pitman, 1992), 177–98.

268 Paris Museum and Historical Society: Mrs. Sarah Carruthers, teacher's certificate (provisional), 1 January 1855; Mrs. Sarah Carruthers, teacher's certificate (female, first class), 24 September 1855; Prentice, *School Promoters*, 112.

269 Prentice, *School Promoters*, 109; Maas, *Helpmates*, 27–30. On similar developments in Britain, see Davidoff and Hall, *Family Fortunes*, 289–93.

270 See 1859 diary, entry for 18 February.

271 Prentice, *School Promoters*, 113.

272 For example, see 1859 diary, entries for 1 January, 1 April, and 7 May; 1869 diary, entries for 5, 27, 29 January, 13 February, and 9 March. See discussion of affluence in "A Canadian's Story" at pages 12–13.

273 Holman, *Duty*, 164; Davidoff and Hall, *Family Fortunes*, 155, 162.

274 See 1859 diary, entries for 16, 17, 22 February; 14 March; 1, 6 April; and 1 May. See 1869 diary, entries for 1 January and 1 April.

275 Holman has observed that these lectures fell into two categories: one focused on science and geography, the other on art, history, and philosophy. See Holman, *Duty*, 125–26.

276 See 1859 diary, entries for 18, 25 January, 9 February, and 1, 22 March.
277 See discussion of temperance reform below at note 406.
278 See 1859 diary, entry for 11 February; Holman, *Duty*, 125–26.
279 Holman, *Duty*, 150, 158, 166, quote from 159.
280 Davidoff and Hall, *Family Fortunes*, 90, 357. See also McKenna, *A Life of Propriety*, 60; discussion of domesticity at page 25.
281 Prentice, *School Promoters*, 114; quote from Holman, *Duty*, 166. See discussion of the ranking of other women in female life writing at page 18.
282 Holman, *Duty*, 161. See 1859 diary, entry for 19 March.
283 Holman, *Duty*, 162. See 1859 diary, entry for 9 February.
284 Holman, *Duty*, 163. See 1859 diary, entries for 11, 12, 18 May. See discussion of feelings in life writing at page 20.
285 Holman, *Duty*, 164.
286 See 1859 diary, entry for 10 February.
287 Holman, *Duty*, 167.
288 See 1859 diary, entry for 18 February; 1869 diary, entries for 30 April and 1 May.
289 See 1859 diary, entry for 5 May. Sections of the original six acres at Rose Hill would remain in the Armstrong family until 1994. For a discussion of the status attached to living in a large brick or stone house on a spacious plot of land, see Katz, *People of Hamilton*, 28.
290 Davidoff and Hall, *Family Fortunes*, 370–75; Holman, *Duty*, 167.
291 See 1859 diary, entry for 18 February.
292 See 1869 diary, entry for 1 July.
293 See also Mary's notice of other gardens in 1859 diary, entry for 7 May.
294 Katz, *People of Hamilton*, 28; Holman, *Duty*, 151. See discussion of household above at note 92.
295 Katz, *People of Hamilton*, 28, 34–36.
296 Philip, Mary, Mary Ann, Thomas, Samuel, Mary's help girl, and the hands Patrick and Alick.
297 See Katz, *People of Hamilton*, 236, 305, and A. Prentice, "Education and the Metaphor of the Family: The Upper Canadian Example," *History of Education Quarterly* 12, no. 3 (1972): 281–303. The blending of ideas of household and family had deep roots in English aristocratic culture. For example, see K. Mertes, *The English Noble Household, 1250–1600* (Oxford: Blackwell, 1988).
298 Ryan, *Cradle*, 157, 182.
299 Most families that Maas studied had at least six children. See Maas, *Helpmates*, 31, 115. In regard to family size as an indicator of social status, see also Palmer, *Working-Class Experience*, 83. See discussion of family relationships at page 28.
300 Davidoff and Hall, *Family Fortunes*, 328.
301 Katz, *People of Hamilton*, 231. See Mary's reference to "hired boys" in 1859 diary, entry for 11 February.
302 Westfall, *Two Worlds*, 70.
303 Marks, *Revivals*, 23–24; Davidoff and Hall, *Family Fortunes*, 76, 108. See discussion of church activities at page 62.
304 Of course, it does not follow that church attendance was solely a middle-class phenomenon. Marks has pointed out that religious involvement and concern with respectability were not just middle-class characteristics, and that some labourers and wealthy skilled workers also sought respectability through church involvement. See Marks, *Revivals*, 28, 31, 35. Davidoff and Hall have argued that the church's meritocratic, rather than aristocratic, appeal could de-emphasize class distinctions within a congregation. See Davidoff and Hall, *Family Fortunes*, 77, 83.
305 Marks, *Revivals*, 22, 33, quote from 22. See discussion of faith and respectability at pages 57–58.

306 Marks, *Revivals*, 32–33, 49–50, quote from 32. See discussion of feminized religion at pages 59–60.

307 See, for example, 1859 diary, entries for 12, 16, 19, 23, 27, 31 January.

308 Marks, *Revivals*, 61, 79; N. Semple, "The Impact of Urbanization on the Methodist Church of Canada, 1854–1884," *Canadian Society of Church History Papers* (1976), 242.

309 Van Die, *Evangelical Mind*, 183.

310 See 1869 diary, entry for 1 January.

311 See pages 41 and 44.

312 See discussion of gender ideology at page 25, and discussion of women's status by association at pages 41 and 67.

313 Holman, *Duty*, ix.

314 Holman, *Duty*, 28–49, 75–76, 50–52, 74, quote from 50.

315 In 1868 and 1870 he was listed in the city directory as a solicitor with offices at 74 Church Street and a residence on William Street, at Yonge Street, in Yorkville. In the assessment roll for 1868 Samuel Wickson is listed as a barrister, with land on William Street owned by his father, James Wickson, totalling forty-plus acres and valued at $950. See CTA: Samuel Wickson entry, Village of Yorkville Assessment Roll, 1868, p. 17, line 388, Series 746, Files 2 and 3; *1870 Directory*, 142; *1868–69 Directory A*, 367, 383.

316 In 1851 Arthur married Anne Mary Harris, daughter of the Reverend James Harris, but was widowed, and he later married Mary Ann Thomas, who was his wife by 1859. By his second wife he had at least one son, named Paul Giovanni Wickson, who became a noted Canadian painter. In 1859 Arthur and Mary Ann lived at 393 Yonge Street. In 1868 Arthur lived with his wife at 162 Mutual Street, at the corner of Gould Street. In 1870 he lived at 21 Grenville Street. In England, he was minister of the Horsley-Down Congregational Church. He died in 1913. See T. Hodgins, ed., *The Canada Educational Directory and Calendar for 1857–78* (Toronto: Maclear, 1857), 89–90; C.T. Bissell, *University College: A Portrait, 1853–1953* (Toronto: University of Toronto Press, 1953), 3–9; J.R. Robertson, *Landmarks of Toronto*, vol. 3 (1898; reprint, Belleville: Mika Publishing, 1974), 2–4; Wallace, "U.C.'s First Registrar"; T.B. Wilson, ed., *The Ontario Register, Volume 5, 1981* (Lambertville, New Jersey: T.B. Wilson, 1981), 209; University of Toronto Archives: *Annual Announcement of the Toronto School of Medicine, Twenty Seventh Session, October 1, 1869, to April 1, 1870* (Toronto: Globe Printing, 1869), 67, P1978-0070.(03); "University of Toronto," *Globe*, 6 June 1863; *1859–60 Directory*, 204, 258; *1869–69 Directory A*, 367; *1870 Directory*, 142.

317 See "A Canadian's Story" at page 10.

318 For example, see 1859 diary, entry for 6 January. Thomas first attended school in Yorkville and then spent three years at the Toronto Academy. Following this period of education he "was engaged on his father's farm" until he made his failed attempt at the meat business. See Mulvaney and Mercer, *History of Toronto and County of York*, vol. 2, 211–12. See discussion of Thomas's relationship with his grandfather at pages 29–30.

319 Prentice, *School Promoters*, 114; Ryan, *Cradle*, 169. See also A. Smith, "The Myth of the Self-Made Man in English Canada, 1850–1914," *CHR* 59, no. 2 (1978): 194–97.

320 The 1859-60 directory only listed a very small number of butchers. See *1859–60 Directory*, 218. I am grateful to Ruth Wickson Newman of Parry Sound, Ontario, for the additional information that Mary's brother William Orme Wickson was also a butcher in the St. Lawrence Market in 1862; however, I have not been able to confirm this in other sources. I am also grateful to Professor Edward Alfred Allworth for the information that from 1865 William Orme Wickson is listed in census record for Wayne County, New York State, where his brother George Guest Wickson lived before moving to California c.1881. William Orme Wickson died in Williamson, Wayne County, in 1906.

321 Burley, *Particular Condition*, 91; Holman, *Duty*, 35; Davidoff and Hall, *Family Fortunes*, 208.

322 Davidoff and Hall, *Family Fortunes*, 209, 217–18.

323 See "A Canadian's Story" at page 6.

324 See 1859 diary, entry for 19 March. See also *1859–60 Directory*, 17, 204.

325 Burley, *Particular Condition*, 34.

326 The partnership had dissolved and Philip Armstrong was back on his own by 1860. See AO: *G.R. Tremaine's Map of the City of Toronto* (1860), A-10; *1861 Directory*, 301.

327 The first record of John McCarter is in the 1850–51 city and county directory, where he is listed as living in Toronto, south of Dundas Street. He is first listed as a butcher in 1861. In 1867 his residence is listed as being in the township of York. See *1850–51 Directory*, 94; *1861 Directory*, 229, 302; *1864–65 Directory*, 328; *1867–68 Directory*, 174, 368.

328 See "A Canadian's Story" at page 10.

329 *1859–60 Directory*, 218.

330 Burley, *Particular Condition*, 94.

331 In the 1856 directory John Wickson is listed as a butcher in the St. Lawrence Market, as is Philip Armstrong. Mary's brother James is listed as a butcher at 79 Richmond Street. See *1856 Directory*, 259; AAFP: Wickson folder; WFP: Calendar "100th Anniversary of the founding of the business John H. Wickson" (c.1934).

332 AO: *G.R. Tremaine's Map of the City of Toronto* (1860), A-10. See also *1859–60 Directory*, 204. John Wickson had married Eliza Chilver in 1837, and they had several children, including John Rusby Wickson and Henry. Rusby, who was close with the Armstrongs, turned twenty-one in 1859 and lived on Victoria Street. John built a summer residence in the 1860s on the north side of Eglinton Avenue, between what is now Bathurst Street and Old Forest Hill Road. John named his residence "Forest Hill" after the surrounding environment. He could not have known at the time that he had chosen what would become the name for the village of Forest Hill, which in 1923 was incorporated as a separate municipality within York Township. See T. Frayne, "Forest Hill: Where a nice Tudor home comes with a neat $285,000 price tag," *Toronto Daily Star*, 14 November 1970, 7; W. French, *A Most Unlikely Village: An Informal History of the Village of Forest Hill* (Toronto: Ryerson Press, 1964), 5; AAFP: Wickson folder.

333 See 1859 diary, entry for 16 February.

334 In the 1867 Yorkville assessment roll, John Wickson has seventy-eight-plus acres on Yonge Street, and three acres cleared on New Kent Road. The New Kent Road property, including John's slaughterhouse, was valued at $1,200. The next year, this property was valued at $1,600. John is listed in the 1868–69 city directory as living at Russell Hill Road and Davenport Road and running his butcher business with his son Henry who boarded with him. John did quite well financially, leaving an estate worth over $51,000 upon his death in 1900. See CTA: John Wickson entry, Village of Yorkville Assessment Roll, 1867, p. 16, lines 382–83, Series 746, Files 2 and 3; John Wickson entry, Village of Yorkville Assessment Roll, 1868, pp. 17–18, lines 386, 404, Series 746, Files 2 and 3; *1859–60 Directory*, 204; *1868–69 Directory A*, 367. For the information on John's estate I am again grateful to Ruth Wickson Newman of Parry Sound, Ontario.

335 Mary recorded a farmer bringing cattle to the Rose Hill property (probably for slaughter) on 10 January 1859; *1846–67 Directory*, 3.

336 I.R. MacLachlan, *Kill and Chill: Restructuring Canada's Beef Commodity Chain* (Toronto: University of Toronto Press, 2001). I am grateful to Professor MacLachlan for bringing his study to my attention. See also Kealey, *Toronto Workers*. For studies of similar trades, see, for example: I. McKay, "Capital and Labour in the Halifax Baking and Confectionery Industry during the Last Half of the Nineteenth Century," *Labour/Le Travailleur* 3 (1978): 63–108; J. Burgess, "Work, Family and Community: Montreal Leather

Craftsmen, 1790–1831" (Ph.D. diss., Université du Québec à Montréal, 1986);
J. Burgess, "The Growth of a Craft Labour Force: Montreal Leather Artisans,
1815–1831," *Canadian Historical Papers* (1988): 48–62.

337 I am grateful to Professor Gregory Kealey and Robert Dennis for bringing studies of
Chicago to my attention. See J.R. Barrett, *Work and Community in the Jungle: Chicago's
Packinghouse Workers, 1894–1922* (Urbana: University of Illinois Press, 1987); R. Hal-
pern, *Down on the Killing Floor: Black and White Workers in Chicago's Packinghouses,
1904–54* (Urbana: University of Illinois Press, 1997); L.C. Wade, *Chicago's Pride: The
Stockyards, Packingtown, and Environs in the Nineteenth Century* (Urbana: University of Illi-
nois Press, 1987). See also S. Giedion, *Mechanization Takes Command: A Contribution to
Anonymous History* (New York: Oxford University Press, 1948); S. Milton, *The Killing Floor:
The First World War and the Emergence of the South African Beef Industry, 1902–24* (London: Institute of Commonwealth Studies, University of London, 1993).

338 *1862–63 Directory*, 133; *1864–65 Directory*, 345. See also Maple Leaf Foods, "Our History," http://www.mapleleaf.com/about_mlf/our_history.asp (accessed 7 February
2003).

339 The numbers of butchers appearing in directories for given years are as follows: 1856
(66), 1861 (114), 1862 (75), 1864 (98), 1865 (107), 1867 (53), 1876 (146). These
numbers may not accurately reflect the total number of butchers in the city, but they
do provide a useful rough guide. They probably also reflect overall population growth.
See *1876 Directory*, 392–93; *1867–68 Directory*, 368–69; *1865 Directory*, 44–46; *1864–65
Directory*, 328; *1862–63 Directory*, 247; *1861 Directory*, 301–302; *1856 Directory*, 258–59.

340 The districts of York North, York West, York East, Toronto West, and Toronto East were
examined. See National Archives of Canada, "Federal Census of 1871 (Ontario Index),"
http://www.archives.ca/02/02010803_e.html (accessed 27 September 2002).

341 Davidoff and Hall, *Family Fortunes*, 101, 208, 215–16; Burley, *Particular Condition*, 76.
See discussion of business partnerships at pages 52-53.

342 Judging by his surname, John McCarter's national origin was probably either Irish or
Scottish. He has not been located in the census material and his religious affiliation
is unknown.

343 Burley, *Particular Condition*, 76; Ryan, *Cradle*, 138.

344 Westfall, *Two Worlds*, 30–49. See also Van Die, *Evangelical Mind*, 14–36. Greven examines evangelical, moderate, and genteel protestant temperaments in America from the
seventeenth to the early nineteenth century. See Greven, *Protestant Temperament*, 17,
22–142, 330.

345 Westfall, *Two Worlds*, 9, 83–109, 123.

346 Westfall, *Two Worlds*, L, 52–53, 67–68; Van Die, *Evangelical Mind*, 15.

347 Westfall, *Two Worlds*, 9, 123.

348 Originally located elsewhere in Yorkville and called the Wesleyan Chapel after its
opening in 1841, the church had moved in 1854 to Bloor and Gwynne Streets and
changed its name to the Yorkville Wesleyan Methodist Church. It assumed the name
Central Methodist Church around 1865. Samuel Wickson was involved as a trustee on
the board of the Central Methodist Church from 1876 to 1879. Its congregation eventually amalgamated with that of St. Andrew's United Church across the street at 117
Bloor. See UCCA: St. Andrew's United Church (Toronto, ON) fonds, fonds no. 2505,
fonds level description (administrative history); St. Andrew's United Church (Toronto,
ON) fonds, board and committee records, trustee minutes, fonds no. 2505/1, location no. 77.705L — box 1 — file 5, title page, provisional meeting of the trustees of Bloor
St. Methodist Church, 11 March 1876; Robertson, *Landmarks of Toronto*, vol. 4, 350-53.

349 UCCA: Paris Congregational Church (Paris, ON), fonds, congregational minutes,
church book, fonds no. 1448, location no. 77.209L — box 1 — file 1, council minutes,
31 May 1865. See discussion of Rev. Arthur Wickson's career at page 51. See Sarah

Wickson Hamilton obituary, *Brantford Expositor,* 26 August 1918, 2. I am grateful to Marg Deans for this last reference.

350 GAFP: marriage certificate of Thomas Armstrong and Fidelia Maughan, 1863; declaration of Samuel Wickson under the Canada Evidence Act, 6 March 1908, "In the matter of the marriage of Thomas Armstrong with Fidelia Jane Maughan." See "A Canadian's Story" at page 10.

351 See 1859 diary, entries for 27 February and 25 April.

352 Van Die, *Evangelical Mind,* 36; Marks, *Revivals,* 24.

353 Marks, *Revivals,* 24.

354 Van Die, *Evangelical Mind,* 22–23; Greven, *Protestant Temperament,* 64–65. For a description of the ordination of Mary's brother-in-law Rev. Richard T. Thomas, which included a personal account of his conversion and his ceremonial questioning by Rev. Arthur Wickson, see "Death of a Congregational Minister," *Star Transcript,* 28 August 1895, 2. I am grateful to Marg Deans for this reference.

355 Family tradition holds that in 1877, while Thomas was away seeing patients during an epidemic, the local Anglican minister, Canon Osler of St. John's Church, York Mills, greatly helped Fidelia Armstrong and her sick children, two of whom died, and one of whom was buried by Osler. Out of gratitude for the minister's kindness, the family converted to the Anglican Church in 1877. However, joining the local Anglican congregation would also have been a keen business move for a doctor eager to find new patients in the community. I am grateful to my father, Dr. Andrew Armstrong, for this story and suggestion. See Mount Pleasant Cemetery, Toronto, Ontario: Interment Register no. 1, Interment numbers 68 and 188.

356 In the 1851 census Mary is listed as an "Independent" (Congregationalist) and Philip as a Wesleyan Methodist, but in 1861 both are listed as Wesleyan Methodists. From Mary's diary it is evident that she had probably converted to Methodism by 1855. See 1859 diary, entry for 9 February at page 99; LAC: Philip Armstrong household, 1851 Census York Twp. (Part 1), York Co., Canada West, enumeration district no. 1, p. 177, line 1, LAC microfilm C-11760; Philip Armstrong household, 1861 Census York Twp., York Co., Canada West, enumeration district no. 3, p. 95, line 18, LAC microfilm C-1090.

357 See 1859 diary, entry for 23 April. See also LAC: Sarah Hamilton household, 1881 census, Province of Ontario, enumeration district no. 160 North Brant, sub-district D, Town of Paris, division no. 2, p. 29, lines 20–24, LAC microfilm C-13264. I am grateful to Professor Edward Alfred Allworth for this reference.

358 Davidoff and Hall, *Family Fortunes,* 76–77. See discussion of religion with regard to social network and community at pages 61–62.

359 See discussion of status and religion at page 49.

360 Westfall, *Two Worlds,* 69–71, 73–75, quote from 69.

361 Westfall, *Two Worlds,* 72–73.

362 Westfall, *Two Worlds,* 76–79.

363 See 1859 diary, entry for 23 April. Interestingly, St. James' is an Anglican cathedral, and it appears that on this occasion, English national sentiment overcame denominational affiliation, which only augmented Mary's enjoyment of the service. See section on national identities at pages 68–74.

364 See for example, 1869 diary, entries for 1, 20 January, 13 February, and 1, 12, 30 March.

365 See 1859 diary, entry for 10 April.

366 Huff, *British Women's Diaries,* XIX–XX.

367 See 1859 diary, entries for 20, 21 January, 12 March, and 28 April.

368 Davidoff and Hall, *Family Fortunes,* 89.

369 See 1859 diary, entry for 1 May.

370 Davidoff and Hall, *Family Fortunes*, 77, 90; Maas, *Helpmates*, 100.

371 See 1859 diary, entry for 12 January.

372 See 1859 diary, entry for 8 April.

373 Strong-Boag, *Woman with a Purpose*, xiii.

374 See 1859 diary, entry for 14 April.

375 Marks, *Revivals*, 31.

376 Marks, *Revivals*, 69. See also B. Welter, "The Feminization of American Religion, 1800–1860," in *Dimity Convictions: The American Woman in the Nineteenth Century* (Athens, OH: Ohio University Press, 1976), 83–102.

377 Marks, *Revivals*, 32, 49–50; Davidoff and Hall, *Family Fortunes*, 108–113. See discussion of male Christian values at page 50.

378 Davidoff and Hall, *Family Fortunes*, 90, 107; quote from Marks, *Revivals*, 30.

379 See 1859 diary, entry for 24 April.

380 Marks, *Revivals*, 31.

381 See 1859 diary, entry for 12 May.

382 Marks, *Revivals*, 93. See, for example, 1859 diary, entry for 1 May.

383 Davidoff and Hall, *Family Fortunes*, 416.

384 Holman, *Duty*, 100, 105–106, 111, quote from 105–106. See discussion of middle-class formation at page 40.

385 Quote from Davidoff and Hall, *Family Fortunes*, 416.

386 See discussion of religion and status at pages 49–50.

387 See 1859 diary, entry for 25 April.

388 Davidoff and Hall, *Family Fortunes*, 108. See also Holman, *Duty*, 111.

389 See 1859 diary, entry for 20 February.

390 See "A Canadian's Story" at page 4.

391 Reverend Dr. Adam Lillie, who had married Philip and Mary, attended the council meeting where Edward Ebbs accepted the church's call to become its new pastor. See AAFP: Armstrong and Wickson folders; UCCA: Paris Congregational Church (Paris, ON) fonds, congregational minutes, church book, fonds no. 1448, location no. 77.209L—box 1—file 1, council minutes, 27 July 1858.

392 AAFP: Wickson folder, M. Deans, Wickson-Hamilton family history file and genealogical table (2003).

393 UCCA: Paris Congregational Church (Paris, ON) fonds, congregational minutes, church book, fonds no. 1448, location no. 77.209L—box 1—file 1, council minutes, 31 May 1865. See "A Canadian's Story" at page 14, and discussion of extended family relations at page 31.

394 On church and community, see Marks, *Revivals*, 52; Davidoff and Hall, *Family Fortunes*, 99.

395 See the advertisement in the *Christian Guardian*, 20 April 1859, 63, and the article recounting the services in the same, 11 May 1859, 74.

396 Van Die, *Evangelical Mind*, 15.

397 See discussion of respectability and religious practice at pages 57–58.

398 Westfall, *Two Worlds*, 76.

399 See discussion of voluntary societies in "A Canadian's Story" at pages 11 and 14.

400 *1859–60 Directory*, 215.

401 See 1859 diary, entries for 10, 12 January, and 24 February. For comment on the meetings see the advertisement in the *Christian Guardian*, 5 January 1859, and the article about the meeting under "City Items" in the *Christian Guardian*, 12 January 1859, 6.

402 Marks, *Revivals*, 54, 79; Davidoff and Hall, *Family Fortunes*, 108; Ryan, *Cradle*, 186.

403 Quote from Holman, *Duty*, 111; Marks, *Revivals*, 53; Ryan, *Cradle*, 186. See discussion of the femininity of religion at pages 59–60.

404 Marks, *Revivals*, 75; Ryan, *Cradle*, 211; Maas, *Helpmates*, 35–36.

405 See 1859 diary, entry for 24 February.

406 Holman, *Duty*, 132–34, 139–40.

407 A legislative committee, formed in 1856, found that 88,945 people had signed a peti-
tion in support of prohibition. See J. Noel, *Canada Dry: Temperance Crusades before
Confederation* (Toronto: University of Toronto Press, 1995), 113, 144–50.

408 Marks, *Revivals*, 93.

409 Holman, *Duty*, 135.

410 See 1859 diary, entries for 5, 12, 19 April; advertisement in the *Globe*, 5 April 1859, 3;
"Mr. Peter Sinclair's Lecture," *Globe*, 6 April 1859, 2.

411 See discussion of lectures at page 47.

412 St. George's Society of Toronto, *Report of the committee for 1867* (Toronto: St. George's
Society, 1868).

413 See 1859 diary, entries for 14, 15, 26 February and 1 March.

414 See 1859 diary, entry for 1 March. See also discussion of Mary and Philip's marital relationship at page 27.

415 See 1859 diary, entry for 24 February. See also discussion of gentry emulation at page
44.

416 See 1859 diary, entry for 23 April.

417 Holman, *Duty*, 121–25. See discussion of cultivation and respectability at page 47.

418 See 1859 diary, entry for 28 April; YDMIS advertisement in the *Globe*, 27 April 1859,
33.

419 Fair, "Gentlemen," 185–210.

420 In 1850 he won a total of £2 5s, taking third place for his peas, second for his rutabagas, third for his turnips, third for his beef ox, and second for his beef cow. In the 1852
show, other competitors included Robert Baldwin, a liberal politician who advocated
reform, and George Allan, a member of the legislative council, or upper house of the
government, and namesake of Allan Gardens in Toronto. At the 1859 ploughing
match, almost twenty ploughs competed, and Allan promised to provide a silver cup
for which the ploughers would compete at the next match. See "County of York Agricultural Show," *Globe*, 12 October 1850; "Prize List," *Globe*, 25 September 1852; "York
Ploughing Match," *Globe*, 7 April 1859, 2. See also 1859 diary, entry for 6 April and
note 124.

421 In 1855 Philip was a judge in the "fat and working cattle any breed" competition, and
in the "fat sheep" competition. See "Provincial Agricultural Exhibition Prize List," *Globe*,
1 October 1855. In 1862 Philip was listed as a member of the THS. He was also present at the 1860 annual meeting of the Board of Agriculture as one of the delegates
"from County and Electoral Division Agricultural Societies, and from Horticultural
Societies." See *Canadian Agriculturalist* 12, no. 20 (15 October 1860): 533. See also
Toronto Horticultural Society, *Annual Report of the Managing Committee of the Toronto
Horticultural Society for 1861* (Toronto: Roswell & Ellis, 1862).

422 See "A Canadian's Story" at page 10. A posthumous biography of Philip records that
at various times he was also president of the West York Association and a member of
the Art Association, the York Pioneers, and an organizing member of the Philharmonic
Society. See Mulvaney and Mercer, *History of Toronto and County of York*, vol. 2, 211–12.
See also *1866 Directory*, 466; *1870 Directory*, xxv; *1873 Directory*, 310; *1876 Directory*, 464;
1877 Directory, 512; *1878 Directory*, 540; *1879 Directory*, 506; O.C.J. Withrow, *The
Romance of the Canadian National Exhibition* (Toronto: Reginald Saunders, 1936),
53–62; P.F. Dodds, *The Story of Ontario Agricultural Fairs and Exhibitions, 1792–1967* (Picton, Ontario: *Picton Gazette*, 1967), 190–95; P. Crawford, "The Roots of the Toronto
Horticultural Society," *OH* 89, no. 2 (June 1997): 125–39; D. Bain, "George Allan and
the Horticultural Gardens," *OH* 87, no. 3 (September 1995): 231–51.

423 Holman, *Duty,* 83, 100–103.

424 AO: *Illustrated Historical Atlas of the County of York,* xiii, atlas 79.

425 Holman, *Duty,* 100–103.

426 Mulvaney and Mercer, *History of Toronto and County of York,* vol. 2, 211–12.

427 Maas, *Helpmates,* 66; Russell, *Attitudes,* 106, 162–63. See discussion of women's status derived from male family members at page 41, and discussion of status amelioration at pages 43–44.

428 See "A Canadian's Story" at page 14.

429 See discussion of social mobility at page 41.

430 Holman, *Duty,* esp. 98ff; Marks, *Revivals,* esp. 22–97. See also Davidoff and Hall, *Family Fortunes;* Ryan, *Cradle.*

431 This was presumably the St. Lawrence Market in the city where her husband had his business. See discussion of market attendance at pages 34 and 38.

432 See 1859 diary, entries for 10 January and 4 March.

433 See 1859 diary, entry for 26 April; 1869 diary, entries for 27 January and 2, 13 February.

434 See, for example, E. Gellner, *Nation and Nationalism* (Oxford: Blackwell, 1983), 1–7; A.D. Smith, *The Ethnic Origin of Nations* (Oxford: Blackwell, 1986), 129–73; B. Anderson, *Imagined Communities* (London: Verso, 1983). For a summary of Anderson's argument, see J. Tomlinson, *Cultural Imperialism* (London: Pinter, 1991), 81–82, cited in K. Wilson, "Citizenship, Empire, and Modernity in the English Provinces, c.1720–1790," *Cultures of Empire: A Reader,* ed. C. Hall (Manchester: Manchester University Press, 2000), 159–60.

435 A.D. Smith, *National Identity* (London: Penguin, 175).

436 For a description of the Manchester School of imperial history, which has been inspired by J.M. Mackenzie, see C. Hall, ed., *Cultures of Empire: A Reader* (Manchester: Manchester University Press, 2000), 21. For a discussion of imperial history in general, see Hall, *Cultures,* 16, 20–23. For a definition of "culture" as used in this context, see Hall, *Cultures,* 10–11. See also E. Said, *Orientalism* (London: Routledge, 1978); J.M. Mackenzie, *Propaganda and Empire* (Manchester: Manchester University Press, 1984); J.M. Mackenzie, *Imperialism and Popular Culture* (Manchester: Manchester University Press, 1986); J.M. Mackenzie, *Popular Imperialism and the Military, 1850–1950* (Manchester: Manchester University Press, 1992); C. Hall, *Civilising Subjects: Metropole and Colony in the English Imagination, 1830–1867* (Manchester: Manchester University Press, 2002), 9.

437 M.L. Pratt, *Imperial Eyes: Travel Writing and Transculturation* (London: Routledge, 1992), 6–7ff. See also Hall, *Cultures,* 26.

438 S. Mills, *Discourses of Difference: An Analysis of Women's Travel Writing and Colonialism* (London: Routledge, 1991); S. Mills, "Knowledge, Gender, and Empire," in *Writing Women and Space,* ed. A. Blunt and G. Ross (New York: Guilford Press, 1994), 29–50; S. Mills, *Gender and Colonial Space* (London: Institute of Commonwealth Studies, University of London, 1995).

439 F. Parkes, *Wanderings of a Pilgrim in Search of the Picturesque,* ed. S. Mills and I. Ghose (Manchester: Manchester University Press, 2001), 16.

440 Smith, *National Identity,* 175.

441 Hall, *Civilising,* 400, 423, 428.

442 Hall, *Civilising,* 65.

443 Maas, *Helpmates,* 41, 44, 171; Conrad, "Sundays," 4. See also E.O. Hellerstein, L.P. Hume, and K. Offen, eds., *Victorian Women* (Stanford: Stanford University Press, 1981), cited in Maas, *Helpmates,* 41 n. 133.

444 Anderson, *Imagined Communities.* See also Tomlinson, *Cultural Imperialism,* 81–82, cited in Wilson, "Citizenship," 159–60.

445 Wilson, "Citizenship," 160–61.

446 Maas, *Helpmates,* 41, 44, 171. See discussion of gender ideology at page 25.

447 Wilson, "Citizenship," 161–62.

448 See 1859 diary, entry for 14 March.

449 Quote from 1859 diary, entry for 5 March. See also 1869 diary, entry for 18 January.

450 See announcements in the *Globe,* 27 April 1859 and 4 May 1859, for Philip's sale of lots at Rose Hill on 5 May 1859. See also his advertisements for the ploughing match in the *Globe,* 31 March 1859.

451 For example, see Mary's comments on the execution of criminals, 1859 diary, entry for 3 March, and the question of the location of government, 1859 diary, entry for 14 February. See also Wilson, "Citizenship," 161–62.

452 Van Die, *Evangelical Mind,* 9.

453 Quote from G.C. Spivak, "Three Women's Texts and a Critique of Imperialism," *Critical Inquiry* 12 (1985): 243–61, cited in Hall, *Cultures,* 26.

454 See discussion of temperance lectures at page 65.

455 Maas, *Helpmates,* 138

456 See 1859 diary, entries for 1 January, 10 February, and 24 May.

457 See discussion of Arthur's career at page 51.

458 Hall, *Civilising,* 402, 424–25, 436.

459 See discussion of YDMIS at page 66.

460 See 1859 diary, entry for 28 April. The patriotic song was probably a musical adaptation of the Eliza Cook poem "An Englishman." Cook was a British poet who lived from 1818 to 1889. See entry for "Cook, Eliza," in Dictionary of National Biography, supplement, vol. 2 (London: Smith, Elder, 1901), 53–54.

461 See discussion of St. George's Society at page 65.

462 See 1859 diary, entries for 29 January and 8 April.

463 See 1859 diary, entries for 4 March and 19, 28 April.

464 Though "race" is now considered to be a social construct, I choose to use this term (rather than "ethnicity") because its socially constructed meanings are central to my analysis. See Hall, *Civilising.* On some aspects of "race" in Canadian history, see J.W. St. G. Walker, *"Race," Rights, and the Law in the Supreme Court of Canada: Historical Case Studies* (Waterloo: Wilfrid Laurier University Press, 1997); J.W. St. G. Walker, *The Black Loyalists: The Search for a Promised Land in Nova Scotia and Sierra Leone, 1783–1870* (Toronto: University of Toronto Press, 1992).

465 Marks, *Revivals,* 65.

466 See 1859 diary, entry for 1 May.

467 Hall, *Civilising,* 401, 424–25, 436–37.

468 Hall, *Civilising,* 402, 424–25, 430, 437.

469 Hall, *Civilising,* 429–30, 439.

470 Hall, *Civilising,* 429. See discussion of Fenian Raids in "A Canadian's Story" at page 13.

471 Prentice, *School Promoters,* 77.

472 Russell, *Attitudes,* 191; Holman, *Duty,* 17, 159.

473 See 1859 diary, entry for 28 April.

474 John White, *Sketches from America* (London: S. Low, Son, & Marston, 1870), cited in Holman, *Duty,* 159.

475 See Wilson Benson's immigrant experience as described by Katz in *People of Hamilton,* 99, 109.

476 See 1859 diary, entry for 13 May.

477 See discussion of Mills and Ghose's work on women as spectators of empire at page 69.

478 See Conrad, Laidlaw, and Smyth, *No Place Like Home*; Carter, *Small Details*; K. Carter, *Diaries in English by Women in Canada, 1753-1995: An Annotated Bibliography* (Ottawa: Canadian Research Institute for the Advancement of Women, 1997).

479 Huff, *British Women's Diaries*, xiii-xv.

480 See 1859 diary, entry for 6 January. She seems to have made and backdated her short entries for 1, 3, 4, 5 January on this day.

481 For a discussion of entry formats, see Huff, *British Women's Diaries*, xv-xvi.

482 For a discussion of entry formats, see Huff, *British Women's Diaries*, xv-xvi.

483 Huff, *British Women's Diaries*, xiii-xv.

484 Culley, *A Day at a Time*, 15-17. See also Fothergill, *Private Chronicles*, 4-5.

Notes to Diary of Mary Armstrong 1859

1 The spelling of this word is unclear.

2 Philip Armstrong (1808-1879), Mary's husband.

3 i.e., Primitive Methodists.

4 Samuel Wickson (1828-1910), Mary's brother.

5 Thomas Armstrong (1838-1929), Mary and Philip's son.

6 John Wickson (1817-1900), Mary's brother.

7 Sarah (Wickson) Carruthers (1824-1918), Mary's sister. She married a Mr. Carruthers of Toronto. See entry for 24 May. She would later marry Norman Hamilton in 1865.

8 Arthur Wickson (1825-1913), Mary's brother.

9 James Wickson (1794?-1869) and Jane (Tuesman) Wickson (1789?-1875), Mary's parents.

10 It is uncertain who these people are. There are twenty-seven people named Ross in the 1856 directory, and nobody named Hausman. However, there is a Francis Hauman in the 1859 directory, a comb maker who lived on Sydenham Street in Yorkville. As well, in 1865 a carpenter named James Ross lived on New Kent Road in Yorkville. He seems to have died before 1868, as the directory for that year lists a Mrs. Ross, widow, at the same address. See CTA: James Ross entry, Village of Yorkville Assessment Roll, 1865, p. 20, line 349, Series 746, Files 2 and 3; *1856 Directory*, 241; *1859-60 Directory*, 91; *1868-69 Directory A*, 382.

11 John Rusby Wickson (1838-1916) and Emma Wickson (1841-1896), children of John Wickson and Eliza (Chilver) Wickson (1818-1890). Rusby was a butcher at the St. Lawrence Market. See the section on occupation and trade in "A Diarist's World" at pages 50-55.

12 Arthur Wickson and his wife, Mary Ann (Thomas) Wickson.

13 It may be that Miss Robinson is the daughter of Isaac Robinson, who is mentioned later in the 1859 diary (see notes 26 and 110). There was also a Rev. J.B. Robinson on the committee of the Canadian Congregational Theological Institute in 1857-58 with Arthur Wickson. See Hodgins, *Canada Educational Directory and Calendar for 1857-58*, 90. "R. Robinson" was listed as second vice-president of the Yorkville Temperance Society in 1859. See *1859-60 Directory*, 281. Miss Givens may be the daughter of Dr. H.H. Givens, living at "Pine Grove, near north road, Givens St.," as listed in *1856 Directory*, 147.

14 Mary Ann Pallett (1848?-?), daughter of Robert Pallett and Anne (Armstrong) Pallett (1830?-1855). Mary Ann is Mary Armstrong's step-granddaughter.

15 The omnibus was a horse-drawn bus that ran between St. James' Cathedral and the Yorkville post office every fifteen minutes.

16 i.e., 1858.

17 i.e., 1857.

18 Probably Walter MacKenzie, a barrister living in Yorkville. See *1856 Directory,* 189.

19 A farm hand.

20 Philip Armstrong, Mary's husband. Mary refers to Philip as "Mr. Armstrong," "Pa," or "Papa"; she refers to her father as "Father." See discussion of Mary and Philip's marital relationship in "A Diarist's World" at page 11.

21 There is a sale on 5 May.

22 These lessons were probably in Latin or Greek, which Thomas would have required for medicine. James Wickson, Mary's father, was a butcher by trade but also had some education. See discussion of Thomas's relationship with his grandfather in "A Diarist's World" at pages 29 and 51-52.

23 Thomas attended the Toronto School of Medicine from 1859 to 1862. His instructor was William Thomas Aikins, also a senator of the University of Toronto, who is mentioned a number of times in this diary. One of Aikins' account ledgers from 1862 lists "amounts due" and a number of individuals in alphabetical order, presumably students. One Armstrong owing five dollars is crossed off. This may be Thomas Armstrong, though the address is listed as 105 Sayer Street. At any rate, a publication of the School of Medicine lists "T. Armstrong" of Yorkville as a student for the 1861-62 session. See University of Toronto Archives: *Annual Announcement,* 67, P1978-0070.(03); University of Toronto, Thomas Fisher Rare Book Library: account ledger for 1862, W.T. Aikins Papers, Academy of Medicine Collection, Box 3 (miscellaneous).

24 Mr. Sugden frequently ran an advertisement in the *Globe* offering vocal instruction. See *Globe,* 10 January 1859 and 4 May 1859.

25 See comment on Yorkville Church in "A Diarist's World" at page 56.

26 Probably Isaac Robinson mentioned above in note 13 and below in note 110.

27 This is another piece of property owned by Philip. It is uncertain where it is located; perhaps immediately south of what is now Mount Pleasant Cemetery, between Yonge Street and Mount Pleasant Road. See AO: *Illustrated Historical Atlas of the County of York,* 19, atlas 79.

28 Perhaps a neighbour or shopkeeper.

29 Reference to this meeting does not appear in the *Globe*; however, see below, note 34.

30 "Daguerreotype" is a type of photograph invented in 1839 by Louis Daguerre.

31 This was the coldest day in Toronto history, the mercury registering -26.5°F (-33°C). See M. Filey, *A Toronto Almanac* (Toronto: Mike Filey, 1984).

32 This was a meeting of the Wesleyan Methodist Missionary Society, Canada Conference. The Reverend Richard Jones was chairman of the Toronto District. On 5 January announcements were made of the anniversary meetings of the various branch societies. The Adelaide Street Church branch met on Monday, 10 January, at 7 p.m. Interestingly, the Yorkville Church branch met on Wednesday, 12 January, and Thomas and Philip seem not to have attended this gathering, though James Wickson did (see below at note 36). A newspaper article written two days after the meeting read: "The first of the Missionary Meetings for this city was held in the Adelaide St Church on Monday evening. Jas. Howard, esq., occupied the chair. The extreme cold somewhat diminished the attendance; but the meeting was the right kind; highly interesting and profitable." See the advertisement in the *Christian Guardian,* 5 January 1859, and the article about the meeting under "City Items" in the *Christian Guardian,* 12 January 1859, 6. See also discussion of the missionary society in "A Diarist's World" at page 63.

33 William Orme Wickson (1830-1906), Mary's brother. See "A Diarist's World" above, note 320; see below, note 125.

34 The election of school trustees is announced in the *Globe,* 6 January 1859, 2, and 11 January 1859, 2. A summary of the results of the election is made in the *Globe,* 13 January 1859, 2.

35 i.e., at the Yorkville Church.

36 See above, note 32.

37 Jane Wickson, Mary's mother.

38 Probably Dr. J.H. Richardson of the Toronto School of Medicine, who is also mentioned as one of James Langstaff's professional associates in Duffin. *Langstaff,* 265. See also the faculty list in University of Toronto Archives: *Annual Announcement,* 67, P1978-0070.(03).

39 Anne Mary was probably the first wife of Mary's brother Arthur Wickson.

40 Perhaps this is the Dr. W.J. Scott mentioned in Godfrey, *Medicine for Ontario,* 30.

41 Edward Taylor, husband of Hannah Wickson, James Wickson's sister. Hannah and Edward Taylor were married in Surrey, England, in 1821 and had at least six children. See AAFP: Wickson folder.

42 It is uncertain who this is; perhaps a family friend.

43 This entry is illustrative of Professor Jacalyn Duffin's point that in the nineteenth century "illness was a social occasion." See Duffin, *Langstaff,* 37–40.

44 Mary Ann (Thomas) Wickson, Arthur Wickson's second (and present) wife.

45 William Orme Wickson (see notes 33 and 125) and George Guest Wickson (1821–1905), Mary's brothers.

46 James Wickson (1816–?) and Jane Wickson (1823–1903), Mary's brother and sister.

47 No advertisement for this lecture could be found in the *Globe.* It was probably held at the Temperance Hall on the north side of Adelaide Street between Bay and Yonge Streets. Daniel Wilson was professor of English and History at University College, University of Toronto, where Arthur Wickson was classical tutor and registrar from 1856 to 1863. See Wallace, "U.C.'s First Registrar," 224. For Temperance Hall location, see AO: *Illustrated Historical Atlas of the County of York,* 10–11, atlas 79. For information on Wilson, see Bissell, *University College,* 28, 38–39, 42–50.

48 William Pallett (1851?–?), brother of Mary Ann Pallett, William and Mary Ann are the children of Robert and Anne (Armstrong) Pallett.

49 Merino sheep yield long, fine wool, which can be combined with cotton to make a soft material like cashmere, or which can be made into a fine woollen yarn. Mary is probably preparing to knit a garment out of this material.

50 A two-wheeled one-horse carriage.

51 It is uncertain where this property is.

52 A light sleigh.

53 No advertisement for this lecture could be found in the *Globe.* Henry Holmes Croft was a professor of chemistry at University College at the University of Toronto. The Croft Chapter House there was named after him. Croft was also a faculty member of the Toronto School of Medicine and second vice-president of the Toronto Horticultural Society in 1859. See Bissell, *University College,* 5, 35, 40–41; E.C. Guillet, "Varsity's First Chemistry Professor," in his weekly column, "Old Times in Ontario," *Toronto Daily Star,* 31 March 1960, 30. See the article on horticultural society in the *Globe,* 24 February 1859, 3. See also the faculty list in University of Toronto Archives: *Annual Announcement,* 67, P1978-0070.(03).

54 Wife of the Honourable Peter Boyle de Blaquière, member of the legislative council (upper house) of the Province of Canada. All members were permitted to use the style "Honourable." The lower house was the legislative assembly.

55 Rev. Edward Ebbs, the husband of Jane Wickson, Mary's sister.

56 A farm hand.

57 Wife of Edward Hooper. The Hoopers were the Armstrongs' neighbours immediately to the north. Edward Hooper built Farnham Lodge in 1844. See Martyn, *Aristocratic Toronto,* 104–109.

58 The Provincial Lunatic Asylum was located at 999 Queen Street and was opened in the early 1850s. In 1853 the decision was made by the board of trustees to close the

Toronto General Hospital on King Street and build a new one, which was opened in 1856. It was located in the east end on a block bounded by Gerrard, Spruce, Sumach, and Pine Streets. See Godfrey, *Medicine*, 182; AO: *Illustrated Historical Atlas of the County of York*, 10–11, atlas 79; *Plan of the City of Toronto* (Toronto: James Bain, 1858?), C-295-1-163-0-27; W. Cosbie, *The Toronto General Hospital, 1819–1965* (Toronto: Macmillan, 1975), 63–67.

59   Perhaps this was the lecture given by Mr. McLachlan, which was announced a day in advance in the *Globe*, 1 February 1859, 2.

60   See discussion of the St. George's Society in "A Diarist's World" at page 65. Mr. Carter was the conductor for concerts put on by the St. George's Society. He is also listed in the 1859 directory as a music professor, living on College Street in Yorkville. See advertisement, "St. George for Merry England!" in the *Globe*, 23 February 1859, 3. See also *1859–60 Directory*, 239; St. George's Society of Toronto, *Report of the committee for 1867*.

61   A cow.

62   Mary probably used the symbol ÷ to stand for shillings, which is normally rendered /–.

63   The New York (or simply "York") currency standard converted the Spanish dollar into 8s. Since there were 20s to £1, and £1 at the New York Standard was equal to $2.50, then a "York Shilling" was equal to 12.5¢. A wide variety of coins circulated in the colony; local banks had been issuing their own notes since 1830, and official Canadian coins were first issued in 1858. A decimal system of money was adopted in 1857, but the use of the imperial system persisted for many years. See McCalla, *Planting the Province*, 245–46. See also F.H. Armstrong, *A City in the Making: Progress, People, and Perils in Victorian Toronto* (Toronto: Dundurn Press, 1988), 11.

64   This lecture was given by Dr. John Collett of New York at the Temperance Hall. He gave a series of lectures on anatomy, physiology, and health from 4 to 11 February. See advertisements in the *Globe*, 2 February 1859, 3, and 8 February 1859, 3, which give the subject of that night's lecture: "Heart and lungs, circulation of the blood, nature and properties of air, causes of bronchitis, consumption, etc." His lectures cost twenty-five cents admission, or a reduced rate of one dollar for the whole series of lectures.

65   It is uncertain who these ladies are. No Stonehouses are listed in the 1856 directory, and there are four Charltons. However, in the 1859 directory there is an Isaac Stonehouse living at 135 Brock Street. See *1856 Directory*, 119; *1859–60 Directory*, 185.

66   A hired "help" girl.

67   Dr. John Rolph founded the Toronto School of Medicine in 1843. It was incorporated in 1851, and in 1854 it became the medical department of the University of Victoria College, then based in Cobourg, Ontario. In 1856 Dr. W.T. Aikins led a group of rebellious faculty from Victoria University to re-establish the Toronto school, and Aikins adopted the name "Toronto School of Medicine" for his Richmond Street school. See Cosbie, *Toronto General Hospital*, 49–50.

68   Sarah (Wickson) Carruthers. She was perhaps in England to study art at this time. She would compete as an artist upon her return to Canada. See "A Paris Artist," *Brant Review*, 8 March 1883, 1. I am grateful to Marg Deans of the Paris Museum and Historical Society for reference to this article.

69   Liddy, the hired "help" girl.

70   This is the Reverend H.J. Grasett, M.A., Rector of St. James' Cathedral. He was also a member of the Board of Trustees incorporated in 1847 for the Toronto General Hospital. See GAFP: marriage certificate of Robert Pallett and Anne Armstrong, 1848; Cosbie, *Toronto General Hospital*, 51–52. Grassett is also mentioned in several marriage notices as the performing minister in Wilson, *Ontario Register*, 185, 195–96, 214.

71   No record of Anne (Armstrong) Pallett's death can be located. This reference would imply that she died in the summer of 1855.

72 The Yorkville Church moved in 1854 to Bloor Street and Gwynne Avenue and changed its name to the Yorkville Wesleyan Methodist Church. Mary is referring to the first anniversary of the new church. See UCCA: St. Andrew's United Church (Toronto, ON) fonds, fonds no. 2505, fonds level description (administrative history). See discussion of church in "A Diarist's World" at page 56.

73 It is uncertain who Mr. Walker is, though he is probably a neighbour. The 1856 directory lists twenty-one Walkers. See *1856 Directory*, 237.

74 Again, it is uncertain who this individual is. Probably she is a neighbour, perhaps related to Dr. Wilson, who gave some of the evening lectures that Mary refers to. However, the 1856 directory lists 51 Wilsons. See *1856 Directory*, 242–44.

75 Philip's first wife (and Anne's mother) was Mary (Calvert) Armstrong, who died in 1836. See comment on Philip's first wife in "A Canadian's Story" at page 6.

76 Mary Ann was about age seven in 1855. She was recorded as aged four in the 1851 census (actually taken in 1852). See LAC: Robert Pallett household, 1851 Census, York Twp. (Part 1), York Co., Canada West, enumeration district no. 1, p. 9, line 47, LAC microfilm C-11760.

77 Probably the Dr. S.J. Stratford mentioned in Duffin, *Langstaff*, 28.

78 William Pallett, about age four in 1855. He was recorded as aged one in the 1851 census (actually taken in 1852). See LAC: Robert Pallett household, 1851 Census, York Twp. (Part 1), York Co., Canada West, enumeration district no. 1, p. 9, line 47, LAC microfilm C-11760.

79 George Guest Wickson, Mary's brother. However, it is uncertain who Biddy is; perhaps "Biddy" is his daughter Eliza Jane (1850–?) or a nickname for his wife, Catherine Ray.

80 Philip was probably singing at the St. George's Society.

81 This lecture was the last given by Dr. John Collett at the Temperance Hall in his series of lectures on anatomy, physiology, and health from 4 to 11 February. The lecture of 4 February was followed by an "extra lecture, to ladies exclusively," and at 8 p.m. on 11 February he gave a lecture "to gentlemen exclusively." See advertisement in the *Globe*, 2 February 1859, 3.

82 It is uncertain who Mr. McCullum is. The 1856 directory lists one McCullen, two McCallams, and two McCallums, but no McCullums. See *1856 Directory*, 190–91.

83 The Provincial Lunatic Asylum was located at 999 Queen Street. See above, note 58.

84 See discussion of the seat of government in "A Canadian's Story" at page 11.

85 The wife of Frederick Widder, a commissioner of the Canada Company. See discussion of gentry emulation in "A Diarist's World" at page 44. See also entry for 21 February below and note 99.

86 Dr. W.T. Aikins, head of the Toronto School of Medicine. See above at notes 23 and 67.

87 Henry Holmes Croft. See above at note 53.

88 i.e., 1819.

89 i.e., 1821.

90 This was in the Camberwell/Walworth area of Surrey, England.

91 A woman's coat of the Regency period; cf. stole, redingote.

92 Local schools in Camberwell, but not the school of the three sisters, are discussed in Dyos, *Victorian Suburb*, 163–68.

93 Probably off of Rosemary Road, between Old Kent Road and Camberwell Road in north Camberwell. The Rosemary Branch Tavern was located in the area, and its landlord, James Smith, owned nineteen acres of land that had belonged to the Shard estate and were gradually developed over the course of the century. See Dyos, *Victorian Suburb*, 104–105 and street plan in back cover slot.

94 A type of vine.

95 A hired "help" girl.

96 It is uncertain who Holmes is; perhaps he is a cabman. The 1856 directory lists eight people named Holmes. See *1856 Directory*, 159.

97 i.e., Morpheus, god of sleep and dreams.

98 See above note 32, and discussion of missionary societies in "A Diarist's World" at page 63.

99 See above at note 85. The house was located on the north side of Front Street, near Brock Avenue.

100 Unclear spelling. This could be "Duemih," "Daenish," "Danish," or perhaps "Flemish."

101 There are no Siddons or Seddons listed in the 1856 directory. In the 1859 directory there is a Silvanus Sedon, a pensioner, who lived at 487 Richmond Street West. See *1856 Directory; 1859–60 Directory*, 173.

102 Unclear spelling. This could be "Baygam" or "Baggour"; it is uncertain who this couple is.

103 Probably Paul Giovanni Wickson (1858–1922). A notable Canadian painter, he grew up in Toronto and moved to England with his father about 1872. There he studied art, and he returned to Canada about 1884 and settled in Paris, Ontario, with his wife, Elizabeth Hamilton, the stepdaughter of his aunt Sarah. Sarah Wickson's second husband was the wealthy businessman Norman Hamilton (1806–1874), who in 1844 built his home, "Hillside," in Paris; it still stands and is now known as "Hamilton Place." He was twice a widower, and Sarah was stepmother to his daughter, Elizabeth. Paul specialized in painting horses and farm animals, though he also did a number of portraits. Some of his paintings hang in the Paris branch of the County of Brant Library; some are privately owned by descendants of his relatives; some are held at the University of Toronto; and one in particular, *The Country Doctor*, is owned by the Toronto Academy of Medicine. A copy of this painting appears on the cover of Duffin's book *Langstaff*. This painting may be a portrait of Paul's cousin, Dr. Thomas Armstrong. I am grateful to Marg Deans of the Paris Museum and Historical Society for much of this information. See also Duffin, *Langstaff*; E.C. Guillet, "Artist Enriches Historical Scene" in his weekly column, "Old Times in Ontario," *Toronto Daily Star*, 15 October 1960, 13.

104 This lecture was not advertised in the *Globe*. Professor Meredith was likely Edward A. Meredith, who lived on the east side of Yonge Street in Rosedale. See *1856 Directory*, 180.

105 Probably the University of Trinity College, which had a medical school. In 1850 King's College closed, and the secularized University of Toronto took its place. Bishop Strachan founded religious Trinity, which was opened in 1851, and many of the old King's College faculty, supporters, and students defected from the University of Toronto to Strachan's new university. In 1853 the University Act created University College as the instructional part of the University of Toronto. Thomas's uncle, the Reverend Arthur Wickson, was appointed in 1856 as a classics tutor and registrar at University College. See Bissell, *University College*, 3–9. See discussion of Arthur's career in "A Diarist's World" at page 51.

106 John O'Leary and James Fleming were executed at the same time on 4 March 1859 for separate knifepoint killings. A large number of women witnessed the execution at the old jail. The *Globe* published a detailed account of the prisoners' last hours, their confessions, and their executions on 5 March. The writer noted: "The most noticeable fact [about the crowd outside the jail], perhaps, was the large number of females present. Old women with grey hairs, mothers with babies in their arms, young women and girls, all were represented." It seems that other women in the city echoed Mary's concern for the doomed boys. See "The Wellington-Street and Georgina Murders," *Globe*, 5 March 1859, 2. See also Kyte, *Old Toronto*, 188; discussion of current events in "A Diarist's World" at pages 21–22.

107 Robley Dunglison (1798–1869), *Medical Lexicon. A new dictionary of medical science containing a concise account of the various subjects and terms* (Philadelphia: Lea & Blanchard, 1839). Thomas's instructor, W.T. Aikins, studied under Dunglison in Philadelphia from 1849 to 1850. See Duffin, *Langstaff*, 24.

108 This Mr. Sanderson is likely Rev. R.S.G.R. Sanderson of the Wesleyan Methodist Book Room on the north side of King Street East. His residence was on Bloor Street, in Yorkville. See *1856 Directory*, 216.

109 It is uncertain where Mary Ann Pallett attended school.

110 Probably Isaac Robinson; cf. Isaac Robinson in Errington, *Wives and Mothers*, appendix 2, 203.

111 Joseph Webb was a pastry cook at 14 Agnes Street; he is listed in the *1859* directory. In the 1856 directory there is a Thomas Webb listed as a baker and confectioner on Yonge Street. See *1859 Directory; 1856 Directory*, 239.

112 i.e., Rev. Arthur Wickson and his wife, Mary Ann (Thomas) Wickson.

113 There is no mention of a lecture for this evening in the *Globe*.

114 i.e., Mary Ann Pallett.

115 Jane (Wickson) Ebbs, Mary's sister.

116 Overshoes.

117 i.e., Paul Giovanni Wickson.

118 It is uncertain who this Mr. Mason is. Eight Masons appear in the 1856 directory. See *1856 Directory*, 179.

119 i.e., Paris, Canada West.

120 There is no mention of a lecture for this evening in the *Globe*. Mr. Hodgens is likely J. George Hodgins, M.A., who was deputy superintendent of education for Upper Canada and lived on Pembroke Street. See *1859–60 Directory*, 96.

121 A frustratingly ambiguous reference to Philip's family.

122 Philip was very involved with agricultural and horticultural societies. See below, note 124, and discussion of agricultural societies in the "A Diarist's World" at page 66–67.

123 This lecture was apparently given by Peter Sinclair, a travelling temperance lecturer from Edinburgh. An advertisement appearing in the *Globe* on 5 April announced his lecture that evening at Temperance Hall on Temperance Street, in connection with the Temperance Reformation Society. The Honourable Robert Spence chaired the lecture, and admission was 12.5¢. The following day a brief article appeared in the *Globe* describing the content of the lecture and remarking that there had been "a good attendance." Sinclair was doing a series of lectures in Toronto during the month of April. See advertisement in the *Globe*, 5 April 1859, 3; "Mr. Peter Sinclair's Lecture," *Globe*, 6 April 1859, 2. See also discussion of temperance reform in "A Diarist's World" at pages 64–65.

124 See discussion of agricultural societies in "A Diarist's World" at pages 66–67. Philip, as president of the County of York Agricultural Society, entered an advertisement in the *Globe* on 31 March that announced a ploughing match of the "United Townships Agricultural Society" to be held on 6 April at "Mr. Snyder's farm, Yonge St [at Eglinton Avenue]." On 7 April an article appeared in the *Globe* describing the previous day's match: "The … ploughing match took place yesterday … in the presence of a large and respectable company. The Hon. G.W. Allan, MLC, Mr. Howland, MPP, and Major Campbell, MPP, were on the ground. Nearly twenty ploughs were entered for the competition ....The Hon. Mr. Allan promised a silver cup, to be competed for at the next match. Later in the day, a numerous company sat down to a substantial dinner at Prospect House, the President of the Society, Mr. Armstrong, in the chair…. Amongst other suggestions which he made was one in favour of a monthly meeting of the Society for discussion." See Philip Armstrong's advertisement in the *Globe*, 31 March 1859, 3, and "York Ploughing Match," *Globe*, 7 April 1859, 2.

125 It is uncertain where William Orme Wickson is in 1859; he may be in England or in New York State. See "A Diarist's World" above, note 320.

126 It is uncertain where the library is; perhaps in the Town Hall.

127 This is Margaret Bowes Taylor, widow of Samuel E. Taylor, merchant, of 28 Richmond Street. See her death notice in the *Christian Guardian*, 30 March 1859, 51. She died on 28 March. On 27 April the Wesleyan minister, Rev. Jonathan Scott, put a notice in the *Christian Guardian* asking for relatives, ministers, and friends of Mrs. Taylor to send him "correct copies" of her letters, prose or poetry, and any "authentic facts" so that he might compile them into "an intended biographical volume," which she had asked him to prepare. See "The Late Mrs. Margaret Taylor of Toronto," *Christian Guardian*, 27 April 1859, 67.

128 Another lecture in Sinclair's series; see above at note 123. The lecture began at 3 p.m., and Sinclair attended the Temperance meeting at the Temperance Hall on Temperance Street at 7 p.m. See advertisement in the *Globe*, 12 April 1859, 3.

129 See above at note 118.

130 A "melodeon" is a small reed organ.

131 This would date her departure for England at around August 1858.

132 It is uncertain who Mr. Buckam is; however, I am grateful to Marg Deans of the Paris Museum and Historical Society for the suggestion that this might in fact be David Buchan, a prominent Baptist and sometime bursar of the University of Toronto.

133 Evidently this was Malcolm Cameron, the businessman, politician, and temperance advocate. See "Malcolm Cameron," *Dictionary of Canadian Biography*, vol. 10 (Toronto: University of Toronto Press, 1966), 124. Cameron chaired some of Sinclair's lectures. See advertisement in the *Globe*, 5 April 1859, 3.

134 In a March newspaper article Colonel Playfair is mentioned as lecturing on temperance in a meeting of the Cadets of Temperance at the Temperance Hall on Brock Street. The 1858–59 directory indicates that the Coldstream Section Cadets of Temperance met at the Brock Street Hall. The Cadets of Temperance and Daughters of Temperance were groups for children and women that were affiliated with the chief group, the Sons of Temperance. In the article on Playfair, allusion is made to the obligations of his "civil and military career," and that as "parliamentary duties [called] him to the house," he resigned as chairman of the group. See "The Festival of the Cadets of Temperance," *Globe*, 16 March 1859, 3. See also *1859–60 Directory*, 281; Noel, *Canada Dry*, 144–45.

135 It appears that Mr. Briscoe was a vocalist in the St. George's Society. His name appears in the advertisement for the 1 March concert put on by the society. See the *Globe*, 23 February 1859, 3. William Briscoe is listed in the 1859 directory as a carriage builder living at 125 Queen Street West. See *1859–60 Directory*, 31.

136 A poisonous Eurasian ornamental shrub.

137 Hybrid garden primroses.

138 St. James' Cathedral at King Street and Church Street, built between 1849 and 1853. See P. McHugh, *Toronto Architecture: A City Guide*, 2nd ed. (Toronto: McClelland & Stewart, 1989).

139 i.e., Mr. Sugden.

140 Like William Briscoe above (see note 135), Mr. Baxter and Miss Kemp were vocalists in the St. George's Society. Their names appear in the ad for the 1 March concert put on by the society. See the *Globe*, 23 February 1859, 3.

141 Alfred George Wickson and Agnes Rebecca Wickson, born 22 November 1858. The infants would both die in August 1859. See AAFP: Wickson folder.

142 Greenwich is to the east of Walworth and Camberwell in Surrey, England, and Old Kent Road is a main street in the area.

143 Rev. T.S. Ellerby was the pastor of the First Congregational Church on John Street. In January he gave lectures on Christianity at the Zion Chapel at Adelaide and Bay

Streets. See his advertisement in the *Globe*, 8 January 1859, 3. See also Robertson, *Landmarks of Toronto*, vol. 4, 474.

144 Mrs. Lillie was probably the wife of Reverend Dr. Adam Lillie, who lived on Carlton Street in 1859. Rev. Lillie was the Congregational minister who had married Philip and Mary in August 1837. He was also a senator of the University of Toronto. See entry for Lillie in *1859–60 Directory*, 116. See also University of Toronto Archives: *Annual Announcement*, 67, P1978-0070.(03), 11.

145 This party was advertised in the *Globe* as "The complimentary soiree of the Yorkville Debating and Mutual Improvement Society to the gentlemen who delivered the late course of Lectures in connexion with the society." The party was held at the "New School House, Yorkville" at 7 p.m., and tickets went for fifty cents each according to the advertisement placed by George Severn, the secretary of the society. See the *Globe*, 27 April 1859, 33. Mary makes no indication as to which of her relatives that attended the party were involved with the society.

146 This is perhaps F.T. Roche, the chief clerk in charge of the Patent Branch, Union Lands Department, listed in the 1859 directory. See *1859–60 Directory*, 166.

147 See advertisement for a temperance lecture given by the Reverend J.C. Ash in the *Globe*, 9 March 1859, 2.

148 Daughter of John and Eliza Wickson.

149 It is uncertain who Mr. Wadsworth is.

150 Mary Ann (Thomas) Wickson, Arthur's wife.

151 This was the dedication ceremony for Cooper's Church, Davenport Station. Services began at 10 a.m. and the last one of the day began at 6:30 p.m. The church structure was described as "unique and simply expressive," the walls "of stone and brick," with "a basement for Sabbath School and other purposes … nine feet high." George Cooper, Esq., and his wife, Mrs. Cooper, of Dundas Street, were the primary benefactors of the new church. "Crowds of worshippers covered the road leading to the church" and the building was filled to capacity. "At least two hundred visitors were entertained during the day" under the "hospitable roof of Davenport House." See the advertisement in the *Christian Guardian*, 20 April 1859, 63, and the article recounting the services in the same, 11 May 1859, 74.

152 William Jay, *Morning and Evening Exercises* (London: Bartlett, 1845). This is a collection of devotional exercises written by William Jay (1769–1853), an Independent/Congregationalist divine who spent most of his adult life and ministry in Bath, England.

153 See announcements in the *Globe*, 27 April 1859 and 4 May 1859.

154 Walter Rose. The brick house referred to is Rose Hill, built in 1836. This house gave its name to the area, and Philip and Mary advertised their property in the *Globe* as being located on Rose Hill, Yonge Street. The house was built by the tanner Jesse Ketchum, who gave the property and new house to his daughter Anna. In 1836 Anna Ketchum married Walter Rose, a private banker. When Walter Rose died, the property was sold to Joseph Jackes. See Martyn, *Aristocratic Toronto*, 65–66.

155 The 1859 directory has several Bains, but none listed as a Major. See *1859–60 Directory*.

156 Thomas was born in 1838. In 1859 Arthur and Mary Ann lived at 393 Yonge Street. See *1859–60 Directory*, 204.

157 Anne (Armstrong) Pallett.

158 Mary Ann (Thomas) Wickson, wife of Arthur Wickson.

159 Paul Giovanni Wickson.

160 The spelling is unclear here.

161 Forest Hill was the name John Wickson gave to his summer residence on the north side of Eglinton Avenue at Bathurst Street. In 1923, when Forest Hill was incorporated into a separate municipality within York Township, the name of Wickson's residence

was chosen for the Village. See French, *Most Unlikely Village,* 5. See also Frayne, "Forest Hill," 7.

162 It is unclear who Lilly is; perhaps Mary Ann Pallett or a pet.

163 There are two Captain Dicks in the 1859 directory: James, living at 325 James Street, and Thomas, living at 399 Queen Street West. See *1859-60 Directory,* 61.

164 i.e., Sunday school and Mr. Armstrong. "SS" could also designate "Sabbath school" or "Sunday service."

165 Lyons, New York State.

166 i.e., Niagara Falls.

167 The Yonge Street Agricultural Society, of which George P. Dickson was president, held their annual spring show on Victoria Day. Their announcement in the *York Herald* on 8 April 1859, page 2, remarked: "There is a faint probability that the local militia may be called out to muster on that day, if so, of course the public will receive timely notice, should the society think fit to alter the day. We sincerely hope such an useless Government requirement as the 'Muster' will not interfere." Interestingly, the No. 2 Troop of the York Volunteer Cavalry was ordered to muster in Yorkville at 10 a.m. on 24 May, "to join in celebrating Her Majesty's Birthday," as directed by the Militia General Order of 5 May. Apparently, this order did not call up enough men to warrant cancelling the society's show, as it went on, the prizes for horses, cattle, swine, fowls, dairy produce, and farming implements being published in the *York Herald* on 27 May 1859, page 2. See also *York Herald* 20 May 1859, 2.

168 Sarah (Wickson) Carruthers, in England at this time.

169 A two-wheeled one-horse carriage.

170 Sugden was probably giving a vocal performance at the hall at the St. Lawrence Market.

171 Perhaps this is Mr. Baxter, a vocalist in the St. George's Society mentioned above in note 140.

Notes to Diary of Mary Armstrong 1869

1 i.e., the storage containers are filled with winter stores. Some excerpts from the 1869 diary were published in L. Heller, "Pioneer had farm at Yonge and St. Clair," *Toronto Star,* 16 June 1982, A30.

2 In the *Globe* on 3 February 1869, page 1, right column, under "City News," an item appears that reads: "Tea Meeting—A social gathering of this description took place last evening, at Queen St Wesleyan Methodist Church, the proceeds being for the benefit of the Trust Fund of the Church." Reverend Mr. Hunter was in the chair, and Alderman Baxter (perhaps the same Baxter mentioned in the 1859 diary in connection with the St. George's Society) led the choir. This may be the chapel fund that Mary is referring to.

3 A dry goods supplier; see entry for January 25.

4 Thomas Armstrong graduated from the Toronto School of Medicine in 1862, and in 1863 he married Fidelia Jane Maughan (1845-1928), daughter of Sophia Riley (1823-1892) and Nicholas Maughan (c.1822-1900). See "A Canadian's Story" at page 10.

5 Probably the Brick Methodist Church in Eglinton.

6 It is uncertain who Miss Watson is.

7 Either Sunday school, Sabbath service, or Sunday service at the Central Methodist Church. See 1859 diary, entry for 22 May and note 164.

8 Thomas and Fidelia lived in Hogg's Hollow (York Mills) at this time. In 1868 Thomas had taken over the practice of retiring doctor George Parsons.

9 Philip Armstrong.

10 Mary's hired "help" girl.

11 An advertisement for Holloway's Ointment appears in the *Globe* on 18 January 1869, page 4.

12 Gibson, Dogson, Shields, and Heward are presumably shopkeepers Mary dealt with on credit.

13 Presumably a store in Toronto.

14 "Meeting," probably for the City of Toronto Electoral Division Society, of which Philip was a director in 1868 and 1869. See *1868–69 Directory B,* 13.

15 Donald and Hall are farm hands.

16 Brougham is a community in Durham region, near Pickering. It was first called Bentley's Corners for a local shopkeeper named Bentley. It was renamed Brougham for Lord Brougham in 1836. Thomas and Fidelia lived there for a time; see below at note 42. See A. Rayburn, *Place Names of Ontario* (Toronto: University of Toronto Press, 1997), 45.

17 Thomas and Fidelia Armstrong's residence in Hogg's Hollow (York Mills, York Township).

18 Thomas and Fidelia's first three children: Philip Maughan Armstrong (1864–1940), Thomas Norman Armstrong (1866–1905), and Albert Eugene Armstrong (1868–1958).

19 Advertisements for Braithwaite's Retrospect appear in the *Globe* on 31 January 1859, page 3, and ten years later on 2 February 1869, page 3.

20 Thomas appears 50 times in the first 1,000 entries in the Mount Pleasant Cemetery burial register of the late 1870s as the attending doctor of the deceased. In 1886 the *Globe* reported that Thomas's income was $1,500. This was in the middle range of the other 30 doctors who appeared on the list, whose salaries varied from $350 to $2,500. Thomas practised medicine until 1907 and lived until 1929, a year after his wife passed away. See AAFP: Armstrong folder; Mount Pleasant Cemetery, Toronto, Ontario: Interment Register no. 1, #1-8315; *Globe* article cited in Godfrey, *Medicine for Ontario,* 141.

21 It is uncertain where this property is. It is mentioned again in the next entry, but nowhere else in this later diary. In the earlier diary it is mentioned on 7 January, 17 February, and 8 March. It was perhaps immediately south of what is now Mount Pleasant Cemetery, between Yonge Street and Mount Pleasant Road. See AO: *Illustrated Historical Atlas of the County of York,* 19, atlas 79.

22 This road is across Yonge Street from the Armstrong residence, Rose Hill. In the 1868–69 directory Joseph A. Simmers is listed as a seedsman living at 47 Cruickshank with his business at 20 West Market Square. In the 1870 directory he is listed as a seed merchant and florist living in Sadowa Villa on Yonge Street in Yorkville. See *1868–69 Directory A,* 334; *1870 Directory,* 121.

23 Philip Maughan Armstrong was born 3 March 1864.

24 In the *Globe* on 6 March 1869, page 1, under "City News," an item appears that reads: "Toronto Electoral Division Society—The directors met at the Agricultural Hall on Thursday evening, and adopted Prize Lists for the Spring and Summer exhibitions, to be held 16 May and 18 July. The Secretary was instructed to communicate with the officers of the Agricultural Societies for the West Riding and the Township of York, and the townships of Etobicoke and Scarborough, inviting them to unite with the City Society for the purpose of a Union Fall Exhibition; and also for the purpose of co-operating in getting up a grand Fall Provincial Ploughing Match; and requesting the societies to appoint delegates to meet with the directors of the City Society." Philip Armstrong was a director of the CTEDS at this time. See discussion of agricultural societies in "A Diarist's World" at pages 66–67.

25 Cooney is a farm hand.

26 Thomas Armstrong.

27 In 1798 Chief Justice John Elmsley built Elmsley House as the first Governor's residence. It burnt down in 1862, and a new Governor's residence was begun in 1866 on Simcoe Street at King Street West. It was finished in 1870 and cost a total of $105,000. See W. Dendy, *Lost Toronto: Images of the City's Past* (Toronto: McClelland & Stewart, 1993), 56–58.

28 Probably the Sunday school from the Brick Methodist Church at Eglinton.

29 This was probably a reception for a visiting speaker advertised in the *Globe* on 10 March 1859, page 2, in a two-day-old advertisement under "Religious Services." It reads: "Temperance Hall—if the Lord will, Mr Henry M. Hooke (of England) will preach in the above hall, tonight (Monday), the 8th instant, at 7:30 pm, and on Thursday and Friday nights, the 11th and 12th instant, in the Town Hall, Yorkville, at 7:30 pm." Philip was probably attending a reception for the speaker the evening before his first lecture in Yorkville.

30 It is unclear where this mill is. It may be at York Mills, as this was near to Thomas's home.

31 Probably Union Station. See Dendy, *Lost Toronto,* 38.

32 This property was to the east of Rose Hill, south of modern St. Clair Avenue, west of modern Inglewood Drive, and east of the ravine. It is mentioned again in this diary on 1, 4, 16 April, and 1 July.

33 James Wickson, Mary's father.

34 Which sister Mary is referring to is unclear.

35 Fidelia was an accomplished vocalist. She sang in Toronto concerts in the 1860s, performing "Gently Falls the Dews" by S. Mercadante at a "Grand Concert" in 1863. In a trio she performed "Eve's Lamentation" by Haydn at a "Music Festival" at Temperance Hall, Clairville, on 8 January 1862. In the flyers and programmes for these concerts she is listed as "Miss Maughan." See AAFP: Maughan folder.

36 The advertisement for this sale appeared in the *Globe* on 27 March 1869, page 3.

37 i.e., bankruptcy sale.

38 David Hume, *History of England* (London: A. Millar, 1754–62).

39 A neighbour to the south at the Hazel Dell property.

40 Presumably a farm hand.

41 No Seagrams can be located in the directories for this time.

42 Thomas and Fidelia first lived near Whitby and Brougham before coming to York Mills around 1867. They were probably visiting friends for this ceremony. See AAFP: Armstrong folder.

43 Allan Gardens, on modern-day Carleton Street at Jarvis Street, opened by the Prince of Wales in 1860. See Bain, "George Allan and the Horticultural Gardens."

44 Mary's birthday is in February and her wedding anniversary in August. This date is close to Philip's birthday (he was baptized on 3 July)—perhaps she is throwing a party for him. If so, it seems strange that she would call it "my party day."

45 James Wickson, Mary's father.

46 Eliza Wickson, wife of John Wickson, Mary's brother.

47 These lists at the end of the diary are not in Mary Armstrong's handwriting. They could be records of prizewinners at agricultural contests judged by Philip Armstrong at some point.

✳

BIBLIOGRAPHY

✳

Manuscript and Printed Sources

Archives of Ontario (AO), Toronto
G.R. Tremaine's Map of the City of Toronto, A-10. 1860.
Plan of the City of Toronto, C-295-1-163-0-27. Toronto: James Bain, 1858?.
Illustrated Historical Atlas of the County of York, atlas 79. Toronto: Miles, 1878.
Series RG 61-64. Toronto Boroughs and York South/Toronto Land Registry Office, Copybooks of Instruments and Deeds, Yorkville and Rosedale deeds. 1799-1868.
Series RG 22-305. York County Surrogate Court estate files.

City of Toronto Archives (CTA), Toronto, Ontario
Series 746, Files 2 and 3 (Village of Yorkville Assessment Rolls, 1865, 1867, 1868).

Cumbria Record Office (CRO), Carlisle, United Kingdom
H. Cunningham, Historical Research Service Report Number CO8/00/235.
Militia records CQ/Mil/1810, Eskdale Ward, Corby Lordship Return.
Militia records CQ/Mil/1813 Eskdale Ward, Corby Lordship Return.
Wetheral Parish Registers, baptisms. 1790–1813, 1813–1837.
Wetheral Parish Registers, burials. 1796–1812, 1813–1834.
Wetheral Churchyard headstone transcripts, 1964, no. 115.

Library and Archives Canada (LAC), Ottawa, Ontario
Canada Census 1851, Canada West.
Canada Census 1861, Canada West.
Federal Census of 1871, Ontario Index, www.archives.ca/02/02010803_e.html.
Federal Census of 1881, Ontario.

Manx National Heritage Library, Douglas, United Kingdom
Braddan Parish Registers, marriages and baptisms. 1787, 1789.

Mount Pleasant Cemetery Records, Toronto, Ontario
Interment Register no. 1.

The National Archives of the United Kingdom (TNA), *London*

Baptism register for Mansion House Chapel (Independent), Camberwell, PRO cat. no. RG 4/4381.

Paris Museum and Historical Society, Paris, Ontario

Mrs. Sarah Carruthers, teacher's certificate (provisional). 1 January 1855.

Mrs. Sarah Carruthers, teacher's certificate (female, first class). 24 September 1855.

United Church of Canada/Victoria University Archives (UCCA), *Toronto, Ontario*

Paris Congregational Church (Paris, ON) fonds, fonds no. 1448.

St. Andrew's United Church (Toronto, ON) fonds, fonds no. 2505.

Yonge Street (South) Methodist Circuit (Toronto, ON) fonds, fonds no. 2528.

University of Toronto, Toronto, Ontario

Thomas Fisher Rare Book Library:

W.T. Aikins Papers, Academy of Medicine Collection, Box 3 (miscellaneous).

University of Toronto Archives:

Annual Announcement of the Toronto School of Medicine, Twenty Seventh Session, October 1, 1869, to April 1, 1870. P1978-0070.(03). Toronto: Globe Printing, 1869.

Andrew Armstrong Family Papers (AAFP), *Toronto, Ontario*

Armstrong Folder:

Armstrong genealogical material.

Maughan Folder:

Flyer for "Music Festival," 1862.

Flyer for "Grand Concert," 1863.

Wickson Folder:

Wickson genealogical material.

M. Deans, Wickson-Hamilton family history file and genealogical table (2003).

Geoffrey Armstrong Family Papers (GAFP), *Toronto, Ontario*

Diary of Mary Armstrong, 1859.

Diary of Mary Armstrong, 1869.

Birth certificate of Mary Wickson, dated 6 July 1825.

Birth certificate of Thomas Armstrong, dated 4 September 1838.

"Chancery Sale of Valuable Freehold Property, Near Toronto, known as the Rose Estate," document dated 22 October 1864.

Declaration of Samuel Wickson under the Canada Evidence Act, 6 March 1908, "In the matter of the marriage of Thomas Armstrong with Fidelia Jane Maughan."

Land indentures (various).

Marriage certificate of Philip Armstrong and Mary Wickson, 1837.

Marriage certificate of Robert Pallett and Anne Armstrong, 1848.

Marriage certificate of Thomas Armstrong and Fidelia Maughan, 1863.

"Plan of the Rose Estate," Dennis and Gossage Provincial Land Surveyors, document dated 18 October 1864.

"York Instrument Number 88196, Memorial of Indenture, Hon. J.C. Morrison to Philip Armstrong," recorded 23 June 1865.

Ruth Wickson Newman Family Papers (WFP), *Parry Sound, Ontario*

Calendar "100th Anniversary of the founding of the business John H. Wickson" (c.1934).

Transcript of indenture between James Wickson, Edward Taylor, and William Maidlow, 21 August 1829.

Periodicals

Brant Review (Paris), 1883, 1884.

Brantford Expositor (Brantford), 1918.

British Colonist (Toronto), 1838.

Canadian Agriculturalist (Toronto), 1860.

Christian Guardian (Toronto), 1859.

Globe (Toronto), 1859, 1863, 1869.

Star Transcript (Paris), 1895.

York Herald (Richmond Hill), 1859.

Other Publications

Armstrong, J., ed. *Rowsell's City of Toronto and County of York Directory for 1850-1*. Toronto: Henry Rowsell, 1850.

Brown, G., ed. *Brown's Toronto City and Home District Directory, 1846-7*. Toronto: George Brown, 1846.

Brown, W.R., ed. *Brown's Toronto General Directory, 1856*. Toronto: Maclear, 1856.

———, ed. *Brown's Toronto General Directory, 1861*. Toronto: W.C. Chewett, 1861.

Butler, S. *The Emigrant's Complete Guide to Canada*. London: N.H. Cotes, 1843.

Caverhill, W.C.F., ed. *Caverhill's Toronto City Directory for 1859-60*. Toronto: W.C.F. Caverhill, 1859.

W.C. Chewett and Co's Toronto City Directory, 1868-9. Toronto: W.C. Chewett, 1868.

Dunglison, Robley (1798-1839). *Medical Lexicon. A new dictionary of medical science containing a concise account of the various subjects and terms*. Philadelphia: Lea & Blanchard, 1839.

The Emigrant's Informant, or A Guide to Upper Canada. London: G. Cowie, 1834.

Hodgins, T., ed. *The Canada Educational Directory and Calendar for 1857-8*. Toronto: Maclear, 1857.

Holden's Triennial Directory for 1805, 1806, 1807. 4th ed. Vol. 2. London: sold by the proprietors, Messrs. Richardsons, H.D. Symonds, printed by W. Glendinning et al., 1807.

Holden's Triennial Directory for 1809, 1810, 1811. 5th ed. Vol. 2. London: sold by the proprietor, printed by J. Davenport et al., 1811.

Hume, David. *History of England*. London: A. Millar, 1754-62.

Hutchinson, T., ed. *Hutchinson's Toronto Directory, 1862-63*. Toronto: Lovell & Gibson, 1862.

Irving, A.S., ed. City of Toronto Illustrated Business Directory for 1865. Toronto, A.S. Irving, 1865.

Irwin, W.H., ed. *Robertson and Cook's Toronto City Directory for 1870*. Toronto: Daily Telegraph Printing House, 1870.

———, ed. *Robertson and Cook's Toronto City Directory for 1871-2*. Toronto: Robertson & Cook, 1871.

Isaacson, S. *A Vindication of the West-India Proprietors*. London: James Fraser, 1832.

Jay, William (1769-1853). *Morning and Evening Exercises*. London: Bartlett, 1845.

Lewis, F., ed. *The Toronto Directory, and Street Guide, for 1843-4*. Toronto: H. & W. Rowsell, 1843.

McEvoy, H., ed. *C.E. Anderson and Co.'s Toronto City Directory for 1868-9*. Toronto: C.E. Anderson, 1868.

Mitchell, J.L., ed. *Mitchell's Toronto Directory for 1864-65*. Toronto: J.L. Mitchell, 1864.

Mitchell and Co.'s General Directory for the City of Toronto and Gazetteer of the Counties of York and Peel for 1866. Toronto: Mitchell, 1866.

1871 Nason's East and West Ridings of the County of York Directory. Toronto: Dudley & Burns, 1871.

Parson W., and W. White, eds. *History, Directory, and Gazeteer of the Counties of Cumberland and Westmorland*. Leeds: W. White, 1829.

Patmore, Coventry. *The Angel in the House*. London: John W. Parker & Son, 1854.

Pigot and Co.'s London and Provincial New Commercial Directory for 1826-7. 3rd ed. London: J. Pigot, 1826.

Pigot and Co.'s National London and Provincial Commercial Directory for 1832-3-4. London: J. Pigot, 1834.

St. George's Society of Toronto, *Report of the committee for 1867 of the St. George's Society of Toronto, instituted for the relief of sick and destitute Englishmen and their descendants*. Toronto: The St. George's Society, 1868.

Sutherland, J., ed. *City of Toronto Directory for 1867-8*. Toronto: W.C. Chewett, 1867.

Toronto Directory for 1873. Toronto: Cherrier, Kirwin, & McGown, 1873.

Toronto Directory for 1876. Toronto: Fisher & Taylor, 1876.

Toronto Directory for 1877. Toronto: Might & Taylor, 1877.

Toronto Directory for 1878. Toronto: Might & Taylor, 1878.

Toronto Directory for 1879. Toronto: Might & Taylor, 1879.

Toronto Horticultural Society. *Annual Report of the Managing Committee of the Toronto Horticultural Society for 1861*. Toronto: Rowsell & Ellis, 1862.

Walton, G., ed. *York Commercial Directory, Street Guide, and Register, 1833-4*. Toronto: T. Dalton, 1833.

———, ed. *City of Toronto and Home District Commercial Directory*. Toronto: T. Dalton & W.J. Coates, 1837.

Secondary Sources

Akenson, D.H. *The Irish in Ontario: A Study in Rural History*. Montreal: McGill-Queen's University Press, 1984.

Anderson, B. *Imagined Communities*. London: Verso, 1983.

Armstrong, F.H. "The rebuilding of Toronto after the great fire of 1849." *OH* 53, no. 4 (1961): 233-50.

———. "The York Riots of March 23, 1832." *OH* 55, no. 2 (1963): 61-72.

————. *A City in the Making: Progress, People, and Perils in Victorian Toronto*. Toronto: Dundurn Press, 1988.

Backhouse, C. *Petticoats and Prejudice: Women and Law in Nineteenth-Century Canada*. Toronto: Women's Press, 1991.

Bain, D. "George Allan and the Horticultural Gardens." *OH* 87, no. 3 (September 1995): 231-51.

Barrett, J.R. *Work and Community in the Jungle: Chicago's Packinghouse Workers, 1894-1922*. Urbana: University of Illinois Press, 1987.

Bissell, C.T. *University College: A Portrait, 1853-1953*. Toronto: University of Toronto Press, 1953.

Blodgett, H. *Centuries of Female Days: English Women's Private Diaries*. London: Rutgers University Press, 1988.

Bradbury, B. "Gender at Work at Home: Family Decisions, the Labour Market, and Girls' Contributions to the Family Economy." In *Canadian Family History: Selected Readings*, edited by B. Bradbury, 177-98. Toronto: Copp Clark Pitman, 1992.

Burgess, J. "Work, Family, and Community: Montreal Leather Craftsmen, 1790-1831." Ph.D. diss., Université du Québec à Montréal, 1986.

————. "The Growth of a Craft Labour Force: Montreal Leather Artisans, 1815-1831." *Canadian Historical Papers* (1988): 48-62.

Burley, D.G. *A Particular Condition in Life: Self-employment and Social Mobility in Mid-Victorian Brantford, Ontario*. Montreal: McGill-Queen's University Press, 1994.

Burstyn, J.N. *Victorian Education and the Ideal of Womanhood*. London: Croom Helm, 1980.

Buss, H. *Mapping Our Selves: Canadian Women's Autobiography*. Montreal: McGill-Queen's University Press, 1993.

Careless, J.M.S. *The Union of the Canadas: The Growth of Canadian Institutions, 1841-1857*. Toronto: McClelland & Stewart, 1967.

Carter, K. "The Cultural Work of Diaries in Mid-Century Victorian Britain," *Victorian Review* 23, no. 2 (Winter 1997): 251-67.

————. *Diaries in English by Women in Canada, 1753-1995: An Annotated Bibliography*. Ottawa: Canadian Research Institute for the Advancement of Women, 1997.

————. "An Economy of Words: Emma Chadwick Stretch's Account Book Diary, 1859-1860." *Acadiensis* 29, no. 1 (Autumn 1999): 43-56.

————. *The Small Details of Life: Twenty Diaries by Women in Canada, 1830-1996*. Toronto: University of Toronto Press, 2002.

Christie, N., ed. *Households of Faith: Family, Gender, and Community in Canada, 1760-1969*. Montreal: McGill-Queen's University Press, 2002.

Clark, A. *Women's Silence, Men's Violence: Sexual Assault in England, 1770-1845*. London: Pandora, 1987.

Cline, C. *Women's Diaries, Journals, and Letters: An Annotated Bibliography*. New York: Garland, 1989.

Cohen, M.G. *Women's Work, Markets, and Economic Development in Nineteenth-Century Ontario*. Toronto: University of Toronto Press, 1988.

Colley, L. *Britons: Forging the Nation, 1707-1837*. New Haven: Yale University Press, 1992.

Collier, F. *The Family Economy of the Working Classes in the Cotton Industry, 1784-1833.* Manchester: Manchester University Press, 1964.

Conrad, M. "'Sundays Always Make Me Think of Home': Time and Place in Canadian Women's History." In *Not Just Pin Money: Selected Essays on the History of Women's Work in British Columbia,* edited by B.K. Latham and R.J. Pazdro, 1-16. Victoria: Camosun College, 1984.

Conrad, M., T. Laidlaw, and D. Smyth, eds. *No Place Like Home: The Diaries of Nova Scotia Women, 1771-1938.* Halifax: Formac, 1988.

Cosbie, W. *The Toronto General Hospital, 1819-1965.* Toronto: Macmillan, 1975.

Cott, N.F. *The Bonds of Womanhood.* New Haven: Yale University Press, 1977.

Cowan, H.I. *British Emigration to British North America.* Toronto: University of Toronto Library, 1961.

Craig, G.M. *Upper Canada: The Formative Years, 1784-1841.* Toronto: McClelland & Stewart, 1963.

Crawford, P. "The Roots of the Toronto Horticultural Society." *OH* 89, no. 2 (June 1997): 125-39.

Culley, M., ed. *A Day at a Time: The Diary Literature of American Women from 1764 to the Present.* New York: Feminist Press, 1985.

Davidoff, L. *The Best Circles: Society, Etiquette, and the Season.* London: Croom Helm, 1973.

Davidoff L., and C. Hall. *Family Fortunes: Men and Women of the English Middle Class, 1780-1850.* Chicago: University of Chicago Press, 1987.

Dearden, J.S. *John Ruskin's Camberwell.* St. Albans: Brentham Press, 1990.

Dendy, W. *Lost Toronto: Images of the City's Past.* Toronto: McClelland & Stewart, 1993.

Dictionary of Canadian Biography. 14 Vols. Toronto: University of Toronto Press, 1966–

Dictionary of National Biography. 63 Vols., Supplement, 3 Vols. London: Smith, Edler, 1885-1901.

Dodds, P.F. *The Story of Ontario Agricultural Fairs and Exhibitions, 1792-1967.* Picton, Ontario: Picton Gazette, 1967.

Duffin, J. *Langstaff: A Nineteenth-Century Medical Life.* Toronto: University of Toronto Press, 1993.

Duffy, E. *The Stripping of the Altars: Traditional Religion in England, c.1400-1580.* New Haven: Yale University Press, 1992.

———. "In the Margins: Medieval Prayer Books and Their Users." Leonard Boyle Memorial Lecture presented at University of Toronto, 20 March 2003.

Dyos, H.J. *Victorian Suburb: A Study of the Growth of Camberwell.* London: Leicester University Press, 1961.

Errington, E.J. *Wives and Mothers, School Mistresses, and Scullery Maids: Working Women in Upper Canada, 1790-1840.* Montreal: McGill-Queen's University Press, 1995.

Fair, R.D. "Gentlemen, Farmers, and Gentlemen Half-Farmers: The Development of Agricultural Societies in Upper Canada, 1792-1846." Ph.D. diss., Queen's University, 1998.

Filey, M. *A Toronto Almanac.* Toronto: Mike Filey, 1984.

Ford, R.A. *Camberwell Green Congregational Church, 1774-1966.* Broadstairs, Kent: Westwood Press, 1967.

Fothergill, R. *Private Chronicles: A Study of English Diaries.* London: Oxford University Press, 1974.

Frayne, T. "Forest Hill: Where a nice Tudor home comes with a neat $285,000 price tag." *Toronto Daily Star,* 14 November, 1970.

French, W. *A Most Unlikely Village: An Informal History of the Village of Forest Hill.* Toronto: Ryerson Press, 1964.

Gagan, D. *Hopeful Travellers: Families, Land, and Social Change in Mid-Victorian Peel County, Canada West.* Toronto: University of Toronto Press, 1981.

Gellner, E. *Nation and Nationalism.* Oxford: Blackwell, 1983.

Giedion, S. *Mechanization Takes Command: A Contribution to Anonymous History.* New York: Oxford University Press, 1948.

Godfrey, C.M. *Medicine for Ontario: A History.* Belleville: Mika Publishing, 1979.

Gorham, D. *The Victorian Girl and the Feminine Ideal.* Bloomington: Indiana University Press, 1982.

Gray, C. *Sisters in the Wilderness: The Lives of Susanna Moodie and Catharine Parr Traill.* Toronto: Penguin, 1999.

Greven, P. *The Protestant Temperament: Patterns of Child-Rearing, Religious Experience and the Self in Early America.* Chicago: University of Chicago Press, 1977.

Guillet, E.C. "Varsity's First Chemistry Professor" in weekly column "Old Times in Ontario." *Toronto Daily Star,* 31 March 1960.

———. "Artist Enriches Historical Scene" in weekly column, "Old Times in Ontario." *Toronto Daily Star,* 15 October 1960.

———. "Toronto Street Railway Started with a Push," in weekly column, "Old Times in Ontario." *Toronto Daily Star,* 9 September 1961.

Hall, C., ed. *Cultures of Empire: A Reader.* Manchester: Manchester University Press, 2000.

———. *Civilising Subjects: Metropole and Colony in the English Imagination, 1830–1867.* Manchester: Manchester University Press, 2002.

Halpern, R. *Down on the Killing Floor: Black and White Workers in Chicago's Packing-houses, 1904–54.* Urbana: University of Illinois Press, 1997.

Hancocks, E. *Potter's Field Cemetery, 1826–1855.* Agincourt, Ontario: Generation Press, 1983.

Harvie, C., and C. Matthew. *Nineteenth-Century Britain.* Oxford: Oxford University Press, 2000.

Havlice, P.P. *And So to Bed: A Bibliography of Diaries Published in English.* Metuchen, New Jersey: Scarecrow Press, 1987.

Heller, L. "Pioneer had farm at Yonge and St. Clair." *Toronto Star,* 16 June 1982.

Hellerstein, E.O., L.P. Hume, and K. Offen, eds. *Victorian Women.* Stanford: Stanford University Press, 1981.

Hoffman F., and R. Taylor. *Much to Be Done: Private Life in Ontario from Victorian Diaries.* Toronto: Natural Heritage/Natural History, 1996.

Holman, A.C. *A Sense of Their Duty: Middle Class Formation in Victorian Ontario Towns.* Montreal: McGill-Queen's University Press, 2000.

Huff, C. *British Women's Diaries.* New York: AMS Press, 1985.

Jameson, A. *Winter Studies and Summer Rambles in Canada.* London: Saunders & Otley, 1838.

Johnson, L. "The Political Economy of Ontario Women in the Nineteenth Century." In *Women at Work: Ontario, 1850–1930,* edited by J. Acton, P. Goldsmith, and B. Shepard, 13–31. Toronto: Canadian Women's Educational Press, 1974.

Jolly, M., ed. *Encyclopedia of Life Writing: Autobiographical and Biographical Forms.* 2 Vols. London: Fitzroy Dearborn, 2001.

Kadar, M., ed. *Essays on Life Writing: From Genre to Critical Practice.* Toronto: University of Toronto Press, 1992.

Katz, M. *The People of Hamilton, Canada West: Family and Class in a Mid-Nineteenth-Century City.* Cambridge: Harvard University Press, 1975.

Kealey, G. *Toronto Workers Respond to Industrial Capitalism, 1867–1892.* Toronto: University of Toronto Press, 1980.

———. *Workers and Canadian History.* Montreal: McGill-Queen's University Press, 1995.

Kerber, L.K. "Separate Spheres, Female World, Woman's Place: The Rhetoric of Women's History." *Journal of American History* 75 (1988): 9–39.

Kyte, E.C. *Old Toronto: A Selection of Excerpts from* Landmarks of Toronto *by John Ross Robertson.* Toronto: Macmillan, 1954.

Langton, H.H., ed. *A Gentlewoman in Upper Canada: The Journals of Anne Langton.* Toronto: Clarke Irwin, 1950.

Little, J.I. "The Fireside Kingdom: A Mid-Nineteenth-Century Anglican Perspective on Marriage and Parenthood." In *Households of Faith: Family, Gender, and Community in Canada, 1760–1969,* edited by N. Christie, 77–102. Montreal: McGill-Queen's University Press, 2002.

———, ed. *Love Strong as Death: Lucy Peel's Canadian Journal, 1833–1836.* Waterloo: Wilfrid Laurier University Press, 2001.

———. "Death in the Lower St. John River Valley: The Diary of Alexander Machum, Jr., 1845–1849." *Acadiensis* 22, no. 1 (Autumn 1992): 122–33.

———. *The Child Letters: Public and Private Life in a Canadian Merchant-Politician's Family, 1841–1845.* Montreal: McGill-Queen's University Press, 1995.

Lonsdale, H. *The Worthies of Cumberland: The Rt. Hon. Sir J.R.G. Graham, Bart. of Netherby.* London: George Routledge & Sons, 1868.

Maas, B. *Helpmates of Man: Middle Class Women and Gender Ideology in Nineteenth-Century Ontario.* Bochum: N. Brockmeyer, 1990.

Macdonald, N. *Canada 1763–1841, Immigration and Settlement.* London: Longman, 1939.

Macfarlane, A. *Marriage and Love in England: Modes of Reproduction, 1300–1840.* Oxford: Blackwell, 1986.

Mackenzie, J.M. *Propaganda and Empire.* Manchester: Manchester University Press, 1984.

———. *Imperialism and Popular Culture.* Manchester: Manchester University Press 1986.

———. *Popular Imperialism and the Military, 1850–1950.* Manchester: Manchester University Press, 1992.

MacLachlan, I.R. *Kill and Chill: Restructuring Canada's Beef Commodity Chain.* Toronto: University of Toronto Press, 2001.

Maple Leaf Foods. "Our History." www.mapleleaf.com/about_mlf/our_history.asp (accessed 7 February 2003).

Marks, L. *Revivals and Roller Rinks: Religion, Leisure, and Identity in Late Nineteenth-Century Small Town Ontario.* Toronto: University of Toronto Press, 1996.

Martyn, L.B. *Aristocratic Toronto: 19th Century Grandeur.* Toronto: Gage, 1980.

Matheson, N. "A Toronto Portrait, 1857." *The Beaver,* June/July 1990, 27-37.

Matthews, W. *British Diaries: An Annotated Bibliography of British Diaries Written between 1442 and 1942.* Berkeley: University of California Press, 1950.

McCalla, D. *Planting the Province: The Economic History of Upper Canada.* Toronto: University of Toronto Press, 1993.

McHugh, P. *Toronto Architecture: A City Guide.* 2nd ed. Toronto: McClelland & Stewart, 1989.

McKay, I. "Capital and Labour in the Halifax Baking and Confectionery Industry During the Last Half of the Nineteenth Century." *Labour/Le Travailleur* 3 (1978): 63-108.

McKenna, K.M.J. *A Life of Propriety: Anne Murray Powell and Her Family, 1755-1849.* Montreal: McGill-Queen's University Press, 1994.

Mertes, K. *The English Noble Household, 1250-1600.* Oxford: Blackwell, 1988.

Miller, A.S., ed. *The Journals of Mary O'Brien: 1828-1838.* Toronto: Macmillan, 1968.

Mills, S. *Discourses of Difference: An Analysis of Women's Travel Writing and Colonialism.* London: Routledge, 1991.

———. "Knowledge, Gender, and Empire." In *Writing Women and Space,* edited by A. Blunt and G. Ross, 29-50. New York: Guilford Press, 1994.

———. *Gender and Colonial Space.* London: Institute of Commonwealth Studies, University of London, 1995.

Milton, S. *The Killing Floor: The First World War and the Emergence of the South African Beef Industry, 1902-24.* London: Institute of Commonwealth Studies, University of London, 1993.

Moodie, S. *Roughing It in the Bush.* London: Richard Bentley, 1852.

Morton, W.L. *The Critical Years: The Union of British North America, 1857-1873.* Toronto: McClelland & Stewart, 1964.

Motz, M.F. "Folk Expression of Time and Place: Nineteenth-Century Midwestern Rural Diaries." *Journal of American Folklore* 100, no. 396 (1987): 131-47.

Mulvaney, C.P., and A.G. Mercer. *History of Toronto and County of York, Ontario.* 2 vols. Toronto: C.B. Robinson, 1885.

Noel, J. *Canada Dry: Temperance Crusades Before Confederation.* Toronto: University of Toronto Press, 1995.

Norris, D.A. "Migration, Pioneer Settlement and the Life Course: The First Families of an Ontario Township." In *Canadian Papers in Rural History,* edited by D.H. Akenson, 130-52. Gananoque: Langdale Press, 1984.

Nussbaum, F. *The Autobiographical Subject.* Baltimore: Johns Hopkins University Press, 1989.

Palmer, B.D. *A Culture in Conflict: Skilled Workers and Industrial Capitalism in Hamilton, Ontario, 1860-1914.* Montreal: McGill-Queen's University Press, 1979.

———. *Working-Class Experience: Rethinking the History of Canadian Labour, 1800-1991.* Toronto: McClelland & Stewart, 1992.

Parkes, F. *Wanderings of a Pilgrim in Search of the Picturesque,* edited by S. Mills and I. Ghose. Manchester: Manchester University Press, 2001.

Pateman, C. *The Sexual Contract.* Cambridge: Polity, 1988.

Payne, R.M. *The Self and the Sacred: Conversion and Autobiography in Early American Protestantism.* Knoxville: University of Tennessee Press, 1998.

Peterson, M.J. *Family, Love, and Work in the Lives of Victorian Gentlewomen*. Bloomington: Indiana University Press, 1989.

Powell, B. "The Diaries of the Crease Family Women." *BC Studies* nos. 105-106 (Spring/Summer 1995): 45-58.

Pratt, M.L. *Imperial Eyes: Travel Writing and Transculturation*. London: Routledge, 1992.

Prentice, A. *The School Promoters: Education and Social Class in Mid-Nineteenth Century Upper Canada*. Toronto: McClelland & Stewart, 1977.

———. "Education and the Metaphor of the Family: The Upper Canadian Example." *History of Education Quarterly* 12, no. 3 (1972): 281-303.

Rayburn, A. *Place Names of Ontario*. Toronto: University of Toronto Press, 1997.

Read, C. *The Rebellion of 1837 in Upper Canada*. Historical Booklet no. 46. Ottawa: Canadian Historical Association, 1988.

Reisner, M.E., ed. *Diary of a Country Clergyman, 1848-51*. Montreal: McGill-Queen's University Press, 2000.

Robertson, J.R. *History of the Brantford Congregational Church, 1820 to 1920*. Compiled by S. Wright. 1920. Reprint, Brant County Branch, Ontario Genealogical Society, 1990.

———. *Landmarks of Toronto*. 4 Vols. 1898. Reprint, Belleville: Mika, 1974.

Rollinson, W. *A History of Cumberland and Westmorland*. London: Phillimore, 1978.

Rosenblatt, P.C. *Bitter, Bitter Tears: Nineteenth-Century Diarists and Twentieth-Century Grief Theories*. Minneapolis: University of Minnesota Press, 1983.

Russell, P. *Attitudes to Social Structure and Mobility in Upper Canada, 1815-40*. Lewiston, New York: E. Mellen Press, 1990.

Ryan, M. *Cradle of the Middle Class: The Family in Oneida County, New York, 1790-1865*. Cambridge: Cambridge University Press, 1981.

Said, E. *Orientalism*. London: Routledge, 1978.

Saunders, A.S. "Yonge Street Politics, 1828 to 1832." *OH* 62, no. 2 (1970): 101-18.

Semple, N. "The Impact of Urbanization on the Methodist Church of Canada, 1854-1884." *Canadian Society of Church History Papers* (1976).

Smith, A. "The Myth of the Self-Made Man in English Canada, 1850-1914." *CHR* 59, no. 2 (1978): 189-219.

Smith, A.D. *The Ethnic Origin of Nations*. Oxford: Blackwell, 1986.

———. *National Identity*. London: Penguin, 1991.

Smith-Rosenberg, C. "The Hysterical Woman: Sex Roles and Role Conflict in Nineteenth-Century America." *Social Research* 39 (1972): 652-78.

———. "The Female World of Love and Ritual: Relations between Women in Nineteenth-Century America." *Signs: Journal of Women in Culture and Society* 1 (1975): 1-30.

Spivak, G.C. "Three Women's Texts and a Critique of Imperialism." *Critical Inquiry* 12 (1985): 243-61.

Stanley, G.F.G. *Canada's Soldiers: The Military History of an Unmilitary People*. Toronto: Macmillan, 1960.

Stauffer, D.A. *The Art of Biography in Eighteenth-Century England* (Princeton, 1941)

Strong-Boag, V., ed. *A Woman with a Purpose: The Diaries of Elizabeth Smith, 1872-1884*. Toronto: University of Toronto Press, 1980.

Tomlinson, J. *Cultural Imperialism*. London: Pinter, 1991.

Tosh, J. *A Man's Place: Masculinity and the Middle-Class Home in Victorian England.* New Haven: Yale University Press, 1999.

Traill, C.P. *The Backwoods of Canada.* London: C. Knight, 1836.

Van Die, M. *An Evangelical Mind: Nathanael Burwash and the Methodist Tradition in Canada, 1839-1918.* Montreal: McGill-Queen's University Press, 1989.

Vickery, A. "Golden Age to Separate Spheres? A Review of the Categories and Chronology of English Women's History." *Historical Journal* 36 (1993): 383-414.

Wade, L.C. *Chicago's Pride: The Stockyards, Packingtown, and Environs in the Nineteenth Century.* Urbana: University of Illinois Press, 1987.

Walker, J.W. St. G. *"Race," Rights, and the Law in the Supreme Court of Canada: Historical Case Studies.* Waterloo: Wilfrid Laurier University Press, 1997.

———. *The Black Loyalists: The Search for a Promised Land in Nova Scotia and Sierra Leone, 1783-1870.* Toronto: University of Toronto Press, 1992.

Wallace, W.S. "U.C.'s First Registrar." *University of Toronto Monthly* 47 (1946-47): 224.

Welter, B. "The Cult of True Womanhood." *American Quarterly* 18 (1966): 151-74.

———. "The Feminization of American Religion, 1800-1860." In *Dimity Convictions: The American Woman in the Nineteenth Century,* edited by B. Welter, 83-102. Athens: Ohio University Press, 1976.

Westfall, W. *Two Worlds: The Protestant Culture of Nineteenth-Century Ontario.* Montreal: McGill-Queen's University Press, 1989.

White, J. *Sketches from America.* London: S. Low, Son, & Marston, 1870.

Wilson, K. "Citizenship, Empire, and Modernity in the English Provinces, c.1720-1790." In *Cultures of Empire: A Reader,* edited by C. Hall, 160-74. Manchester: Manchester University Press, 2000.

Wilson, T.B., ed. *The Ontario Register, Volume 5, 1981.* Lambertville, New Jersey: T.B. Wilson, 1981.

Withrow, O.C.J. *The Romance of the Canadian National Exhibition.* Toronto: Reginald Saunders, 1936.

Wright, D.G. *Popular Radicalism: The Working Class Experience, 1780-1880.* London: Longman, 1991.

Young, A.H., ed. *The Roll of Pupils of Upper Canada College, Toronto: January 1830 to June 1916.* Kingston: Hanson, Crozier, & Edgar, 1917.

✳

Index

❋

Books in the Life Writing Series Published by Wilfrid Laurier University Press